Mary Ettie V. Smith, Nelson Winch Green

Fifteen Years' Residence with the Mormons

With startling disclosures of the mysteries of polygamy

Mary Ettie V. Smith, Nelson Winch Green

Fifteen Years' Residence with the Mormons
With startling disclosures of the mysteries of polygamy

ISBN/EAN: 9783337297985

Printed in Europe, USA, Canada, Australia, Japan

Cover: Foto ©Lupo / pixelio.de

More available books at **www.hansebooks.com**

FIFTEEN YEARS'

RESIDENCE WITH THE

MORMONS.

WITH

Startling Disclosures

OF THE

Mysteries of Polygamy.

BY A SISTER OF ONE OF THE

HIGH PRIESTS.

CHICAGO,
PHŒNIX PUBLISHING COMPANY,
1876.

PREFACE.

THE human mind is peculiarly open to the approach of religious delusion. Man is naturally religious, but prone perhaps to mix with the pure gospels of a pure system, something of a grosser sort, and is inclined to bring the latter down, and to square it with his own poor humanity, when unable to raise himself to the level of an exalted faith. Hence we find the success of these pretenders to new revelations, to be due less to the merit of what they teach, than to the weakness of their victims.

No delusion of this character has for many centuries met with half the success, or achieved a position so threatening and formidable as has the Mormonism of our own day. And no Prophet among the class to which we refer, has entertained the ambitious and aggressive views of Brigham Young, since the advent of Mahomet, whose armed followers overran the fairest portions of the East with the irresistible argument of the "Koran or the sword." And it is perhaps not without reason that the public mind has been suddenly moved to inquire whether the known aims of the successor of Joseph Smith may not point to a similar destiny for this continent. For it is with some concern that we are reminded that in the early years of the hegira, the power and the pretensions of the Prophet of Medina, were much less in fact, than are those of the aspirant to divine honors at Salt Lake to-day.

And while there can be but little doubt as to the result of a conflict, should it come to that, as between the people of the United States and the Saints in Utah, with all the advantages claimed for the latter, from their isolated position, unity of purpose and action, known enterprise, and other admitted elements of strength which would tell in such a contest, yet the question is not entirely devoid of difficulty, with reference to the line of policy the Government at Washington is likely to adopt, in contrast with that which it is believed should be adopted.

This Government, ranking among the first Christian powers of the earth, owes something to civilization and the world as touching the solution of this Mormon question. The assumptions and errors of these " latter day Saints," are too monstrous and radical to pass with a mere rebuke. They should be crushed in the bud, if indeed they have not already passed into a dangerous maturity. They should be torn up root and branch, especially now, when the alternative is held out by the "Prophet" himself, of, "fight or fly."

These men, who have not only set at defiance those acknowledged principles of moral ethics, which for many generations have bound Christendom to a common faith, and worked out for it a high order of civilization, but have repudiated the common instincts of humanity, and the common law also, should not be allowed, even as a compromise, to withdraw from the territory of the United States unpunished.

They should be made to feel the heavy, and resistless arm of the public law. The iron they have meted to others, their defenceless victims, in disregard of law, should be made to enter their own souls, under the sanction of law.

But under our peculiar form of government, undoubtedly the best in the world, a serious difficulty still suggests itself. The outrages in Utah call for an *immediate* remedy. Humanity, racked to its uttermost of endurance, cannot afford to wait the slow process of ordinary governmental action. We have already seen within a few months, an army put in motion, and a Governor appointed for this duty, and the advance of both in the end stayed, for some reason, another year.

When we remember the high character of the present Chief Magistrate of the nation, there can be but little doubt that finally, effective and well judged measures will be taken in the premises; but still the question recurs, why can this not be done now?

Is it only the voice of popular majorities that can move the

Government to action? And is the voice of suffering, though armed with the right, not to be heard, unless it is also armed with might. Must it bear the fearful, and uncertain wand of a balance of power, before it can reach the ear of the politician? Has our nationality come at last, to be but the exponent of a party *only*, and has it nothing left of a sympathy which it should hold in common with all Americans and Christians?

It is not possible that politicians are so lost in schemes of party plunder, as to be blind to the necessity of preserving the Government.

But what need have we for delay in this matter? Is it not time the question were submitted in some form to the serious consideration of the American people, if submitted it must be, before action can be had? Can there be the differential of a doubt, as to what will be the result of such a submission? Indeed is it not already a question of public safety? Can this model system of government survive the shock of so many elements foreign to the aims and scope of its original inception?

Can this people, always liberal and generous, quite up to the verge of safety, escape demoralization while thus trifling with abstractions, which involve the validity of the fundamental law?

Does that "largest liberty," over which we hear the National pride so justly exalt itself, mean the liberty to sweep away the old landmarks of Christendom, and the glorious old common law of our fathers? Is our Bible, and the free institutions which have come down with, and grown up beside it, to be sacrificed to an extreme application of the well approved principles of State Rights, and popular sovereignty? In the splendid machinery of Government which has resulted from the Revolution, and the exalted line of state policy which has grown up under it, did not our fathers bethink them of a sufficient balance wheel equal to the duty of guarding us against the obstructions which bad men and fanatics may choose to interpose to its continued, equal, steady, and general working.

It cannot be supposed, that in the advance made by the framers of our American institutions, it was had in contemplation to retrograde in morals, or in Christian propriety, or to throw away what civilization had already gained for us. But the Mormon practice of polygamy, *is a retrograde*, and hence if our Constitution does not afford a remedy against these evils, and if, from its flexibility, it does not verify the fair promise of its early days, the friends of free institutions may well entertain apprehensions for the future of this country.

But when we look the difficulty fearlessly in the face, the Gordian knot is at once unloosed, for we have in Utah a verification of the truth, that there is in the affairs of men, a certain tendency to a compensation in favor of the right, and *against* the wrong-doer, which cannot be defeated. Hence, admitting for the sake of the argument, that under our liberal system of Government, the practice of polygamy, is among the topics of mere local interest, and subject to the unquestioned decision of the state and local legislature, yet the crimes and scandals, that always must, and as it appears have followed in Utah the violation of those wholesome limitations by which the Christian marriage have been surrounded by a Wise Hand, are *not* exempt from the interference of the law officers of the General Government. But such interference will annihilate both Mormonism and polygamy, since it will *hang all the leaders of any note concerned in these outrages.* And thus we find this question easy of solution, requiring only a firm purpose, and an unrelenting application of justice, on the part of the administrators of public affairs, in carrying out, in a legal manner, acknowledged principles of jurisprudence.

But space will not admit of a full discussion of this important subject here. Trusting these pages may in some measure contribute to a timely and efficient adjustment of the Mormon difficulties, they are now submitted to that umpirage to which an American is always proud to appeal, when questions of great and national interest are under discussion—to the American people.

N. W. GREEN.

INTRODUCTION.

ABOUT the first of March last, the writer of this Narrative was first introduced to the subject of it, by a mutual friend; and listened with astonishment to her extraordinary story. Subsequently much time was spent in weighing, sifting and comparing her statements.

Convinced by this investigation of its entire truthfulness, and recognizing the claim she had upon the public ear, and the claim to be heard in this behalf by the thousands of her sex still in Mormon land, the following pages have been written, and are now offered without apology; albeit but little time has been taken to prepare for the press.

The appearance and general state of mind of Mrs. Smith, at this time, was very peculiar: and not without interest as affording evidence of her good faith. At times timid as the antelope of the mountains among which she has suffered so much, and but partially freed from the thraldom of her Mormon habits of life, she stood braced against all "Gentile" approach, and although she had in theory abandoned her Mormon faith, she had adopted no other in its place. The dread of falling into some new error, rendered her almost inaccessible to truth.

On one occasion, when the Mormon belief in a plurality of gods was under discussion, the fact was stated, that there was but one God over all the universe; she replied with unfeigned wonder, as if the idea was altogether new to her:

"What? Do you believe there is but one God?"

In giving to the world the following narrative, the author fully appreciates the importance of the fact, that its success, and the benefit he deems he has a right to expect may accrue from it to suffering humanity in Utah, will be greatly dependent upon the credence extended to it by the public.

The first questions the honest reader has a right to ask, are these: Is it true? Are these disclosures and revelations made in good faith? Are they really the actual experiences of a woman yet under twenty-nine years of age? A woman educated from childhood in the Mormon faith; familiar with all its details? One who has been a victim to its cruel hardships, and to its practical workings? Has she disclosed to the world what she has actually seen, and felt, and suffered; and nothing more? Is it true, that she has been held a prisoner, in common with many others of her sex, for years in Utah, and that by a singular good fortune, when hope had nearly gone out within her, she effected an escape? And is it true, that to-day she exists as an actuality, courting investigation, and fearing nothing but Mormon intrigue and Mormon assassination?

There is in simple truth an agreement and consistency, upon which the mind intuitively fastens, and upon which it bases its convictions never found in the creations of the imagination. It is with confidence, therefore, that we refer to the internal evidence which this narrative itself affords of its own truth.

The circumstance that real names are given throughout the book, of persons who are still living and who will be likely to make themselves heard, if they have been misrepresented, should furnish another argument in favor of its reliability.

Nothing in the following pages has been written with the design of feeding a morbid curiosity; and whatever has been admitted of fact or form of expression, which possibly may have that effect, has been from necessity, and as growing out of the nature of the subject, and not from any want of respect for that delicate and even fastidious public taste which has ever characterized the people of this country. An earnest desire to subserve the public good, as regards the exposure of these enormities, has been the governing consideration. In fact, many things have been omitted, from a wish to avoid offence in this particular.

We give, in addition, an extract from an affidavit forwarded to the Government at Washington in answer to a communication from the State Department relating to affairs in Utah, as further evidence of good faith on the part of Mrs. Smith:

(COPY.)

Affidavit of Mrs. Mary Ettie V. Smith, relating to certain matters in the Territory of Utah.

"State of New York, } ss.
  Livingston County. }

"Mary Ettie V. Smith, late of Great Salt Lake city, in the territory of Utah; and now of Stuben county, in the State of

New York, being duly sworn deposes and says: That she has been a resident of said Territory for about five years; and has been a member of the community of Mormons for fifteen years: That she is at present twenty eight years of age; that she was a believer in good faith in Mormonism, until she discovered, after going to Utah, the principal business of the Prophet Brigham Young, and the other heads of the Mormon Church to be the commission of crimes of the most atrocious character; among which may be included robbery, murder, and treason to the General Government, and a large number of lesser crimes: and that she was held a prisoner there for a long time, against her wish and consent, after she had expressed a desire to return to the U. S.; and that a large number of persons, particularly women, have been, and are, as she verily believes, so held and restrained, and debarred of the exercise of their personal liberty; and that many of these persons, were they to be assured of the protection of the Government, could and would give such evidence before a legal tribunal, as would, if such tribunal were unawed, and uncontrolled by the Mormons or their influence, lead to the conviction of Brigham Young, and many, and probably most of the heads of the Church, of such crimes as are punishable by death.

"And this deponent further says that as an illustration of the above, she will state, that in the year 1853, she was present when Brigham Young, General Wells, and John and Wiley Norton, discussed and adopted a plan for the murder of Wallace Alonzo Clarke Bowman, an American citizen, at the time engaged in the Mexican trade, and in the quiet and legal pursuit of his lawful business: and that said Bowman was so murdered by direction of said Rrigham Young; and after the manner determined upon as aforesaid. That she saw and recognized his body after his death; and that she cut a lock of said Bowman's hair after his death, and gave the same to Dr Hurt, at the time Indian agent of the Territory.

"That John Norton and James Furguson, now believed to be living at Salt Lake, told this deponent in the presence of various other persons, to wit: Jane Furguson, (wife No. 2 of said Furguson) and others, that they, the said Norton and Furguson shot the said Bowman, in Salt Creek cañon: that a large amount of property was taken from said Bowman, by the said Mormons: and that at this time, said Brigham Young, was governor of the said Territory of Utah.

"That the facts above stated, with reference to the imprisonment, robbery and final murder of said Bowman, can be proved by a large number of reliable witnesses now in Utah; and one besides herself now in the state of New York. That the account given of the same in her Narrative, now about to be published, is substantially true: and that among many others, the following persons would swear to these facts, if properly approached, and well assured of protection against the assassination of the "Danites," to wit: ———: ——— and ——— ——— the two wives of ——— ——— and the mother of ——— ———; (———) and ——— ———, wife of ——— ———; ——— ——— wife No. 2 of ——— ———; ——— ———, and his wife, ·——— ———; and others; all living at Great Salt Lake City.

"This Deponent further says, that she was present at another time, in the year 1851; when the said Brigham Young, governor of the Territory of Utah, 'counseled,' and directed the robbery of a Dr. Roberts; and that afterwards she was present, when the said Dr. Roberts was robbed, at night, on the public highway, in pursuance of the said instructions of the said Prophet and Gov. Young; that said robbery was committed by Captain James Brown, now living at Ogden city, in said Territory, and Hiram Clauson, of Great Salt Lake city; and in presence of Ellen, the wife of said Clauson, and in presence of this deponent; and that she has good reason to fear the said Roberts was afterward murdered by said Brown and Clauson: that she can furnish proof of many similar crimes; an account of which she deems it unnecessary to give in detail at this time; and further this deponent saith not."

(Signed)
MARY ETTIE V. SMITH.

Subscribed and sworn this 21st day of August, 1857, before me.

CHARLES R. KERN,
Justice of the Peace.

CONTENTS

CHAPTER I.
My Birth and Parentage, ... 17

CHAPTER II.
A Storm Gathering, ... 28

CHAPTER III.
Death of the Prophet, ... 33

CHAPTER IV.
Endowments, ... 41

CHAPTER V.
The Exodus, ... 54

CHAPTER VI.
A Night with the Dead and the Wolves, ... 65

CHAPTER VII.
Seeking my Mother, ... 76

Contents.

CHAPTER VIII.
Among the Gentiles. 83

CHAPTER IX.
More Wives, ... 89

CHAPTER X.
Reconciled—Finding my Mother, ... 100

CHAPTER XI.
The Family Broken Up, ... 114

CHAPTER XII.
The Parting—Crossing the Tankio, ... 128

CHAPTER XIII.
Offer of Marriage—Setting out for "Zion," . . . 137

CHAPTER XIV.
Great Salt Lake City, Utah, ... 146

CHAPTER XV.
Church Polity, ... 150

CHAPTER XVI.
Reuben P. Smith's Arrival—Narrow Escape from becoming a "Spiritual," 167

CHAPTER XVII.
"Sealed" to the Butcher for Eternity—A Fearful Discovery, . 180

CONTENTS.

CHAPTER XVIII.
The Escape, ... 193

CHAPTER XIX.
My Father's Friend—Dr. Roberts, ... 198

CHAPTER XX.
Preparing to Entrap an Old Man, ... 209

CHAPTER XXI.
Robbery and Probable Murder of Dr. Roberts, . . . 221

CHAPTER XXII.
Sealed for Time, ... 234

CHAPTER XXIII.
Intrigues of Brigham Young, ... 241

CHAPTER XXIV.
The Story of Wallace Alonzo Clark Bowman, ... 252

CHAPTER XXV.
Fate of Bowman, ... 264

CHAPTER XXVI.
Mormon Jesuitism, ... 278

CHAPTER XXVII.
The Story of William Mac, ... 280

xvi   CONTENTS.

CHAPTER XXVIII.
Milking a Gentile, ... 293

CHAPTER XXIX.
Punishment of Heresy, ... 308

CHAPTER XXX.
Tooille, ... 320

CHAPTER XXXI.
The Flight and Recapture, ... 332

CHAPTER XXXII.
Rope, ... 343

CHAPTER XXXIII.
Going to the Land of my Birth, ... 351

CHAPTER XXXIV.
Crossing the Webber—Perils by the Way, ... 360

CHAPTER XXXV.
Crossing the Plains, ... 370

CHAPTER XXXVI.
Conclusion, ... 383

CHAPTER XXXVII.
Continuation of the Narrative, ... 389

CHAPTER XXXVIII.
Rise, Progress, and Present Condition of Mormonism, . . 409

FIFTEEN YEARS AMONG THE MORMONS

CHAPTER I.

MY BIRTH AND PARENTAGE.

My father, Silas Coray, was one of the four sons of John and Phebe Coray of Providence township, Luzern county, Pennsylvania. My grandfather, John Coray, was accidentally shot by one of his neighbors, and a few years after, my grand mother married James Abbott, and moved to Allegany county, New York, near Arkport. It was but a short time after this event that my father married Mary Stephens, the daughter of Uriah Stephens, a revolutionary pensioner, and one of the six original proprietors of the township of Canisteo, now a part of Steuben county. My parents lived here until after the birth of their first two children, and then moved to Pennsylvania, to occupy the farm my grandfather had left them; but soon returned to New York. His three brothers, John,* David, and Ira, occupied in common the balance of my grandfather's land in Pennsylvania, and by their solicitation,

---

* One of these brothers, my uncle John, is now living with a numerous and respectable family in the town of Burns, Allegany

my father, about this time, purchased the whole property of them, and moved his family onto the old homestead; where had he lived contentedly, he would have saved his family from being scattered, and falling victims to a most fatal and cruel delusion. It was at this place, Providence, Luzern county, Pennsylvania, I was born, January 31, 1829.

My father at this time owned over seven hundred acres of coal land, which has since proved to be very valuable.

When I was ten years of age he sold this fine property and removed with his family to Perry, Pike county, Illinois; where he bought a large tract of land, and soon after, while in the height of his various objects of enterprise, was killed accidentally while drawing a log to a saw-mill; leaving his business in a very unsettled condition, and my mother with nine children then living, two of whom were younger than myself, named as follows: Aurilla, Sarah Ann, Phebe, Howard, George, William, Mary Ettie V., Uriah, and Harriet Elizabeth.

At the death of my father, began that terrible series of misfortunes, a history of which will form the subject-matter of the following pages My father's death occurred in January, 1841.

county, New York. Many members of my mother's family, the Stephens, are yet living in Canisteo, and other parts of Steuben county, New York; and I have many cousins in Pennsylvania, now living. Col. John R. Stephens, my mother's brother, lives upon his estate near Hornellsville, New York; and is well known in that section of the country.

About this time a Mormon Elder, who had been holding meetings in this neighborhood, called upon my mother, and among other things, told her that the Latter Day Saints claimed to be able to heal the sick, and that if she would consent to be baptized, the deafness with which she was afflicted, and which had become a great annoyance to her, would in a very short time be removed; and she would hear again.

Willing at least to try the experiment, she was baptized. The water was very cold, and immediately after her hearing was improved, and soon, it was entirely restored. I feel it my duty to do my mother the justice of stating this very remarkable circumstance, which was the real foundation of her conversion to Mormonism, and of her implicit faith in Joseph Smith, as a Prophet of God; a faith that was never shaken until, years after, she found herself shut up in Utah, a prisoner, and an unwilling witness of abominations which in the States had been disguised.

My mother, who is still living, now understands, that perhaps this *apparent* miracle, was the effect of cold water, or of some other natural though unexplained cause; but at that time, it had with her all the force of a real miracle. It was the voice of God through His Prophet, which she dare not disregard; and accordingly she removed *at once* to Nauvoo, where the Mormons had just laid the foundation for the Temple, taking seven of her children; two of my sisters, having husbands, did not accompany her.

Her entire property, and all papers relating to my father's business, were placed in the hands of Stephen Abbott, a half-brother of my father who had been previously converted to Mormonism.

This was the last trace, or account, or benefit my mother, or any one of our family, ever received of this valuable property, except a small amount of our personal effects, taken with us at the time, which probably went into the hands of Joseph Smith, and was absorbed in the common stock. It was probably a part of the large sum afterwards expended upon the Temple at Nauvoo.

It may appear strange, that my mother so readily gave up her property into the hands of her new friends; but we have already seen that they had, by a pretended miracle, restored her to hearing; and thus, in a double sense, they had obtained a "hearing," and she readily received as infallible, the doctrine of the "immediate second coming of Christ;" and hence, it looked reasonable to her, when they said she would no longer need her property. She had, however, been at Nauvoo but a few months, before she saw the absurdity of this summary disposal of her worldly goods, and returned to Pike county to look after it; but found it sold and occupied by strangers, and out of her reach. She returned to Nauvoo, to make the best of her new religion.

I recollect that I was baptized into the new faith, as were all my brothers and sisters, except my two married sisters, who did not accompany us, and Howard, my second brother, who was a ready penman, soon became a great favorite with Joseph Smith, the Prophet; with whom he spent most of his time as his clerk, and so continued until his death, and afterwards wrote for Brigham Young, and is thus employed now for the latter, at Great Salt Lake City Howard is the author of an history of the Smith family, unfinished at the death of the Prophet, but since published.

I had been baptized by the direction of Joseph Smith, at eleven years of age; and my mother left me temporarily with my brother Howard, through whom all our family were controlled by the Prophet. It was by the advice of the latter that Howard had been married to Martha Jane Knowlton. Some of our neighbors, about this time, began to say that I was old enough to be married. I was but thirteen years of age, and this greatly frightened me, as I verily believed there would be no escape from the will of the Prophet, if *he* should direct me to marry—a thing not unlikely to happen, for he was in the habit of doing thus with others, when he found they were at the age of puberty; and to refuse would be at the sacrifice of my own salvation, unless I could afterwards *obtain his pardon*.

Every effort was made by the Mormons, apparently without the knowledge of the Prophet, to induce my brother to effect a marriage for me, by the offer to him of various presents and other inducements tendered by those who wished to marry me. But he paid but little attention to them, as he had hoped to win higher honors through my marriage. He had conceived the idea of marrying me to one of the Twelve Apostles, as soon as I was old enough to be a mother.

I believed in Mormonism, for I knew no other religion, but I preferred not to marry an old man, but chose to have a husband of my own age, and of my own choice, if I must have one. The Prophet, Smith, had not yet "counselled" me to get married, and I concluded, if an opportunity offered I should surely take the advantage of "Brother Joseph," and run the risk of being forgiven by him.

My sister Sarah had married a Mr. Griffin, and was then living at Nauvoo, both herself and husband having been converted to Mormonism by the apparent miracle of the cure of my mother's deafness.

My sister, who knew what efforts had been made to effect my marriage, became uneasy, and sent for me to come to her house; and I accordingly went, and told her how matters stood; and, among other things, a brother Gully had strongly pressed his matrimonial claims upon my attention. I cried that night till I was quite sick.

My sister told me, if I would not betray her to the Church, she would undertake to find a husband for me, suitable to my age, when I was old enough; but that I was too young now, and that no man should have me for a wife yet, if she could prevent it; that I must go down and ask Howard if I could come and stay at her house until her husband returned, who was at the time absent in Iowa with his brother Henry The latter, who now lives at Scranton, Pennsylvania, knew and must recollect most of the facts I am now relating. To this Howard consented after some delay, and raising various objections; and much elated at my success in escaping for the time the annoyance of old men looking for young wives, I went to her house, where I remained for several weeks.

One day my sister said to me, "Nettie, quite an interesting young fellow has been boarding with us, and if you were two or three years older, you should marry him." I replied, that perhaps I could not get him. "Is he old enough to be my grandfather?" "No, he is not over twenty-four years of age, and is good looking."

I said, "Sarah, when he comes, if he suits me, or comes near to it, I shall try to make him marry me, for fear I shall be 'counselled' by Joseph to marry some man who has a wife already, for I can never consent to have a husband in partnership."*

"Nettie," said Sarah, "if this Mormonism is true, we shall be very sorry if we say much against it; but still I must acknowledge that such a doctrine, if practised much, will cause the women a great deal of sorrow, and add nothing to the happiness of the men."

"I am sure," said I, "they will not enjoy their spirituals over much if they are all like me; I will not tolerate it."

My cousin Emily came in just then, and said, "Nettie, what is the matter? but first come and see my beau;" and going to the window, we saw an old grey-headed man hobbling along—one of the young girl hunters. My cousin was about my own age. She told me her mother wished her to marry Mr. Brown,† her mother's husband, who was a very wealthy old gentleman. When I asked her if she intended to do so, she replied she would not if she could help it, and

---

* Even at this early day, it was understood among us, that spiritual wifeism was practised by the Heads of the Church in secret although it was stoutly denied when questioned by the Gentiles.

† This is the celebrated Captain James Brown, afterwards referred to in this narrative, who was concerned in the robbery and probable murder of Dr. Roberts, near Ogden City, Utah.

asked me to go into the other room: and we had but just seated ourselves, to talk over our mutual troubles, when some one knocked at the front door, for whom my sister opened it, and said, "Good evening, Wallace," and some one replied, "Good evening; I heard Nettie, as you call her, was here." Sarah told him I was in the other room.

When I heard his voice I was very much excited, noticing which, Emily said, "Nettie, what is the matter?" This was heard by Wallace, whereupon he came into the room, accompanied by my sister, and without an introduction, said, "Nettie, I am sorry you are not well; I anticipated having a fine talk with you this evening. I have heard the old men talking so much about you and Emily, that I have come to the conclusion you are worth looking after."

"That old man, Brown," said Emily, "is not satisfied with having my mother, but is determined to add me to the number of his wives, which I am bent upon preventing if possible." and she left the room apparently very much excited.

The case of my cousin, and that of many others which daily came under my observation, made a deep impression upon me, and had probably no small influence upon the step I was about to take.

Wallace Henderson, with whom I was now left alone in my sister's parlor, was five feet ten inches high, had dark brown hair, large black eyes, a high forehead, and dark red whiskers, and a very agreeable address, and on this occasion exerted himself to interest me. He was upon the whole a fine looking boy.

He talked to me of Mormonism, saying it was true; that

the spiritual wife doctrine was true and perfectly right; but that he could never enjoy himself among a crowd of brawling women and noisy children, but said those who can were the ones to practice it.

I then said to him, you really do not think you could fancy such a life, Wallace? To which he replied, "I should be satisfied to get *one* like you, Nettie."

At this point of our conversation, I heard my brother William inquiring of Sarah for me, and being told where I was, he called me out, and said,

"Nettie, I do not want you to have any private conversation with that fellow, or with any other man, without Brother Joseph's permission. He is a stranger to you, and how dare you act thus, after hearing as much as you have about the necessity of marrying a man that can 'exalt' you in the eternal world? How can you think of having private conversation with this trifling scamp, who would not scruple to deceive you, although you think him good looking?"

I replied, "William, I think I can understand why you are giving me this scolding; it opens up to me a clear view of the whole case. You are expecting me to go into the family of one of the 'Twelve Apostles.' Is that it?"

"I can tell you this much," said William, "I have made arrangements with Joseph Smith for your eternal salvation; and you must not deprive yourself of the honor of being the wife of one of the 'Twelve:'" and he said, "come, put on your bonnet, and go home to Howard's."

Sarah, who had listened to all this, said at last, "William, Nettie is too young to be tormented in this way. It is ridiculous. She is just as well with me as with Howard or with you."

"No, she is not," said William; "she must not be indulged in such wicked and jealous principles as you encourage her in."

I submitted, and went with my brother to Howard's, to whom I said, "I am a great trouble to my very religious friends, and a very singular religion I think yours is, too." I went up stairs, and after having a cry over the matter, made up my mind to marry some single man as soon as an opportunity offered: and that I would marry Wallace Henderson if he was in earnest in the encouragement he had given me.

My brother William was gathering wood for Joseph Smith on an island in the Mississippi, and having several men in his charge, was obliged to be absent during the day, and I was left at Howard's.

When he left he said, "Nettie, you must stay here until I come back," I made him no promises; whereupon Howard, who did not justify fully his course in regard to me, said,

"William, you are a tyrant, and you act sillily. She is not going to be deprived of seeing Sarah."

After William had left, I told Howard I was going to Sarah's, and he suffered me to do so.

When I arrived there I found Wallace, who appeared glad to see me, and to whom I told everything; and then he asked me if I would marry so young, and before my mother returned. I told him I would, if I could marry a man that was single, but that I could never endure the spiritual wife doctrine.

"Nettie," said Wallace, "I love, and will marry you tonight, if you are willing. Do you consent?" I did consent, and he kissed me and left, saying he would soon bring some one to marry us.

I told Sarah what I had done, and she did not object, but sat down and gave me much good advice; and soon Wallace came in with Judge Higbee, who married us, January 30, 1843. The day after our wedding I was fourteen years old. My brothers, Howard and William, were so enraged, they did not speak to me for a long time. Although I had married to escape a worse fate, from a sort of necessity, I was very happy, for I soon learned to love my husband, and we should have lived pleasantly, and did, until the spiritual wifeism afterwards stepped between us with its blighting curse

CHAPTER II.

A STORM GATHERING.

I was married in the winter of 1843. At about this time various causes conspired to embarrass and complicate the relation of the Mormons with " the rest of mankind," termed by them " Gentiles." It was well known to me, although young at the time, as it was to every Mormon at Nauvoo, that great numbers of cattle and hogs were in the habit of *wandering* from the surrounding country into the city, and were appropriated by the Saints; and the same with other property that could be concealed. Another thing that increased the prejudice against our community, was the great amount of bogus money afloat about that time, and in some cases traced directly to the Mormons. It so happened that while at Nauvoo, and afterwards, I had an opportunity to know something of this bogus manufacture.

When we were on the route through Iowa, it occurred, that one day, when one of the wagons was upset, the press for making bogus money rolled into sight, and was seen by many Mormons, who till then had not supposed they were one of a gang of counterfeiters. But there is no doubt about the fact that the business of counterfeiting was carried on extensively, and that too under the personal sanction and *blessing* of the Prophet Joseph, and of the Twelve. Most of these Twelve Apostles are now living at Salt Lake, and the same is true to day there, although not done openly, and justified as is the spiritual wife practice. Even this was denied at Nauvoo to the Gentiles, while it was taught us under the ban of secrecy. One thing is certain; *this bogus press was carried, to my certain knowledge, to Salt Lake*, and there is now a man living in Allegany county, by the name of Lewis Wood, who saw it between Nauvoo and Council Bluffs.

It was about this time that Governor Boggs, of Missouri, was shot at St. Louis. It appears the Governor had offended the Mormons very much when the latter were driven from that State in 1838, and I recollect hearing the Prophet say on the stand, that the man who had shot Governor Boggs would have a crown immortal, and it was understood at the time, that O. Porter Rockwell was the person referred to by Joseph.

This O. P. Rockwell is now living at Salt Lake, distinguished by other similar acts, but it was this that first brought him into notice among the Mormons. He was after this known as the chief of the "Danites," a corps of men set apart for such assassinations. In this case Governor Boggs was shot from the outside, through a window; but by good fortune not killed. Another source of revenue at this time was robbing, and "*putting aside*" strangers who were driving cattle to the eastern market, or to the northern settlements. Numerous cases of this kind came to my knowledge after my marriage, in which I *knew* my husband was engaged; some of which the reader will find hereafter narrated.

These cattle, before we left Nauvoo, were slaughtered, and salted to avoid detection, but afterwards, when stolen on the road to the plains, they were put into the teams, or used as necessity required. This cattle stealing was known and counselled by the Prophet. Although at that time I believed him to be a Prophet of God, I now believe he was every way unworthy to be received as such.

To discourage inconvenient scrutiny from visitors at Nauvoo, the Mormons had a custom in vogue among them called "whistling and whittling Gentiles out of town," which was done after this wise.

A company of young men and boys would surround the Gentile who evinced too great a thirst for curious knowledge, and with the greatest gravity whistle in concert, and whittle in careless proximity to his person, following him from place to place, until, annoyed beyond measure, he was glad to escape from the "City of Beauty."

I have often seen this; and after such an exhibition of zeal by the boys, some of the old men of the Church would encourage them by presents, and *promises of heaven*, telling them the time would come when it would be lawful to not only whittle at, but to whittle into the Gentiles in earnest; and the blood-thirsty spirit thus engendered among those boys now exhibits itself in Utah, among the same ones, now grown to be men, by their readiness to shed the blood of the Gentiles at the command of the new Prophet.

The reason given the boys for this "whittling out of town" was, that since the wicked were always liable to be punished, if the "Gentiles" (*i. e.* the wicked) were allowed to remain in the town, the righteous (Mormons) were liable to be punished with them.

A circumstance occurred about this time, which served to scandalize the Church among the Gentiles, and create dissension among the Mormons, and threatened at one time to dismember the Church.

Orson Pratt, then, as now, one of the "Twelve," was sent by Joseph Smith on a mission to England. During his absence, his first (*i. e.* his lawful) wife, Sarah, occupied a house owned by John C. Bennett, a man of some note, and at that time, quartermaster-general of the Nauvoo Legion. Sarah was an educated woman, of fine accomplishments, and attracted the attention of the Prophet Joseph, who called upon her one day, and alleged he found John C. Bennett in bed with her. As we lived but across the street from her house we saw and heard the whole uproar. Sarah ordered the Prophet out of the house, and the Prophet used obscene language to her.

When brother Orson returned a short time after this, and heard the story, he believed his wife rather than the Prophet, and charged the latter with lying. They were both arraigned before the Church, and tried; the husband for "disputing" the Prophet, and the wife for adultery; and both were cut off. The thing grew serious. Pratt was an apostle, and one of the best writers, as well as the best educated man, in the Church. Bennett left Nauvoo, and has never been identified with the "saints" since. Pratt also left, but by the following arrangement returned to the bosom of the Church, and to the favor of the Prophet. He, with his wife, were re-baptized for the remission of their mutual sin, and the Prophet was appeased. Pratt has ever since been one of the pillars of the Church, and at that time would have been an irreparable loss to it.

He had then four wives, but his attachment to his first wife, Sarah, appears to have triumphed over his disgust at her loss of virtue. It is said he very nearly went mad with the trouble growing out of this affair. He afterwards edited a Mormon paper at Washington, known as the "Seer;" and by his glowing descriptions of Utah, has deluded many of the victims of Mormonism to that moral pest-house, who would now gladly escape.

CHAPTER III.

DEATH OF THE PROPHET.

Various causes conspired to increase the storm to such a degree that it finally resulted in the death of Joseph Smith.

Some of these have been referred to in the last chapter; but, probably, the most dangerous element of discord, threatening as it did the internal peace of the Church, grew out of the spiritual wife doctrine; and as some misapprehension as to its origin appears to have obtained currency among the "Gentiles," I deem it proper to state what I know of it.

It has been stated, and generally believed, that this doctrine was first communicated by revelation to Sidney Rigdon. This is untrue, and has grown into public belief from statements of Smith himself, who denied the existence of such a doctrine, when questioned by the Gentiles during his life, even while he was in its practice. In fact, he excommunicated many of his followers who practised it indiscreetly, his brother William among others; and, in order to confine it within controllable limits, and to avoid public scandal, he restricted its practice to the highest dignitaries of the Church; and it was never understood to be a thing of indiscriminate and open practice until after the Mormons crossed the

Missouri, *en route* to the far West. This doctrine was revealed under circumstances of extraordinary import to Joseph Smith, as the "*only* Prophet of God," and was written out at length at the time, and the original writing is now "kept in state" at Salt Lake, and in the personal custody of a member of the Grand Presidency, Heber C. Kimble.

This remarkable document, which has so boldly attempted to rob civilization of her highest achievement, *i. e.* the right of woman to one whole and undivided husband, is said to contain many other radical changes; things which, even among Mormons, it is yet unlawful to whisper; but, when the "sword of the Prophet shall be the law of the world," a day which some Mormons now living hope to see, these mysterious revelations shall be unloosed to "bless" the Mormon world.

The Prophet appears to have encountered an unrelenting opponent in his first and lawful wife, Emma, who discovered by accident this document, and finding it contained new doctrines which threatened to interfere with her domestic rights, attempted to destroy it; but the Mormons claim she was miraculously prevented, and the oracle is still preserved.

Emma attempted, as a last resort, to poison the Prophet, and though she failed in that, she soon found sympathy and support among the disaffected within the Church.

The Prophet had sent some time before this, three men, Law, Foster and Jacobs, on missions, and they had just returned, and found their wives blushing under the prospective honors of spiritual wifeism; and another woman, Mrs. Buel, had left her husband, a Gentile, to grace the Prophet's retinue on horseback, when he reviewed the Nauvoo Legion. I heard the latter woman say afterwards in Utah, that she did not know whether Mr. Buel or the Prophet was the father of her son. These men established a press in Nauvoo, to expose his alleged vicious teachings and practices, which a revelation from Joseph destroyed. The press was thrown into the street, and the material scattered.

This provoked a conflict with law officers of the State. Sheriffs and constables searched the city for the Prophet, and Hiram, and others of the leading ones, but for a long time they evaded them. The Prophet fled across the Mississippi, to Iowa, and took refuge with the Indians.

A circumstance occurred in the midst of the excitement, which I think was not rightly understod by the Gentiles.

A sheriff in pursuit of the Prophet, whose name I do not now recollect, was murdered by the Mormons, and thrown into the Mississippi. His friends supposed he had been drowned accidentally, for this was the story circulated by those who murdered him. Things were assuming a bad shape. The Prophet's wife Emma, stirred up the people by the story that the Prophet was a coward, and had forsaken his people.

Historians of these events tell us that the Governor of Illinois persuaded Joseph Smith, and his principal Apostles to surrender themselves to the law officers, and tendered to them his official protection. But there is always an undercurrent in history, a knowledge of which is necessary to a right-estimate of the facts, which is only to be found in the domestic lives of the great actors upon the stage of life. Emma, who wished to destroy the Prophet, wrote to him reproachfully, for his cowardice; and denouncing him as an impostor, and asked him to give a proof of his mission, by facing the enemies of the church.

This had the effect she had expected and desired. The Prophet returned to Nauvoo, and was arrested, with his brother Hiram, John Taylor, Willard Richards and others, and all were lodged in Carthage jail.

But the excitement among the Gentiles was at its height. The idea had obtained credit, that the Governor would protect the Prophet, and screen him from justice. A mob gathered at Carthage, on the 27th of June, 1844, and took the matter into their own hands. John Taylor, late editor of the "Mormon," a paper published in New York city, escaped with a slight wound; his watch having intercepted a ball, which otherwise must have passed through his body. He gave us a detailed account of the end of the Prophet.

He said Hiram fell dead at the first shot from the mob, through the window; Joseph, who was sitting upon the window-sill, received a shot which wounded him, may be mortally. He then turned quickly to Hiram, and seeing he was dead, exclaimed, " My Lord, my God, have mercy upon us, if there is any God ;" and fell out of the window, where he was soon riddled with balls.

When the dead bodies arrived at Nauvoo, the spiritual wives of the late prophet, before unknown with certainty, now disclosed by cries, and a general uproar, their secret acceptance of the new doctrine. One of them, Olive Frost, went entirely mad; but his own wife Emma, appeared remarkably resigned. She afterwards married a Gentile, and disavowed Mormonism.

The bodies of the Smiths were brought to Nauvoo, and buried in the cellar of Joseph's house, although the ceremony of burying their empty coffins was performed at the "grave." The death of the prophet was a terrible blow; and the problem whether the Church would be annihilated by it, or not, was destined to turn upon that of a choice of a successor, to which there were many aspirants. William Smith, the only surviving brother of the dead Prophet, founded a strong claim upon the fact of his being the next of kin; Lyman White, Gladden Bishop, James Strang, John E. Page, Sidney Rigdon, and many others were candidates.

Brigham Young, already a rising man among the adherents of the new faith, was absent upon a "mission" at the time; but his return was daily expected. He was President of the "Quorum of Apostles," and next to the Prophet, had been perhaps the most popular of the leaders, with the people. It has been stated, and generally believed, that Brigham Young was elected Prophet, and Head of the Church, by the college of Apostles. This is not true. Although that body undoubtedly favored the elevation of the President of their quorum, they had no such power invested in them. The election of all officers in the Church, from the Prophet down to the lowest, is a question to be submitted to the whole body of the people. Sidney Rigdon was making a strong effort to get a special convention, hoping thereby to secure his election before the return of Brigham Young; and in fact succeeded in getting it called. The people had assembled upon a day fixed for that purpose. In those days, the advent of a steamboat on the Mississippi was always an event. One had been anxiously expected for several days, which it was hoped would bring "Brother Brigham." After the convention had been organized, most of the candidates presented their claims by a personal address; and the last speaker, Sidney Rigdon, had risen to address the excited assembly, and was risking everything upon a strong, last appeal to the people, in his own behalf, who were now about to decide whether he (Rigdon) should be a Prophet, and a Mormon, or an apostate.

He had nearly finished, and the friends of Brigham Young were wild with vexation, for Rigdon was evidently gaining upon the popular feeling. Just then the cry came up from the river, that a boat was in sight, and when it arrived, Brigham proved to be on board. When on shore, he came at once to the convention, and advanced to the stand, with the air of a prophet, and the lofty bearing of one who bore in his person the fortunes of an empire. He was at that time under forty years of age, with a handsome and pleasing face, and an open and frank address; he possessed the rare faculty of inspiring enthusiasm in others, without allowing it to overpower himself.

By a short and well-timed speech, in which he referred feelingly to the dead Prophet, he frankly presented his claims to the succession. The effect was instantaneous, and permanent. He was elected President of the Church of Latter Day Saints, and a Prophet of God; and from that day to this, has ruled the Church with an untrammelled absoluteness, unknown to any other human government. This will appear the more remarkable when we state that he is, with all other officers of the Church, liable to be removed twice each year; *i. e.* the 6th of April and October; when each are reëlected, or others in their stead, when disaffection exists as to any one of them; the whole being governed by the voice of the people. A perfect democracy in its original sense.

The defeat of Rigdon and Strang ended their belief in Mormonism, and each went off to found a new order upon their own hook; as did also most of the other defeated candidates. Success has however attended the lead of none but Brigham Young, who was followed by all those whose orthodoxy was then undoubted.

The new Prophet declared openly in favor of the spiritual wife dogma, as soon as he could do so safely, which formed the first great feature of his administration. His energy and personal influence soon infused new life within the Church, and served to calm the opposition from without. His fair beginning promised a peaceable and successful future, but the schismatics who had left, and who were for the most part opposed to the new doctrine, were fanning anew the fires of persecution among the Gentiles. The Mormons were soon convinced that the coming storm, the mutterings of which they heard in the distance, would render necessary another remove, and it was reluctantly decided to make a final exodus to the great West—to seek a home among the rocks and mountains in the heart of the great plains, west of the Mississippi

It was now early spring, and every preparation was made that promised to expedite this migration. A crop was planted with a view to removal immediately after the harvest; and seeds gathered for future planting in other soils. The great Temple was yet unfinished, but a prediction of the dead Prophet had foretold its completion, and the utmost exertion was made to effect its verification before the coming fall; and this, under the energetic leadership of Brigham Young, was fully accomplished, even to the last ornament. But another and stronger motive impelled to the finishing of the Temple. The late apostasies from Mormonism had shown the necessity of some stronger tie than mere religious zeal to bind the saints together.

Since the Heads of the Church had left Kirtland Ohio, they had possessed no Temple, with "upper rooms" of the required sanctity and seclusion, in which to celebrate the dark and mysterious rites of the "*endowment*," and every effort was made to finish the Temple for the observnce of these ceremonies, before the final exodus.

CHAPTER IV.

ENDOWMENTS.

By early winter, the "upper rooms" of the Temple, set apart for the mysteries of the Endowments were finished, and the persons in the different quorums accounted worthy, were sent for, to receive the "fullness of that blessing."

None but those of approved integrity, and of undoubted orthodoxy, who have paid their "tithing," can travel this "Mormon road to Heaven," as it is called. This "tithing," in its fullest sense, implies a tenth of all one's property and income, and one-tenth of the time to be spent in labor on the public works, or money to hire a substitute.

There are many things about these initiations which I do not feel at liberty to disclose, as I have received them as religious mysteries, at a time I believed they were true— when I knew no other religion. Indeed, my whole knowledge of religion, until within a few months, has been associated with these ceremonies, as opening the only road to heaven. They have taught me to believe my chief duties as a woman, in this life, consisted in having a great many children; and my prospect for happiness and "exaltation" in the next world, to be greatly enhanced, by being one of many fruitful wives of one man; and that even my salvation depended upon the pleasure of the Prophet, or on that of a spiritual husband, and I had never heard a true account of that beautiful story of a free salvation through Christ, of which I am now anxious to know more.

Those things in the following ceremonies, which I have neglected to disclose, are such as, while they would only gratify the morbid curiosity of some readers, and offend the good taste of others, are forever sealed within my own breast by a solemn obligation of secrecy, and must so remain until I can see how their disclosure can contribute to the public good: a reason for silence on those points, which all conscientious people will, I think, duly appreciate; and yet I am free to acknowledge, that I have had some difficulty in settling with my conscience the exact point at which my disclosures should end; and the difficulty has not been lessened by the instruction and advice kindly given me by several distinguished ministers of the Gospel, that I ought to feel myself at liberty to make an unreserved disclosure of the whole matter. I have, however, thought it safest to give my conscience the benefit of the doubt, where there has been any question as to what I ought to do; and hence the following is all I have to disclose upon this part of Mormonism at present:

My husband, who was a member of the fourth "Quorum of Seventies," and myself, were called to the Temple to receive our "Endowments."

We ascended the first stair, at the head of which Brigham Young met us. He took me by both hands, and led me to a door at the left, and whispering in my ear a pass-word, left me to go in, and afterwards did the same with my husband, who was directed to enter a door at the right.

The room I had entered was nearly filled with women: no men were in this room; and no women were in the room at the right, where Wallace had entered. Here we were undressed and washed in a large tub of warm water, by a woman who is "ordained" to that office, and then anointed with "consecrated oil," by another woman, also "ordained" for that particular duty.

Two high priests were in an adjoining room, consecrating this oil, and handing the same into both rooms as it was needed, which was poured from a horn over our heads, and a lengthy prayer was then said over us. Every part of the body being in turn the special subject of this prayer, that we might become as little children, even as Adam and Eve were when placed in the Garden of Eden, and many other matters of a similar bearing, which I cannot now recollect, although I witnessed the ceremony many times afterwards.

We were then dressed with a white night-gown and skirt, and shoes of bleached drilling, and with our hair loose and dripping with consecrated oil, each received a new name, and were instructed that we were never to pronounce this name on earth but once: and that, when we came to enter within the "Veil," hereafter described.

The same process is gone through with in the men's washing-room, except that they wore nothing but shirt and drawers, and when all was ready in both rooms, each party was piloted by one of their own sex into a common room, fitted up to represent, and called the Garden of Eden. On this occasion there were about forty persons of both sexes. The room into which we were taken was very large, the walls were hung with white muslin, and was fitted up with boxes, containing a great variety of trees, designed to represent the Garden of Eden. All the trees were in life, and presented a very fine appearance, and we were marched round the room among them in slow and solemn procession.

It is required that each candidate be perfectly clean in dress and person, and a filthy thing is here regarded an abomination.

A circumstance happened at this initiation which will illustrate how readily propriety is sacrificed to their ideas of orthodoxy. It appears that a large Irishman, who, though a good Mormon, had not lost his native propensity to "bulls," had come into the wash-room for his "Endowments," either thoughtlessly or ignorantly, with shirt and drawers not over clean. He had, however, put on a clean "dickey," but this would not pass after his anointing, and being the last one washed, and the procession ready to move into the Garden of Eden, he threw on his clean dickey, and marched in and received, to use his own words, "Me Enduments, with nary an onclane rag abute me," having on, in fact, nothing but his dickey.

But to continue. The first thing we saw in the centre of the "Garden" was the "devil," dressed in black muslin, in conversation with "Eve," the latter being tempted to partake of the forbidden "*fruit*," to which she finally *yielded*. Eve then went to Adam, with an offer of the "fruit," who, after much resistance, "he likewise fell;" whereupon the "Lord" came into the "Garden," with a glittering white robe, bespangled with every kind of brilliants that could send back a flash of light, from whose face Adam, and Eve, and the "Tempter" fled away hiding among the trees; but finally the first two confessed their "crime," and the "Lord" pronounced a curse upon them and upon their race, copied from Genesis, and the devil crawled out of sight upon his face. The Lord then put aprons upon Adam and Eve, and upon us all, made of white linen, illustrated by means of green silk, to represent fig-leaves. We were then led out again, each to our respective rooms, and thus ended the "first glory."

I deem it proper, and a duty I owe my sex, *to hand down to infamy* the names of the women I have seen not only then, but since, represent "*Eve*" in the "Garden of Eden," the more so, because the persons whose names I am about to mention appear to have performed it willingly and with "*pleasure.*"

Eliza Snow, who was one of the wives of the Prophet Joseph, and now a wife of Brigham Young "for time," as it is termed, which means she will be Joseph's wife again in heaven, performed this part more than any other woman. Now at fifty years of age, she is even yet very beautiful, and she may be said to perform *infamously* well. I have also seen Mrs. Buel, mentioned heretofore, do the same. She is the woman whose husband lived at Lima, Ill., when Joseph seduced her from him. I have also seen Mrs. Knowlton in the same capacity She is the mother of my brother Howard's wife, Martha

Martha is a good and pure woman, and will not submit to the double wife *practice*, although she is forced to acknowledge, in common with all Mormon women, that it is right in *principle*, each week when she is questioned, as they all are, by the "teachers." When my brother Howard one time brought home another wife, Martha fought her out of the house, and he was forced to console himself with one. But when I left Salt Lake last year, he was courting *two sisters*, whom he intended to take home, thinking they would together be able to hold the balance of power in Martha's household. I presume she will in the end submit, as that is sure to be the fate of most Mormon women.

"Satan" is generally represented by Judge Phelps, for whom I have no words sufficiently hateful. Levi Hancock also often performed the same. And "Adam" by Orson Hyde and Parley P. Pratt. I have no doubt but these characters have been represented by others, but these are the persons who generally do it. The whole room was hung with white cloth, and behind one side of the "Garden of Eden" there was no wall but the curtain, with an arrangement of "peep-holes," where Mormons who have before taken their Endowments may witness it again. Brigham Young was in the practice of sending for various ones among the women to that room, where he examined them as to their pass-words and grips, and forced them to witness again the "temptation." I was often sent for afterwards at Salt Lake on such occasions.

The character of the "Lord" was always represented by "Brother Brigham," if he could possibly be there—if not he deputized some one; but Brigham never played the "Devil," or "Adam" on these occasions.

I think I need not inform my readers how heartily the women mentioned as "Eves" at these infernal rites were in secret despised and hated by the great mass of the Mormon *women:* especially Eliza Snow. Though forced to treat them well in society there, I take pleasure in letting them know the opinion that obtained among their own sex, and which would have found an expression of universal disgust from those of their associates, if it were not crushed into silence by the overshadowing power of the Prophet.

We were now undressed again, and each put on the "*garment,*" which is so arranged as to form a whole suit at once; and the "robe," which is a strip of white muslin, say three-fourths of a yard wide, and long enough to reach to the feet, gathered in the middle, and tied by a bow, to the left shoulder, and brought across the body, and the edges fastened together on the right side, with a belt around the waist of the same. Over this was put the apron we had received in the "first glory;" and the women wore what is called a veil made of a large piece of book muslin, reaching nearly to the floor, and gathered up at one corner to fit the head. The men wore a kind of turban, made of the same material, otherwise men and women were dressed alike. Thus disguised, it was quite impossible for us to recognize each other

We were next led into what is called the Terrestrial Glory where Brigham Young received us, and after a long effort to explain the disgusting scene in the "Garden," as necessary to our future exaltation, he gave each a pass-word and grip necessary, he said, to admit us into the "Celestial Glory;" where our (*i.e.* Mormon) "god" dwells. Some say this is Adam; and some that Joe Smith is to be our "god," and afterwards, Brigham Young intimated, that he (Brigham), was the medium of our salvation, and that Joseph was his "god." They do not all agree upon this point; but they do agree upon another thing, and that is that there are many gods, and they do not acknowledge the one Triune God of the Bible, but that every *man* will sometime be a "god;" and that women are to be the ornaments of his kingdom, and dependent upon him for resurrection and salvation; and that our salvation is dependent upon the recollection of these passwords; that when we get to Heaven, these pass-words will open the door to us if we can recollect them; but even then, Brigham's permission is necessary before the women can enter. The absolute truth of which theory I have never doubted until within a few months.

From this we pass, after being armed with the pass-words and grips, to another room, where is an altar, before which, if any wish, they are "sealed"—that is married. The name of this I do not recollect, but it is the third "Glory." We arrived finally, where a veil separated us from the "Celestial Glory." A man behind the veil examined us, as to the passwords and grips Brigham had given us, and to whom we gave our "new name," received at the first anointing. Holes through the veil enabled him to see us when we could not see him, and also, to cut with a small pair of scissors, certain marks, beside others, the Masonic square and compass, upon the right and left breast of our "garments," and upon the right knee, a gash, deep enough to make a scar, by which we were to be recognized as Mormons. This gash upon the right knee is now often omitted, because many of the women object to it. We were then admitted into the "Celestial Glory," where, seated upon a throne, in great state, was a person representing "our god." This was a gorgeously furnished room, illustrating by earthly signs a heavenly glory. This ends the first "anointing."

The time occupied in this initiation is about ten hours. Two days in the week are set apart for this purpose, and sometimes group after group succeeds each other, and the initiation is continued all day, and not unfrequently long after midnight.

Arrived at this point, the candidate is prepared to proceed to the "second anointing." This I have never received, and for various reasons, not the least of which was, that very few have received this as yet, and will not until the new temple at Salt Lake city is finished. I had also heard it hinted, that the "second anointing" was administered without clothing of any kind; and moreover, as it will be seen hereafter, I had reason to doubt somewhat, though not entirely to discard Mormonism.

It was a noticeable feature, that the outside show of some of the regalia and furniture connected with these "Endowments," were made to conform to those of Masonry; and Mormons are anxious to have the "Gentiles" associate all they know of these beastly "Endowments," with Masonry, or as being a modified form of it, made eligible to women, as a blind to cover the real objects of this "Institution;" and I have noticed by the public prints, since my arrival in the States, that this was the opinion entertained among those "Gentiles" supposed to be best informed upon this subject But this is but a mere blind; and the real object of these mystic forms is no way connected with, or borrowed from Masonry. Now, in conclusion of my disclosures upon this part of my subject, associated as it is with hateful memories of that peculiar kind, most distasteful to the recollection of a pure woman, I deem it my duty, in compensation for what I have felt compelled to omit of the foregoing, especially of that never to be forgotten scene in the " Garden of Eden," to state, that the "*moral*" and *object* of the whole is, socially, to unsex the sexes;   *   *   *   *   *   *   *

*   *   *   and when I call the attention of the reader to the fact, that while I have described the *dress* of all the parties to this inhuman display, and ocular demonstration, I have *not* mentioned the *dress* of "*Adam* and *Eve*," nor the nature of the "Fruit" by which each was in turn tempted; I think he will admit, that while I have said *enough*, I have also left more unsaid than the imagination, held with the loosest possible rein, would be likely to picture ; and I have only to add, that the reality *is too monstrous for human belief*.* And in view of the above *facts*, penned under emotions too deep for tears; facts, the truth of which, not only

* It would seem to be a misfortune, that a false estimate of propriety should be allowed to interpose a barrier against the exposure of these Mormon debaucheries. But as Mrs. S——, from conscientious scruples, and a doubt as to the good to be accomplished by a more full disclosure, preferred silence, we leave this subject as it is.

myself, but thousands of outraged women in Utah, would, if once freed from the fear of actual death, substantiate by their oaths; the truth of which I should attest by my blood, if within reach of Mormon assassination, may I not be permitted to appeal to the Christian mothers of the world, in behalf of those women, now shut up at Salt Lake, and in behalf of their daughters, just budding by flocks and whole broods into the new existence of womanhood, to be prostituted under such a system? Will this Christian land; will the mothers of Christendom not put forth an effort to save them? Above all, will not this great people, through its government, interpose the strong arm of the public law; backed, as it must be, by armed men, to open the doors to over fifteen thousand women imprisoned, for the crime of being women; and for the purpose, now not disguised, of raising up, in the shortest possible space of time, a race of swift, and *armed* witnesses, to defend and propagate this new faith—a faith resting upon no better foundation than the mere dictum of a pretended Prophet, whose dying words proved his disbelief in a God,* and which faith is to-day undisputed, by more than half a million followers?

I shall never forget the feelings with which I left the Endowment rooms, on this occasion. I went immediately to my mother, who, it appeared, had just made the same discovery; and was making an effort to reconcile such practices with her belief in Mormonism. She recounted to me with mournful

* The last words of Joseph Smith were, "My Lord, my God, have mercy upon us, *if there is a God.*"

earnestness, the miraculous cure of her deafness, and mentioned a circumstance which had occurred just before the Prophet's death, as follows: It appears the Prophet Joseph had one day broken the leg of my brother Howard, while wrestling They were always together, and were both fond of that sport, and on this occasion they had wrestled with uncommon enthusiasm, when, by an unlucky pass, Howard fell with a broken leg. It was immediately set by the "Prophet," with the assistance of one of his wives, with but little pain, as Howard alleged. It was then anointed with consecrated oil, and was well in so short a time, that it had at least the *appearance* of a miracle. Howard to this day claims he experienced no pain of any amount, and *believes yet* that Joseph healed it.

With all these astonishing evidences before us, how could we doubt Mormonism. These facts were *known* to us, and an account of many other similar cases were circulated, and believed among us. How could we accept the Prophet in one particular, and reject him in another. I often hear persons express astonishment that people can be deluded so easily. If they knew human nature better, they would recollect, that to believe what the best evidence at our command clearly teaches, affords the highest proof of good faith. In this case my mother was unaccustomed to reason, and I was less than seventeen years of age. The influence of the public opinion with which we were surrounded, was all one way. The facts were admitted, and we saw no escape. Mormonism was true; and if so, that was the end of argument.

But the momentary doubt was soon swallowed up by the all-absorbing topic which soon engrossed the Church. The threatening aspect of public sentiment among the Gentiles clearly indicated that it would not brook our delay for another year; and gloomily, our whole community began to close in upon the only apparent salvation for the Church and its Prophet.

CHAPTER V.

THE EXODUS.

The terrible recollection of our last farewell to Nauvoo, and what followed, is still before me, fresh as a thing of yesterday.

A people who could make such sacrifices, in vindication of religious belief, amidst suffering by cold, and hunger, and fatigue, are at least entitled to the credit of being honest when they say they *believed* it true. We had been directed at the close of the harvest to commence drying potatoes, and pumpkins, and beef, and to parch corn, and make strong durable clothing. This was continued until February, 1846. when all appeared to be ready for a general movement.

The Temple was finished and dedicated; and when the final song was sung, and the last benediction pronounced by the Prophet, amidst the tears and the lamentations of strong men, and trusting women, and the last maledictions uttered against the Gentiles, the Temple was abandoned, and the signal given for the commencement of that "exodus," which even to this day, lingers upon my recollection, as among the most wonderful and sublime movements of which the world has any knowledge.

The noise of preparation for the westward march was mingled with the sound of the hammer, which gave the finishing stroke to the Temple, and the last "amen" of the dedication, with the command of "forward," from the captain of "Tens." The movable ornaments of the temple, which had been put up perhaps but an hour since, were taken down, and packed for future use, in ornamenting another Temple in the wilderness. Even the great bell was not forgotten, and is now at Salt Lake, ready to be swung when the Temple there is ready to receive it.

This bell was stolen at St. Louis, by a company of Mormons, under the command of Capt. Mott, and taken to Nauvoo. Whether it was ever known by the owners at St. Louis who took the bell or not, I am not informed; but I was present on one occasion, when this Mr. Mott was telling one of the Heads of the Church about it. Mott pointed to a span of horses, and said, "that is the team that drew the bell we '*selected*,' in St. Louis." It was well known among the Mormons that it was stolen.

The company of ten wagons to which myself and husband were attached, left the city soon after the Prophet and "the Twelve." Each ten wagons were in charge of a captain. My brother William was in the family of Brigham Young, and hence was in the advance; but my mother and the rest of the family were not then ready, and were left to join some other company. I recollect she told me afterwards, she sold her house and lot, worth about $800, for four pounds of pork; of course the Mormon title to the land was not considered good

Our company crossed the Mississippi on the ice the first day, and camped at night at Sugar Creek, in Iowa. This was about the middle of February, 1846. Then commenced a scene of suffering and hardship, among the women and children, which I should now think beyond human endurance.

All night, the wagons came trundling into camp, with half frozen children, crying for food, and the same the next day—and so on the whole line of march.

The weather was not cold for the time of year, but the open sky and bare ground for women and children, in February, is a thing to be endured only when human nature is put to the rack of necessity. Many a mother hastily buried her dead child by the wayside during that winter march, half regretting she could not lie down with it herself, and be at peace.

Our company remained for several days at this encampment, and as company after company passed, I began fully to realize my situation. I was now separated from the rest of my family, for the first time; and left alone with my husband, and I was not certain if my mother had, or would start for the wilderness.

We had a cloth tent, which, if we had been well provided with sufficient clothing, would have made us comfortable.

One night, after we had been here for several days, a heavy snow fell; and we awoke in the morning, to find the snow had broken the tent pole, and ourselves half buried under it. While Wallace was yet engaged in repairing the damage and had removed in part the snow, and put up a new pole, my brother William, of whose whereabouts I knew nothing until now, looked into the tent, and said, "Nettie, you are cold."

I was cold and chilled. The little clothing we had was wet with snow. William had hardly spoken to me until now, since my marriage; and looking round, sadly, he said at length, " Nettie, this is not much like our father's home we have left in Pennsylvania. If we die here, we shall die the death of martyrs." He believed Mormonism was true, and he afterwards *died* a martyr, while I *lived* one.

Our company was that day reorganized, and we moved on ward. For a few days, I rode in the wagon of the Prophet by his invitation, and by an arrangement made by Wallace and William, as I could ride more comfortable thus. Brother Brigham, upon hearing me ask William if he had left my mother and the children at Nauvoo, to be murdered by the mob, directed him to go back for them. He accordingly returned to Nauvoo. When we had arrived at Sheridan River, William left us, and I rode again with my husband.

Thus the march was continued, in companies of ten wagons each; and as we were lightly loaded, the stores of the ten families were placed in our wagon; but it made no great addition to our load, for the provisions already began to fail; and after about a month, we were put upon short allowance. The men killed what game they could upon the way, which was but little at that time of the year. It was a weary journey; crossing rivers, and bleak prairies, through Iowa in a westerly direction from Nauvoo. Sometimes short of wood and water, and always short of food. The full history of that sad journey of five months will never be written. Pioneers had been sent on to look out the way, and we followed in the common trail; a long drawn, straggling, struggling train, seeking a home in the wilderness—no one knew where, or when it would be found. This was the beginning of that half nomadic life of suffering and privation, which has at length given character to the Mormons, and rendered them one in purpose, and a strong, isolated people; self-dependent, and quick in resource; asking nothing from, and granting nothing to the rest of mankind, and rough-schooled them to an independence, as surprising as it is perfect.

It was the policy of the Heads of the Church to have the column move on as fast as possible until spring, then to halt at planting time, and put in crops for the coming masses, whose provisions were exhausted. These were called "stakes."

We arrived at Garden Grove, the first "stake" west of Nauvoo, on the first of June, 1846, after having been on half allowance for a long time. Those in front moved on to the "stake" at Council Bluffs. We were directed to make a farm and plant, while part of the men were sent south, into Mercer county, Missouri, to buy provisions. Garden Grove is on Grand River, near the north line of Missouri. After we were established, and David Fulmer was chosen President of the "stake," the Prophet moved on to Council Bluffs.

My husband was chosen among others to go into Mercer county to buy provisions, and left me with his married sister, Mary Allred. My allowance of provisions at this time was very small—a piece of bread and some milk, less than half as much as I needed, was the small share allowed me, *with as many wild onions as I wished.*

We watched the return of the men with great anxiety,

while our stock of provisions grew less and less, till at length our overwrought imaginations pictured our prospects as desperate. To render our condition more gloomy still, it occurred to us that the men had gone into the locality from whence the Mormons had been driven by the Missourians a few years previous, and if they were recognized as Mormons, they would undoubtedly be imprisoned, or perhaps murdered.

After two long weeks, just as we were giving up to despair, the men returned with the grain and provisions they had earned by laboring among the farmers, and some *meat of hogs they had not earned, but taken,* from the neighborhood of the settlements where these hogs were turned loose, and had become partly wild. The Mormons considered it right to take anything they could from the Gentiles, as they held themselves to be the only people of God.

I have no recollection of having enjoyed so great a feast as on the return of the men with the provisions. I ate all I wished the first time for over four months. We lived a short time in our tent, which we had pitched in a small wood near the river. Our bed consisted of two quilts and one blanket, and we had a few tin dishes, which made up our stock of "furniture;" and yet, strange as it may seem, when not actually starving, we were very happy and contented, for up to this time my husband had been very kind and attentive, and I had so much confidence in him that I felt no fear he would take another wife. I was happy, too, in the expectation of soon being a mother, and my husband engaged his niece, Jane Henderson, to stay with me. Our neighbors had assisted Wallace in building us a nice log cabin, about one mile from the other houses at the "stake," on the bank of the river. Into this we soon moved. I have no hesitation in saying this was the most beautiful and romantic spot of earth I have ever seen before or since. Our cabin was surrounded by a heavy growth of timber, and each tree was entwined by the climbing rose or entangled masses of the wild grape: and the whole scene was a blooming labyrinth of wild flowers and graceful foliage, enlivened by the twitter of birds, the noisy whiz of the pinnated grouse, and every variety of game, bounding from the thickets or along the graceful banks of Grand River. The wild turkey and deer were abundant, and the only disagreeable neighbors we found here were the wolves and the owls. The first often frightened us at night by their threatening howls, while the latter rendered the night hideous and lonely beyond measure by their unearthly hooting from two oak trees that overhung our little cabin. Indeed, these two oaks appeared to be the centre of a vast circle of owl society, for from far up and down and over the river, and from the far-off depths of the heavy timber, and over the little prairie near by, came back a quick response from owl throats, in every variety of pitch and measure, from the hoarse bass to the tremulous treble, until the flower-enamelled wilds about us fairly trembled with the crash of answering hoots and gibberings; and then as suddenly all was still again, and when half lost in slumber, perhaps, again to be startled by a repetition of the dismal concert. I have since then felt the loneliness of the wild prairie and the great deserts of the West, as well as the unmitigated solitude of the Rocky Mountains; but I am of the opinion that perfect solitude cannot exist where owls do not hoot at night.

But my dream of personal security was soon to be disturbed in a way I little suspected. I had noticed my husband had treated his niece Jane uncommonly well, and one day I saw him with her in the door-yard in close conversation. He took her hand, whereupon she ran into the house, and coming to me, threw her arms round my neck, and said,

"My dear aunt, do not be offended at me, I could not help it."

"Help what?" said I.

"Did you not see uncle Wallace?"

I replied that I did, but that he was only in fun.

"Oh! no he was not. He says he wants me for a wife, and I will not remain here for another day."

My readers will understand that it is not an uncommon thing for Mormons to marry their nieces, and even their half sisters. For instance, it often happens that when a man has several wives, their children, having a common father, will intermarry.

Wallace soon came in and sat down by me, with a thoughtful and troubled air, and after an interval of silence he kissed me. I repulsed him for the first time in my life, saying he was false to me, that he loved me no longer, to which he replied,

"Nettie, I am satisfied with you, I want no other—and if I was not attached to you, I should know what to do. But that is what embarrasses me. If I hated you, I should take another wife at once, as I must do in the end. living as I do among this gang of Mormons. I am enlisted, and it is more than my life is worth to attempt to leave them. Indeed I could not do so now and live, as I know too much about them—more than you imagine. But here is the trouble, I can no longer endure being the butt of ridicule among the men for having but one wife. You may as well understand the whole case at once. I have concluded, as between the two evils, to bring home another wife. I do not care who. If you have a choice, select one, and I will always recognize you as the first and principal wife. I must stop the mouths of the croakers, who would sacrifice everything to their spiritual wifeism."

Who can imagine the horror with which I listened to what, at the time, seemed the end of human hope with me. I had married Wallace to avoid this most dreaded evil, and I was now to be sacrificed.

Where was my mother now? or a brother? I was alone. To whom should I fly? At last I appealed to him—to my husband—and threw myself upon his generosity. I pointed him to the suffering and privation of the last five months, the cold and hunger I had endured, my age, and to the fact, that though but a child myself, I was soon to be a mother, and prayed that he would, at least for the sake of the one unborn, delay the terrible step for a while. The big tears rolled down his sun-browned face, and he trembled with emotion. I knew a terrible struggle tore his breast, and I gathered calmness to abide the issue. It was a fierce contest, and I felt my fate hung upon the result. I awaited the end, and it came but too soon.

He grew calm at length, and after a long period of troubled thought, rose and said, as he stepped to the door,

"Jane, you may stay with your aunt to-day: to-morrow is our wedding. I have your father's consent, and it is all arranged. The sooner it is over now the better."

I saw he was about to leave the cabin. With one wild bound I sprang upon him, with the intention of holding him by force, but he met me with a look that told me all was over; and quick as the lightning's flash, I spurned him with all a woman's hate, and shaking him off, dashed with what speed my condition would allow in the direction of the river, with what intention I knew not, but I have still a recollection of throwing, as I ran, my whole soul into one wild yell of horror, as a last adieu to home, for in the excitement of the moment I had no wish to return to it. My next recollection of this unnatural scene was upon waking up the next morning, as if from some horrible dream. I found Wallace and Jane by my bed, apparently greatly alarmed at my condition.

Wallace showed the greatest sincerity in his expressions of sorrow, and plead strongly for pardon—promised never to bring, or again attempt to bring, home another wife.

I cannot now tell whether his unfeigned distress gave me most pleasure or pain. I was weak and exhausted, and wished not to live. It occurred to me that if my child should be unfortunately a girl, it would be better for me to die now than to be the instrument of giving life to another victim to the cruel fate which awaits all Mormon women.

Wallace reproached himself as being my murderer, and in the excess of his anguish cursed Mormonism as having led him into every possible crime—that it had lured him on to a fate which he could not bear, and from which he dare not fly. He really moved my pity. I asked him if he would take the measures to find my mother. He said if I would allow him, my wishes should be his law. He made no conditions, but his surrender was perfect, and volunteered to go to his " bride's " father and break off his engagement at once and entirely. Hope, which had so lately seemed impossible to me, once more lighted my future. I required no pledge but *sincerity*, and waited with alternate hope and fear while he was gone to undo his marriage engagement.

When he returned, he said it was all arranged with " her " father, and the " Heads " of the Church; and that now I should have no more trouble with him upon the subject of spiritual wifeism, and I accepted in good faith his promise.

THE EXODUS.

CHAPTER VI.

A NIGHT WITH THE DEAD AND THE WOLVES.

How quick the lights and shades of life succeed each other. The day which succeeded our reconciliation was, I think, the happiest of my life.

I had a long talk on the bank of the river, with Wallace, alone, in which he renewed his promise to take no wife but me. And to put me more fully at my ease, he explained by reference to our "Endowment vows," described in the fourth chapter of this narrative, why he had felt it his duty to take, in obedience to the commands of the Church authorities, another wife as he had; and in the end, offered up a fervent prayer for my recovery, and that I might yet be satisfied with the plan of salvation through the "Prophet."

It is strange, that at this time I did not observe that in his prayer he still recognized the double wife doctrine; but I was too happy to escape the evil upon any conditions, to look closely into the argument of the case. All I asked was my own husband, and this granted, I was willing to admit in theory the whole of Mormonism.

It may be interesting to my readers to know that on this occasion, when we had just escaped having *another* wife in the house, I was barefooted, and had not a sign of a bonnet, and for want of a more suitable dress, I was sitting on the bank of the river, with my husband, in my night-gown, and he was dressed in buckskin hunting shirt, and pants and moccasins. And yet, this was the happiest day of my life. As we were to make a holiday of it, after dinner we all went to the river, fishing. While there, Wallace saw a deer on the other side, and leaving me with Jane, he got his gun from the cabin, and shot it. The deer, with the fine lot of fish we had caught, marked the day, one of good cheer and plenty. In a few days more, I was the mother of a fine boy. Wallace was kind to me, and was much pleased with his child.

Several weeks passed thus calmly, in which I was uncommonly happy, but I began to observe something wrong with Wallace. He would walk the house in an unsocial manner, or sit as if brooding over some great sorrow, for hours.

I said to him one day, in order to draw him out, that if he would promise to give me the child, and allow me to go untrammelled, he should have as many wives as he pleased; and as he made no reply, I gave the baby to Jane, and asked him to go with me for a walk, to which he replied, "I cannot, I am perfectly wretched, knowing as I do, that I can never be contented with you, or make you so, while resting under my present obligations to the Mormons. We have been deceived. You do not know it, but I do. I have taken solemn oaths to support the doctrines of Mormonism; I have been over persuaded, and led on, till I dare neither retreat nor go forward."

And he wept like a child. I thought then, and think still,

that Wallace Henderson was honest in the beginning, and that whatever were his faults afterwards, they were chargeable to the cruel impositions of a false church. This I say, in this connection, because hereafter I may have no heart to say anything in his favor. I said to him, "you are mad." He was looking pale, and haggard, and said,

"I was about to tell you all, but here comes *that girl's father.*"

I saw Mr. Hawkins coming to the door; I took the baby and went to the bank of the river, as I did not wish to hear what he had to say.

This Mr. Hawkins was the father of another girl the Mormons wished my husband to marry, and I presumed his errand was to induce Wallace to be sealed to her at once. He remained a long while, and when he went away I saw Wallace take a seat on the door-sill, thoughtfully and much troubled. I sat upon the bank of the river until it was quite dark, and I did not notice at the time that my baby was not well wrapped up. Finally, Wallace started from his reverie, came to me, and kindly asked why I did not come in, and why I had left my own house. I saw by his manner that Mr Hawkins had not succeeded in his aims and I was happy again.

We went to the house, and Wallace appeared in better spirits than usual. Jane had built a fire, and the supper was soon ready, and the blanket hung up at the door, for we had no other as yet. I told Jane, as I was now nearly well, she could go home in the morning, and I would try to get on without her. I wished to remove every possible hinderance to our good understanding.

The child cried most of the night, but appeared better in the morning, and Jane went home.

We lived very pleasantly for a few days. Wallace was contented and happy, but other troubles were in store for us—for me. Our child, which had not been well since that night on the bank of the river, and which took cold there, was taken sick, and although we prayed, and used all the means prescribed by the "Church," which are anointing with "consecrated oil," and prayers—it died. This was a terrible blow to me. I *felt* the child had gained by the change, but I was not reconciled. I had clung to it as something that I could hold to my heart, in undivided love, in place of my husband; for I began to understand that sooner or later, I must give him up.

My aunt and other women came the next day and made my dead baby a shroud, and laid it out upon a chest. It had no coffin yet. When all this was done, each took leave, and left us alone. There was a great deal of sickness at the time, and most of them had some one at home requiring attention. I was too much absorbed in my grief to notice how things went. My child was not to be buried until the next day. Though dead, it was mine yet another night, and I clung to it.

My aunt would have remained with us, but her daughter Phebe, even then, lay at the point of death. And Wallace told her he did not wish to be unreasonable, and he should not leave me; so she went, apparently having done for us all *necessity* demanded at her hands. Although, before dark, it seemed to me awful, that we were to pass the night alone, young as we both were, with our first child dead in the house; yet long before morning came, I would have given all my interest in this world for even a faithful dog as a companion.

It will be recollected from what I have said in the chapter preceding this, that our cabin was over a mile from the main "stake," and of course was that distance from any other human dwelling. It was also near one of the thickest coverts for every kind of wild game; and when it is understood that most of the country in that part of Iowa is open prairie, the intelligent woodsman will see at once, that the vicinity of our dwelling must be a resort for whatever beast of prey migh* chance to be an inhabitant of the country. It was a beautiful night. The moon shone clear and calmly down among the newly budding trees, and opening flowers of spring. Not a breath of air stirred the half-grown leaves of the forest, or rippled upon the bosom of the river. But teeming nature, once again wakened from the long sleep of winter, was vocal and noisy with its new life. The owls were never so clamorous or dismal as on that night, and the wolves made the distant welkin ring with their angry howls; and a thousand wild voices were awake that night, and blending with the solemn moaning of the river currents, until then always pleasant to me, to crush my sinking heart. Oh! who knows how much the heart can bear and not break? I had not spoken, or looked away from my dead child, since my aunt had left. It lay upon the chest under the open window, and the pale moon shone in upon its little face, now cold and wan. We had no door, and no glass in our one window, as there was none in the country, and neither could be except by a blanket. Wallace had neglected from day to day to make a loor as the weather did not render one absolutely necessary.

Somewhat along in the evening, William Hickman, one of the "Danites," came to the cabin door, and asked for Wallace, and seeing there was some trouble with us, came in and inquired what was the matter. He had not heard that our child was dead. Hickman said: "This will make it bad for us; but what a splendid night for our expedition, and things are in such a shape we cannot put it off?"

Wallace pointed to our dead baby, under the open window, and made no reply.

"Yes," said Hickman, "I see that is serious. But we must go." Then turning to me, said, "Nettie, you are a 'brave,' are you not? You will not be afraid, will you? If you exercise a little judgment, you will see that circumstances alter cases, and there are lives dependent upon this mission."

Wallace told him he could not go; he said that would be too cruel. Hickman then turned to me, and said, "You must not talk of bravery again."

I had listened to this conversation unmoved till now. It seemed as if nothing else could have drawn me from my one crushing sorrow. I called the wretch's attention to the howling of the wolves, to my dead baby, to my feeble health, having scarcely recovered from the sickness of childbirth and lastly to my own age, being but little over seventeen. I think I called him some hard names; and asked him, if when he said "some lives depended upon the mission," he did not mean, that the object of the "mission" was to *take the lives of some 'Gentiles.'*" I appealed to them both as *men*, for protection as a woman; an appeal which I have since heard, is never disregarded by Christian men.

Hickman, although somewhat embarrassed, said they would fasten the door, as well as they could, but Wallace *must go*, and it was time they were there already; and, taking him by the arm, hurried him away, *and they left me alone with my dead child.* Great God, what a night!!"

If the peril had been any the less real, I think I must have gone mad. As it was, long after the footsteps of the base men who had just left me had died away; and after I had sat cowering half dead with fear, by the side of my child, for a length of time which I have no means of measuring, I was startled into a full sense of my real situation, by an increased howling among the wolves; and which appeared to close in upon the cabin from every direction. I was certain, and could not be mistaken. They increased in number, and every moment came nearer. Oh! then the howling was terrific.

For a few moments I was paralyzed. The clear, calm moonlight fairly recoiled and trembled as howl answered howl, first on this, then on that side of the river, and up and down, and everywhere. Strange as it may seem, my chief and first fear was, that my *dead child* would be *torn* by them, and *devoured.* Then I thought nothing of my own personal danger. But I soon bethought me what to do, and action was relief

My pent up soul put forth its strength, to save my dead child. My first movement was to put out the lights, probably the very worst thing I could have done. Next, I fastened down the blanket as well as might be, at the door and window. I had nothing with which to barricade them.

I saw very soon my folly in having blown out the lights; for, within ten minutes, the wolves were howling in the open moonlight, near the cabin, and I could hear and see them snarl and snap each other; and quickly they were nearer and nearer the door, and *disputed with each other for a place at the entrance.*

Oh, horror! That was a terrible moment. I screamed, and beat against the blanket, to frighten them back. This would succeed for a moment, but other wolves would return to be driven off in the same way.

Time sharpened my wits, and I actually grew self-possessed as my chances of escape lessened. A minute then was equal to an hour of ordinary thinking. I knew where to lay my hand upon a board. It was near my child. I screamed, and drove them off the door-step; and then, before they could return, I laid the corpse upon the board, and lifted it over head upon the joist, which I could just reach from the chest; and *that* was out of danger. But the wolves were back again, mad and more furious than before; I drove them with a will back once again, and then it took me but a moment to draw myself up to, and on the joist, and I was safe, at least I believed so, with my child, and the event proved it true.

There was no chamber floor nor ladder, and how I got up I could not tell afterwards. I watched my child, the long,

long night, sitting upon the joist, and when the wolves threatened most to come in, I yelled them away, or at least I imagined I frightened them. One thing is certain, none passed the blanket, although more than once I saw it move in the moonlight, and could hear their sharp, quick snuffing near it, as if smelling the way in.

It was a long, dreary night; but strange as it may seem, I suffered comparatively nothing from fear, until I found myself apparently beyond the reach of the wolves; then my mind took in the whole position of affairs, in one terrible review; and even magnified the danger still pending—I imagined, at first, it would be possible for them to gain the roof, and reach us in that way, as they well might have done, if the roof had been as frail as coverings to temporary buildings of this kind sometimes are.

A few hours before daylight, they were more furious than ever, and I expected were about to choose some new point of attack. But they did not.

The early morning light came at length, by degrees, and although it was a long time before it revealed the difference between that and the moonlight, inside the cabin, yet I knew it had come; because the wolves dropped off, one by one, and finally all was silent outside; and the calmest and sweetest spring morning I had ever seen, ushered in by the song of birds, came to my relief. Oh! it *was* a relief, and I was not mad; and my dear child was by my side. And then the tears, for the first time, during that long night, came to my eyes—to bless me, and I wept, in sad and calm reconciliation, to the death of my child. A resignation I had not felt before

I have since recognized in this, a Hand of which Mormonism had given me no account, and does not acknowledge, at least not in the beautiful sense of the Bible.

After I was fully reassured, and had dried up my grateful tears, I began to cast about for the best method of getting down; and just at that point Wallace came home. He looked haggard and guilty. His first words were those of apology, and he begged earnestly for pardon. He assisted me down. I had no words for him then; I needed rest, and singularly enough, I soon found a kindly relief, in a calm sleep, from which I awoke refreshed, but little before noon.

CHAPTER VII.

SEEKING MY MOTHER.

THE men came to bury my child. I was too weak to go to the grave, so I took leave of it at home, with a calmness which would have been impossible for me the day before; regretting most that I was not to be buried with it.

When it was all over, I had a long talk with Wallace. I told him what my convictions were; that I thought him a villain, that I felt myself not only the victim of his sensuality and selfishness, but that he was governed neither by the laws of God nor man, and was wanting in honor; and when he attempted to justify himself, I gave him to understand, that it was of no particular consequence what he said, for his conduct was beyond the limits of endurance.

This conversation gave me great pain, because I was even then greatly attached to him; and had not entirely abandoned the hope, that his faults were more chargeable to the influence of Mormonism, than to his own bad heart. He protested, that if I could once understand his position, I would not condemn him

He proposed we should move to the stake, near the other dwellings, to which I consented gladly, as I should there be not only safe from the wolves, but should be most likely to get some word from my mother; to find whom now became the absorbing object of my life, as I believed she would not only take me home, and protect me against Wallace, or at least against his taking another wife, but that she would help me expose, as I knew she could not justify, some new enormities of Mormonism, which I had discovered since we had parted. It will be recollected, that I was not yet past the age when the child goes to the mother for the cure of all its woes. We therefore moved up to the "stake" immediately.

I asked Wallace, a few days after, where he went the night he left me with the wolves, and went with William Hickman.

Wallace finally told me the whole story, as follows: saying he would trust my honor not to expose him.

I have to state in the first place, that there were two roads leading through Iowa to Council Bluffs. One passing by our "stake," Garden Grove, and another parallel to it, six miles to the north. The one on which we lived, and had travelled when we came out, was called the Southern road; and was mostly travelled the previous year. But that spring, most of the travel, whether by Mormons, or other emigrants, was on the Northern road.

Wallace said, "the President of the 'stake,' David Fulman, had received the information, that a Gentile family by the name of Martin, were about to pass Garden Grove, on the Northern road, and that they had a great many cattle and horses. This Martin was a man of wealth, who was on his way across the plains, probably going to California.

"The 'Danites were therefore directed by Fulman to intercept him, and take Martin's stock and tie them in the timber, where he would be unable to find them; and when he had passed on, they could be brought out, which *we* accordingly did—Hickman and myself, with some others. I have one yoke of oxen, and David Fulmer has one, and the rest was distributed among the men as they had need. Isaac Allred has also one yoke of the oxen."

I asked Wallace if he thought that right. He said, "the Mormons believed, and it was undoubtedly true, that those who were not for us, were against us." In reply to another question, he said, "If the emigrants, when they lose their cattle, go on, and do not run against their fate by making us too much trouble, in looking for, or in the attempt to recover them, they are not harmed; *otherwise they are put out of the way.*"

We had been at the "stake" but a few days, when I had the good fortune to hear from my mother.

It will be recollected that my brother William had been sent back by Brigham Young to Nauvoo for her, the previous spring, and now we heard by a nephew of Isaac Allred, who had travelled with them part way, that they would probably pass Garden Grove the next day; though they would come no nearer than six miles of us, as they were to continue on the Northern road. My mother and William were not aware that we were at Garden Grove. I was anxious, and determined to go to the road the next morning, to meet them. Wallace asked me if he consented to take me there, if I would promise to come back. I told him I would not. We then had a long discussion, in which he told me, he did not wish me to leave him; that he dare not leave the Mormons, or refuse to sustain all their requirements; and that he had sworn to do so. He said it would cost him his life to refuse. That as soon as he could, he would take me away from them. He was willing I should see my mother, but that I must not leave him; and that by the next day, Isaac Allred would be back from Missouri. Allred had intended to bring back a horse, and if he did, we could get it, and overtake my mother, as they would travel but slowly. "Yes," said I, "a stolen horse, which I will not ride, if I never see my mother again." Wallace admitted it would probably be a stolen one. It happened there was not a single horse at the "stake," at the time.

The weather was very beautiful the next morning, and I persuaded Wallace to start with me on foot to the upper road. I represented to him that I had often walked twice that distance, when coming from Nauvoo, when I had nothing to encourage me on, and now, the wish to see my mother, was a sufficient inducement for any effort.

We therefore set out early, in fine spirits, following the river, and wading across it at the first shallow place. This was not unpleasant, as the weather was warm. We got along very well for about four miles, when I became so exhausted, that I could go no further; and we rested for half an hour, with our eyes anxiously fixed in the direction of the road, grudging the delay of a moment; and then went on with more ease, until we came at last to the well worn track. We eagerly looked each way. The eye could command a view of several miles forward and back on the road, over the open prairie. But no team in sight. None—no moving thing. Hope sank within me. We sat down and waited a long time, and still there was nothing to be seen on the trail to the east, from which they must come, if not already gone by. This was a great disappointment. I urged Wallace to remain all night, as they might possibly pass before morning.

He said we could not, as there was danger from the Indians; and besides, we were not prepared to camp out. It was hard to give up the cherished hope of finding my mother, and of going on with her. I was determined, in case we met with the success we expected, not to return to Garden Grove, as I had nothing to call me back, where there was every thing to make it unpleasant to me. Both the girls Wallace had thought of marrying lived there yet.

Wallace at length took hold of me, and pulled me up, and we started back—on my part most reluctantly. It was like going to the grave.

We had gone but a short distance when the sky became overcast, and threatened rain. But we hurried on. We were anxious, if possible, to reach the ford we had crossed in the morning, before it was too dark to find and pass it; but what with the approaching night, and gathering clouds, it was soon dark, and then the rain set in, and we had no light but the successive flashing of the lightning.

We had evidently delayed too long at the road. I became perfectly exhausted, and I sat down in the dark, the rain falling in torrents, unable to move another step. We were now in a grove of timber, and had been guided by the tops of the trees and the noise of the river, in keeping a direct course down the stream, as we dare not venture too near the bank.

Wallace said, it would not do to sit down, and he took me upon his back and carried me a long way, until he made a misstep, and fell, and we both found ourselves rolling upon the ground together, though unhurt. There we sat until the rain ceased, and we were then enabled to make our way very well by starlight, with none the less ease for being well rested.

We soon found we were going astray, as we were out of hearing of the river, but imagined we could hear it off to the right, and by going in that direction we found it. When we arrived at the bank, we ascertained there was no crossing-place at that point. The banks were high, and the water roared wildly, and was rendered still more terrific by the mystery of the darkness. We now bethought us, that perhaps the rain had raised the stream somewhat, which, if so, would render it unsafe to cross. Wallace directed me to sit down and rest, while he examined the bank below. He was gone some time, and returned without finding a place where he could get to the water. He then went up the stream some distance, and had the good luck to find a low bank, and a ford near by. He waded over the river, and then back, to satisfy himself there was no deep holes; then called to me to come up, as he dare not leave the place, for fear of losing it in the dark. On account of the distance, and the roaring of the water, I could not understand what he said, but went to him, fearing he had met with some accident.

I was so lame, and overworked by the long walk of the

day, and stiffened by the rain, that I was under the necessity of resting several times before I arrived where he was, but felt myself greatly encouraged to hear of the discovery he had made.

He wished to carry me over, but I dare not risk him in the dark; and although he insisted upon doing so, I persuaded him it was safer to walk together, and take hold of hands, and thus we should be a mutual help, which would leave him his whole strength to stem the current, which had grown very strong since the rain. Thus we started into the water, holding each other by the hand. The water, most of the time, came just up to my arms, and it was with the greatest difficulty I kept my footing. But I held to my husband, who advanced carefully and surely, and we gained the other side in safety, greatly to my satisfaction. I then sat down upon the bank, while Wallace went to examine the locality. He came back soon, saying, as near as he could make out in the dark, we were not far from the old cabin, from which we had moved a few days since. This was the place where I had spent the night alone with my dead baby and the wolves. Wallace said we would go there and pass the night. He had by chance some matches with him, with which, if they were not ruined by the water, he could light a fire. Luckily his opinion proved to be correct, and we soon found the cabin, where we arrived glad enough. I was nearly as well pleased for the time as if I had found my mother.

Wallace soon had a cheerful fire, and although we found no bed or food there, we were soon warm, grateful, and happy. He spread his coat upon the floor for me, and I laid down, and dropped asleep. But he allowed me to lie but a short time, as he said I had better get up and dry my clothes, as I was liable to take cold.

Wallace had been patient, and kind with me, during our tiresome adventure, which I appreciated very highly. When I attempted to get up, I found it impossible at first to move my stiffened limbs. But by rubbing, and getting warm by the fire, I was better after a little. Long before we got fully dry, we were both asleep, and did not wake till the sun shone into the door the next morning. I found it impossible to walk, and Wallace, after putting on a fire, went to the "stake," and brought some breakfast, and a tin cup of warm tea, which greatly revived me. He also brought his oxen and sled to take me home; and just as we were about to start, Isaac Allred came by, on his way down the river, for a hunt, and offered to take me home on his horse. Wallace insisted I should ride—placed me on his horse, and Allred took me home, where I arrived, well satisfied with finding myself once more safely housed, and contrary to my expectations, I experienced no great inconvenience from our adventure. I was in a few days quite well again.

CHAPTER VIII.

AMONG THE GENTILES.

My husband, a few days after this, said to me, "A great many Mormons have gone to Missouri, for the purpose of earning provisions, and the like, to bring into the 'stake,' and I think of joining them in the enterprise. What do you say to going with me, and we shall both get some kind of employment until winter?"

I gladly embraced the opportunity to get away from Mormonism. I told Wallace I would like to go, but that I would never return. He said if I should hint at such an intention before I left, we should not be allowed to go. That our lives would be worth but little. "I should not dare to make such a remark unless I was ready to die; and when in Missouri, it will be no safer to attempt an escape then than now, as the part of the State where we are going to is full of Mormons, though they are not known as such. And if we should attempt to throw ourselves upon the protection of the Gentiles we should be likely to meet the fate of Governor Boggs, who was shot among his friends in St. Louis."

Wallace said further, with much feeling and apparent candor, "Others may perhaps escape from this gang, but I can not. I have gone too far. I have taken other obligations than those of the 'Endowments.' My life, and above all, my peace of mind, is of but little value at the best. You think you suffered too much the night I left you alone with the wolves, but I would gladly have exchanged places with you; for your sufferings ended with the appearance of daylight, while mine continue, as an evil conscience always will, to haunt me still. I try to believe, and I generally do, that the Prophet can pardon all our crimes, as he tells us he can, and will, when committed in the service of the Church. And yet, I recollect, when very young, of being taught that evil should never be done, that good may come of it. And although I know the 'mission' of our Prophet is later than that of Jesus Christ, yet I cannot at all times feel justified in crime, though it be in defence of the Church, or the preservation of the saints. I sometimes wish that murder, and spiritual wife-ism, were not necessary to the success of Mormonism. We will go to Missouri; but, Nettie, you must recollect, it will be useless to attempt an escape, or expect me to, or to hold any conversation upon religious subjects with the Gentiles."

I was greatly disheartened at what he had said, because the idea, that I could not, if I chose, abandon Mormonism, was entirely new to me. We set out within a few days, and when in Mercer county, Wallace found a place to work, at good wages, with a large and able farmer. I took a district school near by, and boarded where Wallace worked. After so many hardships, I was really happy and contented during our stay here. Wallace was very kind, but would not allow me to be intimate with any one, but wished me, when out of school, to remain in my room until he returned from his work, and then we would take walks alone in the woods and fields. The country was sparsely settled, and the inhabitants were large and very wealthy farmers, mostly from the South, and were very kind to us. The name of Wallace's employer was Samuel Porter. Mrs. Porter treated me very kindly, as did her sister Mrs. Duncan, and her daughter Mary Jane. The latter was married during the summer to Saul Litton. They all made me a great many presents, and should this book come to their notice, they will undoubtedly recollect me; and I take pleasure in making this grateful mention of them, as their attention to me was of that kindly and delicate nature, rarely met with, except among truly well-bred people. Their kindness was the more appreciated, as I had been accustomed only to the rude habits of our people.

These ladies offered me a home if I did not wish to return to the Mormons, which I would gladly have accepted if I had deemed it safe for them and myself to have done so.

I had had some conversation with them on the subject of religion, notwithstanding my husband wished to prevent it, and though it was not generally known we were Mormons, they knew our history. Oh! how often afterwards, when camping out upon the bleak prairie, or suffering from hunger, or cold, or the imprisonment of Salt Lake, have I thought of the agreeable summer spent in their society, and wished, oh! how bitterly, I too had received a Christian education, and had been free and untrammelled to do right.

Late in the fall I closed my school, and we prepared to return to Garden Grove with the fruit of our earnings. My husband had treated me so kindly, and had so often promised to take no more wives, that I believed him, and improbable as it was, I returned in the full belief that he would give me no more trouble in that way. We took with us provisions and clothing sufficient to make us very comfortable for the coming winter; but when we arrived at the "stake," David Fulmer directed Wallace to distribute his provisions among the destitute families there, to which he submitted with the best possible grace, as he dare not refuse, although this left us nearly destitute.

As he was under the necessity of supplying the deficiency in some way, he went back to the Desmoines River, in Iowa, with Isaac Allred, to raise money and provisions by labor, or, as I have reason to believe, by some measures less honorable, under the direction of the "Danites," to which clan I believe my husband belonged. He left with me a girl by the name of Ellinor Persons, to whom I became much attached. She was interesting, and became very kind and serviceable to me.

Wallace came back well supplied early in the winter, but rendered his return as unpleasant as it otherwise would have been agreeable, by making an offer of marriage to Ellinor; who was greatly offended, and left us at once. She was a noble girl, and like many other Mormon women, rebelled against spiritual wifeism.

About the middle of the winter we heard from Wallace's father. In the confusion of leaving Nauvoo, we had become separated from him, as we had from my own family. His father was at Council Bluffs, and hearing we were at Garden

Grove, sent Thomas, one of his sons, for us with a team. I had heard nothing as yet from my mother, or from any of my family, and I was glad to go to any place that promised to bring me nearer them.

We started with Thomas in the middle of January, and had a very cold journey. We arrived at Council Bluffs at the end of two weeks, where we were well received by my father-in-law and his family. They lived about one mile from the main "stake," which was called Kanesville. This was the head-quarters of Mormonism at that time. The Prophet was there, and unnumbered hosts of Mormons were going and coming—some forming new "stakes" ahead, or further to the north or south, and others going on to people them; while others still were going on to the far West, to spy out a locality for a permanent home for the Saints. It was yet as uncertain what direction this vast horde would take, as it might be where a swarm of bees just upon the wing would hive. Scouts were sent in every direction, and were returning daily with various reports, and with conflicting recommendations. All was yet uncertain, as the Prophet had not yet spoken. The "oracle" was silent, but would speak in due time, and when the revelation should come, the masses would move. In the mean time, the Prophet's ears were ever open for information of some goodly land, far off and well protected against "Gentile" intrusion, where he could hive the swarming hordes of his people, which an uninterrupted emigration and the swift reproduction of spiritual wifeism were gathering about him at Kanesville.

Those who remained at the "stakes" were busily employed

in raising grain for present use, and to lay up in store for the coming masses, while many, whose "talents" fitted them for the service, were sent back to Missouri, and other points in the States, to buy horses and cattle, and other property with "bogus" money, or to procure them as best they could. This service was mostly performed by the "Danites."

I was glad to hear once more from my mother and family, which I did at this time. It appears they had arrived at Kanesville the previous summer, and had joined a "stake" further north, on the Running Water River, and from there, had moved to Weston, Missouri, where they were supposed to be still. I was anxious to see them, but as I was about to become a mother again, it was impossible for me to undertake such a journey. I had never felt so much the need of my mother as at this point of my life, for I saw that which convinced me that Wallace was about to take another wife.

CHAPTER IX.

MORE WIVES.

In order that my readers may have no difficulty in understanding the true position of the parties referred to in this chapter, and other parts of this book, I have to state, that among the Mormons the act of "making love," as it is termed, is not confined to the male portion of the Church, but that every unmarried woman has the same right, and she is expected to exercise it with the same freedom as the opposite sex, with this difference : that while the female is at liberty to decline an offer of marriage made by a man, he is not at liberty to decline an offer coming from a woman, against whose ability for child-bearing there rests no well grounded doubt, except it may be the single exception, which no Mormon of spirit would be likely to plead in bar of matrimony, viz.: that he has already more wives than he can support. Hence it will be seen the husband may be placed in an unpleasant position by the system of double wifeism as well as the wife, whenever the enamored fair ones may choose to take advantage, in earnest, of this continuous leap-year. And this they often do, without incurring the suspicion of immodesty. It seldom occurs, however, if indeed it ever does, that the subjects of such proposals, made by lady lovers, consider themselves "persecuted;" but it oftener happens that they take advantage of this liberty among the unmarried women to justify themselves within the home circle for bringing home another wife.

We had been at Kanesville but a short time, when I learned one day from Wallace that Harriet, the girl he attempted to marry at Garden Grove, was living with her father near us, and still unmarried.

This gave me great uneasiness, as I saw. he had not given up the idea of marrying her One night he came home, and said he had been to see Harriet, that while passing her father's house she had called him in, and claimed her right of marriage under the principle explained above. In short, had "proposed" in form, and threatened to report him to the Heads of the Church if he did not submit to her reasonable demand.

Wallace sat down by me, and expressed great concern, that, as I was about to be sick, the excitement of his marriage would have a dangerous influence upon me. He said, "I dare not refuse to marry her; the Prophet will take away my license (as preacher), and may be my head. Besides, it is time you had given up these jealous notions. You shall always be mistress here, and Harriet as your servant, and it will make no difference in my attachment to you, or in your rights. You must some day submit, and it will be as easy now as ever."

I rejected his cruel reasoning with what force of woman's wit and will I could, and backed these, in the end, by tears.

I refused to receive another wife into the house, and I think I should have prevented it if no one else had interfered with us; but it is impossible for a Mormon man with one wife to escape from the ridicule of his associates. The next day Wallace was telling some of them what I had said, and they laughed at him beyond measure. Some of them said their first wives had talked in the same way, but came into the arrangement when they found they must. They told him he had nothing to do but to take home his new wife when I was confined, and by the time I was well again he would find me reconciled. Wallace accordingly told me he had concluded to bring Harriet home the next day. He said, "I have waited longer than any other man in the Church would have done for you to become satisfied." And when I told him I thought it would kill me if he did,, he replied, "Then you will die a martyr, and shall wear a martyr's crown."

It was too horrible. I was put to bed immediately, and when I was again conscious of passing events, they told me my child was dead—that its mother's agony had crushed back its little breath before it saw the light. It was some time before my overtaxed and exhausted frame rallied sufficiently to enable me to comprehend the exact state of my household. I soon discovered that Harriet was present, and although she did not presume to approach me, I comprehended she was anxious to treat me kindly, and wished to appease my resentment. It was not many days before I understood, and how I hardly knew, that she occupied a bed within reach of mine, with Wallace. One morning, when I had just opened my eyes, after a calm sleep, which had restored my clouded mind to a clear self-possession, and I was feeling the keenest pleasure in bathing my hand in the warm sunlight which streamed within my reach under the half-drawn window-curtain, my eye fell upon them—upon Wallace and Harriet, in the bed near me, apparently just awake. I think I must have glared upon them wildly, for Wallace was frightened, and when I fell back with a groan after finding myself too weak to rise, he put his hand upon my head, from his place beside Harriet, for he was so near me as that, and said, "Poor, poor Ettie, I am afraid she will never submit to the will of the Prophet. *This doctrine will kill her.*" I mustered what strength I could, and moved beyond his reach to the further side of the bed, and turned my back upon them without a word. From that time I closed my eyes to their movements—I would not see them. I was too weak to contend against numbers, and I could not submit. I sternly strove to calm myself, and I succeeded. I was determined *not to die a martyr.*"

Harriet was greatly humbled and disappointed. She attempted to put herself right with me; she said one day to me, "how can you feel so? I do not towards you. I acknowledge you as first here, and expect to be second to you in Eternity." She said many other things, I do not care to repeat here. I recovered slowly but surely, and was about the house much sooner than I expected.

When I felt equal to the effort, I took occasion to test my influence with Wallace. I asked him if he would take me to Weston, where my mother was supposed to be. He asked me if I would come back, I told him not at once, as I wished to remain awhile. We had a long conversation upon the subject. Harriet was present; I had as yet never recognized her as being in the house. She made some remark to Wallace, to which I replied by asking her what business she had with my husband. This turned the conversation upon her; and I took occasion to administer to her, what force of ridicule I could command. She was soon in tears, I pitied the poor girl, but did not spare. Wallace attempted to interfere, for Harriet's protection, with but small comfort to her. As a compromise, he agreed, as soon as I was well enough to ride, he would take me to Weston.

I was anxious to get away, and the next week we started. Wallace procured his father's horse and buggy, which for that country, was a very comfortable arrangement. Although I was better prepared to receive medical treatment, than to undertake such a journey, we started. Our course was down the left bank of the Missouri River, I soon repented my folly in making the attempt. We had not gone far when I began to feel uncomfortable, and grew sicker every moment we advanced; till at the end of twenty miles, I began to vomit. There was no house near, and Wallace selected a favorable place, by a small streamlet, in a pleasant wood, for an encampment. Taking me out of the buggy, he arranged the seat, and buffalo skin, in such a manner that I could lie down. He then gathered wood, and built a fire, and made me some tea, this revived me very much, and I ate some crackers, and was very comfortable.

He then prepared to spend the night, by securing his horse near by, and feeding him with some grain we had with us, and getting together a good quantity of wood. As we had taken the forethought to bring provisions and blankets, we made a very comfortable night of it. In the morning I felt much better. We were now quite in doubt, whether to return or go on. Wallace was anxious to go back; urging that I needed rest and quiet, before I could perform the journey. I was forced to admit this was perhaps true. On the other hand, I was the more anxious to advance. This was the second time I had set out to find my mother, and I could not bear the thought of riding twenty miles back, however hard it might be to go forward.

We therefore broke up camp, and journeyed on. I soon found I was growing worse. I recollect that my head began to ache, and finally a high fever set in; And I have but little more remembrance of what passed. At intervals, I was conscious of riding, and jolting onwards, and then all was lost to me.

Wallace, as he afterwards said, saw the necessity of hurrying on to some house. How far it might be to one, he had no means of knowing. Towards night, he arrived at the Nishnebatona River, a branch of the Missouri, coming from the north east. There was a ferry kept there by a family living on the other side. The place was known as Allen's Ferry. It was spring, and the streams were high; but after some delay, we were ferried over, and he applied to the family to take care of his wife. He drove up to the door, and his summons was answered by my brother Howard, of whose whereabouts we had heard nothing since our separation at Nauvoo. Howard, who kept the ferry, and Martha his wife, were greatly moved at finding me; especially as I was unable to recognize them. The delirium left me the next day. I had fallen into a calm sleep near morning: and when I awoke I found my brother and Martha near me. I was very near going mad again, before I understood where I was, and how I came there; and when I fully comprehended that I was safe, and with my own family once more, I was very happy.

My first inquiry after regaining my self-possession, was for my mother, whom I had not noticed among my friends. I had suffered so much myself, and had so often barely escaped death since my separation from her, that I felt an undefined fear that she might have fallen a victim, in her old age, to this cruel migration; and I dreaded to make the inquiry. But I was soon happily relieved from further apprehension, by learning she was, as we had heard before, at Weston, Missouri, and was well. This gave me great joy. Howard and Martha were yet looking upon me in astonishment. "How much the child has changed," said Howard, "she was so young and joyous and healthy. What a wreck! Can this be the fruit of Mormonism? Nettie, has Wallace misused you."

I made no reply. My mind turned to the dark past, as to a horror, a bare mention of which might bring it back to me again. I shuddered with such evident fear, that Howard saw the necessity of dropping the subject; and Martha hovered about me, with such kindly and soothing attention, that after giving me some gruel, and bringing some tea, which I tasted; I was soon dozing pleasantly, though but half asleep I tried to keep enough awake, to enjoy my new sense of security My whole soul, unbent its overworked energies; and all my senses nestled themselves into quiet rest. Not an unconscious sleep, but a recuperative unknitting of the mental and physical forces. I fain would have existed always thus. My youth, and flexible constitution, which, though quick to bend, was loth to break, had triumphed, and I needed but this continued quiet, to brace me up again; perhaps for an equally bitter future. I gathered from the whispered invectives in which Martha from time to time indulged against Wallace, that I had been talking in my delirium of him, and of Harriet, and of spiritual wifeism.

Wallace soon came in, and asked if I was better; and as Martha would not answer him, I replied to his question, and he came to the bed. He asked me if I had been telling Martha about Harriet. He appeared very penitent, and begged I would overlook the past. He promised to go for my mother and sister Lizzie, which he said he could do in a little over a week; I urged him to do so. I had been separated from them now over two years.

He set out the next morning for Weston, and I waited his return with the greatest anxiety. After a few days, when I was somewhat restored, I had a long talk and a full understanding with Howard as to my past suffering, and its connection with Mormonism. I told him all. Howard was a conscientious Mormon.

After listening to me with great patience, and thinking the matter over for a long time, he said, "Mormonism is true. Joseph Smith was a prophet of God, else how did he heal my broken leg; and how was my mother healed? How have others been healed, and how have his prophecies been fulfilled? Your husband has not done right. This is not Mormonism."

"But," said I, "Wallace has obeyed 'counsel.' David Fulmer, President of the Stake, has counselled him to steal and rob; and he *has* stolen and robbed. Fulmer has counselled him to take another wife, and he has taken one."

"But," said he, "you will find when you see Brigham Young, that Mormonism differs from that. It is not true that such crimes are countenanced by the Church."

I am satisfied that at that time Howard would have denounced Mormonism, had he known to what it was leading. I am equally satisfied he has since known of the existence not only of these crimes, and their practice by direction or "counsel," as it is called, of the Prophet; but has actually acknowledged the spiritual wife doctrine, by attempting to take another himself; which, up to the time I left Salt Lake, Martha had prevented by driving the "new wife" out of the house.

Wallace returned from Weston without my mother. It was impossible for her to come and see me; but she was well; and had my sister Lizzie with her, as also my youngest brother Uriah. My brother George and sister Sarah had both fallen victims to the hardships of the migration, and were both dead; while William had gone with the Mormon Battalion * to fight for the United States in Mexico, and

---

* The raising of this battalion by the Mormons, at the requisition of the United States Government, was, at the time, and has been since, greatly lauded, as an act of patriotism, often cited as an evidence of Mormon loyalty and good faith. As to which see a well

whether yet alive or not, was at this time unknown to my mother. We soon after heard of his death.

This was the first full and certain intelligence I had received from the family, since our terrible separation at Nauvoo. It was certain two had fallen, and how many more of us were to be overborne by the demands of Mormonism upon us, and its increasing hardships, the future alone could reveal. We now for the first time fully realized the sacrifices we had made for the Church. Our family was widely scattered, and falling victims, one by one, in different localities, yet none bethought him, that Mormonism was a delusion. Wallace represented my mother as mourning the fate of her family, and the loss of her fine property, yet clinging to her belief in the Prophet and his teachings, as implicitly as she did the day she was restored to hearing.

Wallace had promised my mother that he would take me to Weston as soon as I was able to ride, and the prospect of seeing her cheered me and hastened my recovery. Of course he did not tell her how he had treated me, or that he had taken another wife.

---

written and appreciative article, entitled "The Mormons," pages 615-16 of Harper's Magazine for April, 1853.

But Elder Hyde has let us into the secret of this apparent loyalty to the Government, at p. 143 of his book, in the following graphic lines. Speaking of the aims of the Mormon leaders, he says:

"Their design they desire to cloak under a sham patriotism. The United States offered $20,000 bounty money, and Brigham recruited a regiment; persuaded, *commanded* them to leave their families, *many of them perfectly destitute*, and join General Scott's army then in Mexico, *and they obeyed.*"

About a week after this, Wallace asked me, in presence of Howard, when we should go home, and Howard replied that he could go home whenever he chose, but that I was not going with him. Wallace asked me if that was so, and I told him I could not go then, if for no other reason than that I was not strong enough yet; what I should do after that, I could not say. Wallace, therefore, returned to Council Bluffs without me, and I was left with no care upon my hands but my health; which was slowly improving. And yet, as I had not given up my husband entirely, the reflection that he had returned to Harriet, and that she had him all to herself, at times annoyed me. I sometimes felt I was willing to give him up, and tried to convince myself I had done so. But only those who have been similarly situated can appreciate my position.

CHAPTER X.

RECONCILED—FINDING MY MOTHER.

ANOTHER month elapsed before we heard again from Wallace. I had nearly recovered once more my accustomed tone of health, and life was no longer a burthen to me. If my readers will recollect that at this time I was less than eighteen years of age, they will not be surprised that a strong constitution, and a naturally buoyant temperament so soon triumphed over the ills of the past; and I trust my youth and my attachment as a wife, may be deemed a sufficient explanation of the course I afterwards pursued in relation to my husband.

One dark and rainy night, just as the family were preparing for bed, Wallace knocked at the door. Howard opened it, and seeing who it was bid him come in.

I knew his rap almost by instinct, notwithstanding I was determined not to recognize him as my husband. And yet some secret impulse told me, that his appearance at such a time, was an evidence of returning good faith on his part; and my woman's heart secretly, and in spite of my resolution, applauded this act of devotion to me. I felt that could I but know he had given up Harriet, I would gladly receive him back; and then the dark cloud of the past intervened and sealed my lips. When Howard asked him to come in, Martha said, "If he does, I will go out, the trifling scamp. Let him go back to his spiritual mistress. He cannot come here."

I said not a word. My heart and my judgment struggled in opposition for the mastery. Wallace stood at the door, the most forlorn object I had ever seen. He was dripping wet, with the rain still beating upon him. It was one of those cold, chilling storms, which are liable to come any time of the year, creeping into the very bones, which had found him unprepared, as he had no overcoat. Howard faltered about admitting him, and as I did not interfere, he turned to Martha, and said, "I think this man is not as bad as we supposed. It is this Mormonism that has made the trouble; it is hard on women at the best."

"And harder still on the men, unless they are like adamant," said Wallace.

"What shall we do?" asked Howard of Martha.

Wallace then said partly to me, "If we are to separate, I think it necessary to talk it over, and have matters fully understood. I should like to see Ettie alone."

Howard then told him he could go into the front room and say to me what he wished, and that he must then leave, to which Martha tacitly consented. I accordingly went with him. He was greatly distressed. I asked him as to Harriet. He protested he had not seen her since I had; and said he never intended to leave me for her. He gave every evidence of sincerity. Finally, he said, "I wish to know if you intend to return with me. I will ask you to live with me no longer than I treat you well; and when I get another wife, you shall be free to go. I have abandoned Harriet forever, and will take no other wife. Mormonism shall not separate us again."

How could I refuse to accept his promises? I did accept them, and engaged to go back to Council Bluffs with him the next morning; I pitied and believed him. All I had ever asked at his hands was that he should abandon his spiritual wifeism; otherwise, I was content with him. He had not eaten a mouthful since morning, and I offered to get him some supper, but he refused to accept it, and said he would not eat in the house. He then left me.

There was but one other house near, and this afforded him the only hope of getting in for the night. Strange as it may seem, his present suffering endeared him still more to me; and I fain would have protected him from further exposure to the storm, if he had allowed me to make his peace with Martha.

Martha was a good and kindly woman, when excited by no wrong that was crying for redress; but she had a soul of greatness, and a will of iron. I take pleasure in making this mention of her, as she was of great service to me afterwards in Salt Lake, and I would do anything in my power to assist her to escape from the cruel bondage she is suffering in common with all Mormon women there.

Wallace left the house without speaking to the other inmates, giving Martha, as she said afterwards, a look of defiance.

I awoke the next morning early, and joyously made arrangements for the journey. When I told Martha I was about to leave her, and try Wallace once more, she was out of all patience with me, and said I could not fail to regret it, but added, after a moment's reflection, as if she thought she had said too much, "After all, I must acknowledge he is good-looking, and I am sorry I can offer you no greater encouragement."

Howard said nothing, as he had before advised me not to go with him. I was ready for a start when Wallace came, as I knew it would embarrass him if he was delayed, as he was not on speaking terms with the household. Howard and Martha wished us well, and we set out in good spirits. It was fine weather, and the going excellent, and we arrived about three o'clock in the afternoon at the only house between the Nishnebatona and Council Bluffs. We therefore put up for the night; we had driven about twenty miles. The place was off the road in a very pleasant location, and was occupied by an old man and his wife, who entertained us in a very acceptable manner. After a late dinner, we took a walk up the stream, which is known as Key Creek, Wallace taking his rifle. We found the game plenty, and were very successful. I shot two squirrels and, among other things, Wallace shot a wild turkey.

While dressing the next morning, Wallace accidentally left his belt in my room; it was the one he wore around his body under his clothing; which I examined without his knowing it, and found it to contain about three hundred dollars of bogus money. This did not surprise me, as I had suspected it before, and I knew the authorities of the Church, if they did not manufacture it themselves, directed it to be done by others

We had a fine breakfast of the game killed by us the evening previous, and as we had ample time to get home that day, we concluded to have another hunt, as this was a favorable locality for it. Wallace borrowed a horse of the old gentleman, and I rode our pony, and we had a fine ride on horseback over the prairie, and through the timber that skirted the banks of the creek. It seemed to me that I had just escaped from a long confinement in some pent up town. The open sky, and pure breath of the prairie, and the mellow sunlight, cheered my glad soul, now free from anguish.

I shot at a prairie wolf, and wounded it, which we afterwards ran down, and Wallace captured it. This closed our hunt, and at eleven o'clock we continued our journey. We arrived at home in good time that night.

The discovery I had made as to the bogus money in the belt of Wallace, sharpened my curiosity, and I took occasion to watch his movements and all connected with him. I made it convenient, as I had an opportunity a few days after this, to question Joseph Young, brother of the Prophet, about it. I commenced by telling him I thought he had given Wallace more than his share of bogus money. The men who had the management of such matters were generally very cautious about telling the women of t. Brother Joseph, thrown off his guard, replied,

"Did he get me a span of horses?"

I told him I did not know but he bought one for himself.

"Yes, yes," said brother Joseph, thinking I knew all about it, as some of the wives of the Prophet did; "he can sell the bogus any time to the Missourians, if he wishes, and they cannot detect us. If they do, we shall soon be beyond their reach. We must help ourselves this year to a good outfit for crossing the plains; and, next spring and summer, we shall be off and beyond their reach, and they can whistle."

I thus ascertained positively what I had long suspected. I went home knowing that my husband was a thief and a counterfeiter, if not something worse than either; but I could not believe the great body of the Church had endorsed all these crimes; the very enormity of them seemed to prove it impossible; and yet, individuals high in the confidence of the Prophet had, in more than one instance, not only recognized but had counselled these practices.

My life at this time passed very pleasantly, when not embittered by thinking upon what I knew to be the employment of my husband. Our house was the resort of what was called the best society in the Church, and was enlivened by plays and dancing parties, for which the Mormons, as a community, are greatly distinguished. These are recommended to keep up the spirits of the women and, perhaps, to drown the recollection of crimes among the men. But it is proper I should say that, whatever is approved by the Prophet is not regarded as a crime. I was determined, for myself, to put up with everything but spiritual wifeism; and, as long as Wallace did not bring home another wife I was content.

One day, soon after this, a man came to our house, who was unknown to me, and had a long conversation with Wal lace. The subject of their interview seemed to be one of great importance and secresy. After the stranger had left, Wallace told me it was necessary for us to move to St. Joseph, Mo.; that he was going there by direction, and in the service of the Church, and was to keep a boarding-house to accommodate the Mormons in that State, doing business disguised as "Gentiles."

The reader will not be surprised to know, what I soon learned to be true, that this "business" was selling bogus money, and buying with it various kinds of property needed by the Church, and forwarding it to Council Bluffs.

We packed up in a short time, and moved to that place, where we rented a large dwelling near the Court-house. Wallace took with him his sister Abbe, as he said he should be gone from home more or less, and he would not ask me to stay alone with the kind of company we should have at our house. The goers and comers at our boarding establishment purported to be "Gentiles," from various parts of the Union: New Orleans, New York, Boston, and other places, *en route* for California or Oregon, as some of them were; but they were mostly Mormons from Council Bluffs. The latter would land in the night from the river, where Wallace would meet and bring them to our house, and the next morning introduce them as being from some other direction. They would, one by one, privately disperse themselves over the country to prosecute their unlawful traffic, and generally came and went in the night. Our house soon came to be the resort of a precious set of rogues; among whom Wallace was quite at home. Horse thieving and gambling appeared to be a part of the regular business of these men, which they had reduced to a system.

The notorious gamblers of this region, among the Gentiles, somewhat famed about this time, stood no chance with this band of Mormons; for while they were professedly strangers, they had a system of secret signs by which they were under-stood by each other, and they could thus play into the hands of their friends unsuspected.

The horses, and other booty purchased or stolen, was forwarded at once to Kanesville, and was there received by Orson Hyde, who, after assorting it, forwarded it on to the plains, or made such disposition of it as would place it beyond the reach of the Gentiles, in case suspicion should be directed towards them. Orson Hyde is one of the "Twelve Apostles," and is often in the States. There are now many persons living by whom these facts can be proved.

The bogus money used by these men, was mostly made at Nauvoo; but I have heretofore mentioned that the press used in its manufacture was taken west, and on to Salt Lake in the wagon of Peter Hawse, and was at this time at Kanesville. This man, Hawse, is now living on Humbolt River, west of Great Salt Lake City.

Although at this time I was treated kindly by Wallace, I was not allowed to associate with the "Gentiles," or even speak to them. I had no associates of my own sex except Abbe; and forced as I was to know of the crimes that were being daily committed under my own roof, I was nearly wild with horror, not only with the crimes themselves, but with the fear of the detection I felt must surely come sooner or later. It was generally understood, that if we were recognized as Mormons, and our business detected, nothing could save us from the mob, which had driven our Church from the States a few years previous. Our lives must in that case pay the forfeit. Oppressed with all these fearful embarrassments, I besought Wallace to take me to see my mother, who lived but thirty miles from us. He had promised repeatedly to do so, but first one thing, and then another had prevented, and now I was not to be put off. Wallace consented to let me go in the stage alone, as his " business " required his personal attention at home. He gave me to understand, that I would do well to exercise care. Not to associate with " Gentiles " during my absence, or make to them, or any one, indiscreet disclosures of what I knew. "For," said he, "*friends* of the Church will be near you at all times;" and I found this strictly true. I arrived at Weston about four o'clock in the afternoon of the day I left home; and as the stage stopped at the door of the hotel, a stranger presented himself, and asked if Mrs. Henderson was inside. As I answered to that name, he handed me a note from Wallace, as follows: "The bearer is my *friend*, who will take you to your mother's." This "friend" took me to a room in the hotel, and asked me to remain there until he could get a carriage. He very soon returned with one, and set out with me for my mother's, who lived, he said, about one mile from the village. We at length arrived at a long, low house, at which we stopped. It stood upon an elevated spot of ground and near the road. I asked my strange conductor if that was where my brother and sister died. He said, he presumed it was, as my mother lived there. What a tumult of new emotions! I was to find once more my mother, after so long a separation; but I was not to find my sister, nor brother with her; but Lizzie and Uriah were left. The man called at the door, and asked for Mrs. Coray, and when she came, I did not recognize the bent old woman as my mother. She was prematurely bowed by the hardships of the past; and not until we were near each other, was the recognition mutual. Lizzie knew me at once, and I was happy once more with the loved ones of my childhood.

None but a *child* can appreciate the joy I had of pouring into a mother's ear the story of my wrongs, and sufferings. She wished to know at once if Wallace had taken a "spiritual" wife; and I told her all, at least all that concerned myself, and all I dared to tell of the corruptions of the Church.

My story told, with many tears, and listened to with anguish, and her own hardly the less painful to me, tore all our hearts with grief.

Uriah soon came in, and I found him almost a man, whom I had last seen a small boy. It was several days before we had a full hearing of each other's experiences.

When I told mother that I suspected Wallace was a bad man, and was engaged in a manner I dare not whisper even to her, she asked, "has he been killing Missourians? I have heard something of this. They say some of our Church have been seeking revenge upon them; and that some have succeeded in taking it; but I am not at liberty to tell you. I have overheard something that Brigham Young should know; and he must know it, or our Church will be regarded as a band of thieves and murderers."

I saw my mother, like Howard, had full confidence in the Heads of the Church, and I began to fall into their way of thinking, that when the Prophet understood what had been done, and what crimes were being practised in his name, he would condemn and punish the wrong doers. I was satisfied she knew something of which she had given me no hint, and I was sure I had not told her all I knew, for I dare not do it. My mother would not even yield to the belief, that Brother Brigham would in the end approve the spiritual wife doctrine, and she would not acknowledge that Brother Joseph ever did.

I found my mother's life had not been entirely free from adventure since our separation, as the following story told by her will show.

It appears, as before intimated, that after arriving at Council Bluffs, she had moved, with about fifty other families to a "stake" on the Running Water River, to a point some ninety miles northwest of Council Bluffs, where they remained one winter. This is the home of the Puncah Indians, and is a fine open prairie country. They had built a fort on the bank of the river, at a point hemmed in by bold bluffs, which clustered in a sort of circle back and above of the little plain on which the dwellings were built. The latter were arranged in two rows along the river bank. There was no escape by and from the plain on which the little village stood, except up these bluffs, the ascent of which was difficult at the best. The water in the river was deep and ran very swift, so swift, indeed, as to render crossing at this point almost impossible.

"One evening," said my mother, "late in the fall, I was quietly putting things to rights at home, and the boys were yet in the streets, where they had been playing ball until it grew too dark to see, when Uriah rushed into the house, saying, "the bluffs are all on fire." I went to the door, and was startled to find our little settlement in the greatest peril. *The prairies were on fire.* The flames, driven by a fierce wind, had just arrived at the brink of the bluffs, down which they were now tumbling in fearful proximity to our dwellings. We were within a semicircle of fire, every moment narrowing towards the centre, which nothing, to all human appearance, could stay, until checked by its arrival at the river. And the river, we had no means of crossing, as it was too swift and deep. It is impossible to describe the confusion of our little community, thus suddenly awakened from calm security to a frightful sense of impending destruction, which had burst upon us as unexpectedly as it was now inevitable. The first alarm vented itself in a wild yell of horror from an hundred throats. But even these yells were scarcely audible above the loud roar of the approaching flames. A few moments were sufficient to bring men and women to their senses, and then a few cool men suggested, while all were glad to obey in anything that promised succor. There was not room between the fire and the dwellings, or between the latter and the river, to protect ourselves in the usual way, by seting the grass on fire and let it pass, nor *time* for either. Some who were sufficiently daring, conceived the idea of swimming the river, which was perhaps possible for a few, but of course could afford no relief to the women and children, except so far as drowning was better than burning. Others proposed to wet blankets and run through the flames with these over their persons, which was practicable for the strong men, but was not to the great mass.

"The better judgment, and that which prevailed was, not to attempt to save the property, except that which could be easily moved, but to collect all the inhabitants under the bank of the river, which was not high, below where the heat of the dwellings would be felt, as there the exposure would be only to the heat of the grass, and this could last but a few minutes, and then to wet all the blankets and clothing in the river, and cover the living mass with these as best we could.

"This plan it was believed, would save the life of every member of the community, though at the expense of nearly every thing else. Preparations were accordingly made at once. The women and children were got together, with wet blankets and bedding at hand, close to the water's edge, ready for the last emergency. Then prayers were hurriedly said; and astonishing as it may seem, just then the wind veered a little, and then a little more, until it blew down the river, instead of driving on to the dwellings.

"Then every arm was nerved to save the village. The fire was already near a few of the buildings, but by great effort its further spread was stayed. Several men died a few days after, from the excitement and over-exertion in saving the dwellings. The blankets already wet were found very serviceable in protecting the houses.

"The building containing the powder, was but a few rods

from the fire at the moment the wind changed; and thus a greater calamity was perhaps averted, as there was considerable powder in it at the time. I soon after left this "stake," and came here, as I had learned from this how uncertain such a life of isolation might become, under extreme circumstances."

This story of my mother, and others which she told me, illustrated how much she had sacrificed to her belief in the Prophet, but neither of us then imagined that this was but the beginning of our rough experiences in border life.

CHAPTER XI.

THE FAMILY BROKEN UP.

I was very happy with my mother. I was a free and joyous child again, and my mother said, as I was not yet of age, and as Wallace had taken me without her consent, he had no right to me now. We had made up our minds not to separate again, and I wrote to Wallace after I had been at home about four weeks, that he need not come after me, as I did not intend to return to the "boarding"-house. As soon as he received my letter, he came. He arrived at our house late at night, and riding up to the door, struck it with his whip. I knew it was him at once, and went to the door. Without getting off his horse, he asked in a loud, boisterous voice, if I was ready to go home. I thought best to treat him well, and I asked Uriah if he would put Wallace's horse in the barn; and he replied "yes, and himself too, if he wishes, that will be the proper place for both."

Wallace saw by this that my family knew of his past conduct, and did not attempt to conciliate them. The next morning, pleading my promise that I would live with him until he took a spiritual wife again, he claimed that I was under obligations to go home. I dare not explain to my mother fully, how matters stood at the boarding-house, and I thought as we were still among Gentiles, and did not know what course Wallace might take to injure us among them, that I had better return with him, which I accordingly did.

When we arrived at home, we found the house full of boarders—fuller than usual. A mass of goers and comers in masks, whose business Wallace knew, and whom I soon learned to recognize as Mormons, mingled with innocent strangers, ignorant of the risk they ran in coming to our house, which, by this time, had acquired a wide reputation as a general boarding-house. We had plenty of money, and to a degree never before or since known to me, was everything I wished at my command. I should have been well contented had I not known the character of our customers, and the object of our house. Liquors of the rarest brands, and every accompaniment of the most costly entertainments, were served daily at our table. But I am bound to say in simple justice, that these luxuries, and facilities for dissipation, were not for the entertainment of Mormons, who were for the most part men of simple tastes. They were designed to entrap strangers, and to allure their victims, as well as to call there the class of men known as professed gamblers. Wallace, during all this time, and while I knew him, was in no way addicted to strong drink; in fact, I never knew of his drinking at all.

The great body of Mormons were now preparing to move on to the west. Deputations had been sent out, and had brought back glowing accounts of the Utah Valley, which had been selected as the future home of the saints. Great numbers had already gone, and were still going, and my mother had concluded to join the next company, with her family. She therefore found it necessary to go on to Council Bluffs immediately, in order to avail herself of the best facilities for making the journey, as that was the head-quarters of the Church, this side the plains. On her way she called upon us, and I bid her adieu again—for how long a time I knew not. It was a sad thing to part again with my mother, so soon after I had found her. If she went on to the valley, I could not expect to see her until I had made the same journey myself, and I was not sure that I wished to make it.

After this I became more disgusted than ever with our way of life. I went to bed one night, intending to have a talk with Wallace when he came. He did not, however, come in till near morning, and when he did, I told him I could not bear the confusion and wickedness of this kind of company any longer. That if he wished to keep boarders, there were Gentiles enough he could get to make him a good business. But as for the rest, I would expose his villainy if longer continued. Wallace said he was in the service of the Church, and referred me to the revelation of brother Joseph Smith, who authorized the formation of the band of men known as "Danites." That it was necessary, in order to procure an outfit for the poor "saints," now waiting to go on to the valley. That anything that was for the good of the Church, was right. I said so much to him, however, that the next morning he discharged his Mormon boarders, and thus their head-quarters was broken up; at least, I saw no more of them. I had reason to believe that Wallace still coöperated with them.

Wallace came in one day, and said he was going to Jackson county, Mo., upon "*business*" connected with the Church: and as he sat down and counted over a large amount of money, which I knew to be "bogus," I was well satisfied as to its nature. He named several persons who were Mormons, as intending to go with him: and about this time Mr. Mowry, a Mormon from Kanesville brought me a letter from Uriah, saying my mother was very sick: and that if I wished to see her again, I had better come out at once. As Wallace intended to be gone some time, he consented to my going. Accordingly we both left home: he upon his "mission" to Jackson county, and I for Kanesville, in company with Mr. Mowry and his wife, who were on their return. We had a very pleasant journey; Mr. Mowry was an honest Mormon, and believed as I had been taught, that when we were all gathered into "Our Zion," as Utah, it was said would be to us, all the wrongs of which we complained in our present scattered and isolated condition would be righted. I firmly believed at this time, that Joseph Smith was a Prophet of the Lord, and that Brigham Young, as his successor, would not uphold the terrible doctrines now advocated by many, but that when all were gathered together as it had been foretold, he would rule the Saints in righteousness. I had made up my mind to rest my faith in Mormonism upon this; and when I arrived at Salt Lake, if I did not find things as I had expected, I was determined to return to the States, and abandon Mormonism.

Arrived at Kanesville, I found my mother much better, in fact, quite out of danger, and also found my brother Howard there with his family, with whom mother was living for the time My mother was intending to go on to Fort Karney as soon as she was able to travel, and take boarders from among the officers of the United States Army there; which she afterwards did, taking with her Uriah and Lizzie.

Wallace having returned to St. Joseph, sent for me, and I went home, finding quite a number of Gentile boarders in the house.

A little circumstance happened a few days after my return, which, though apparently trivial of itself, yet as it was the prelude to a friendship, which years afterwards ripened into something more than a passing acquaintance, I deem it proper to make mention of it here; although at the time, it made so little impression upon my mind, that it would have been entirely forgotten, only that subsequent events made it of sufficient consequence to be remembered.

It was Sunday and I was alone in the house, and in my own room, which connected with the front hall. I had thrown myself upon a large chest under a window, and had fallen asleep. The weather was very warm. The sash was thrown open, leaving the window, which was closely covered with a thick growth of vines, free for the circulation of the air. The door leading to the hall was partly open, I do not know how long I had slept, when I felt some one touch my hand, and supposing it was Wallace, I told him to pull me up, and he did so: but what was my astonishment, when I looked up, to find in my room, a tall, fine-looking stranger.

He was under twenty years of age, of engaging address; and apologized by saying, he had just landed from the boat, and was looking for a boarding place. That he had noticed our sign, and had rapped, but receiving no answer, had stepped in, as the door was open. I directed him to the parlor, and Wallace soon coming in, he engaged board. He was on his way to California, mostly on account of his health. This was my first introduction to Reuben P. Smith, who years afterwards, at Salt Lake, became my second husband, though at this time, it was apparently the most unlikely thing that could possibly occur.

It was not long after my return from Kanesville before I began to hear stories from various sources, mostly from Gentiles, not very creditable to Wallace.

Although Wallace did not allow me to associate with any other women among our neighbors, yet I heard enough to convince me my husband was not living up in good faith to our mutual understanding of the terms on which I had consented to live with him again.

It was currently reported that during my absence he had lived with a squaw, who was in the habit of visiting our house for food and whatever we had to give her. She was young and pretty, and had the prettiest Indian baby I had ever seen.

A Mrs. Robinson, one of our neighbors, called upon me one day, and told me frankly what she had heard, and said her husband knew some facts which would convince me how the matter stood. I was ready to believe almost anything of Wallace, but this seemed too monstrous, and especially as it had not the sanction of spiritual wifeism to justify it.

I requested Mrs. Robinson to ask her husband to call, which he did, and he gave me such facts, connected with others which I knew, as to place the case apparently beyond the shadow of a doubt. Wallace was supposed to be the father of the Indian girl's pretty baby.

I was now miserable beyond description. I regretted I had not remained with my mother. I was comparatively alone, and I felt he was guilty; but to set the question at rest, I arranged a plan which would detect him if it was indeed so. This was an easy matter, as the squaw was in the practice of coming to the house several times a week. Without wearying my readers with details, it is sufficient that I say my plan disclosed more than I was willing to know, and brought the guilt so home to *him*, that he acknowledged the whole. The Indian girl was his spiritual wife, and her child was his. The Indians, he said, were the sons of the Lamanites, recognized by the Prophet.

The day marked by this discovery ended my relation as wife with Wallace Henderson—a day which he no doubt remembered to the end of his life. I told him what he had to expect from me, and that the thing was ended. That although my family had gone across the plains, that *his* father had not, and he would protect me, as he had repeatedly offered to do. He wept like a child.

I wrote to his father, and told him all I knew of Wallace, and I mentioned his connection with the murder of Brown, the Gentile, at Kanesville, which will be hereafter referred to. I received an answer from his father in a short time, directing me to come to his house at once, and bring his daughter Abbe.

I showed the letter to Wallace and his sister, and the former agreed to send us to him. Although I had made up my mind fully what to do, I found it hard at last to break off forever a relation which, notwithstanding it had been beset with continued hardship and suffering, and by that peculiar neglect, which is the last offence a woman knows how to pardon, yet it had been also mingled at times with joy.

Wallace was more penitent than I had ever known him before, and had I not been in possession of the best possible evidence within my own knowledge, the relation would have been still more difficult to sunder; and if, during the most trying periods of it, I faltered, I had but to remind myself of his squaw spiritual.

Henry Woodard at this time ran a stage from St. Joseph to Kanesville, and arrangements were made with him by Wallace to take us. Reuben P. Smith, before mentioned, who had until now been a boarder with us, was one of the passengers. Before we left, Wallace explained to him that the relation of husband and wife no longer existed between us, and the reasons for it, saying that it had been his fault, that he had lost a good wife by his own folly, but that he had supposed as I was young I would always put up with it, and at parting asked Smith to take Abbe and myself under his care until we arrived at his father's. Smith had concluded to go on to California, and was going first to Kanesville to join, if possible, some of the Mormon companies which were to cross the plains the next spring. Two Mormon women were also in the stage. They were the wives abandoned by William Smith, brother of the "Prophet" Joseph. It will be recollected that William claimed he should have succeeded his brother Joseph as Prophet, and when his claim was rejected by the election of Brigham Young, he apostatized, and taking his lawful wife, left to live with her among the Gentiles. These two were his other wives, now on their way to join the "Saints" at Salt Lake. Elizabeth Pratt was also a passenger, bound for the same place. She was a daughter of Anson, and a niece of Orson Pratt, the latter being one of the Apostles. It will thus be seen that, including the driver Woodard, our party consisted of two men and five women.

CHAPTER XII.

THE PARTING—CROSSING THE TARKIO.

THE morning of our departure from St. Joseph was dark and rainy—a fitting accompaniment to our act of separation. The wind sighed and sobbed in mournful harmony with my own sadness, and the clouds wept as if in sympathy with my full heart. The highest convictions of right are not always sufficient to make the performance of duty easy to us. At the moment of starting, Wallace begged me not to go; and when he saw I could not be moved from my purpose, he asked Smith to befriend me during the journey.

The stage was a covered omnibus, well adapted to our purpose. We drove fourteen miles, and halted for dinner near Savannah, at a farmhouse. I could not eat. Abbe went to the table, and returned to find me crying, and sat down by me and wept also. She was a good girl, little younger than myself, but much younger in heart and in life's rough ways. She held my head, and we sobbed together, and her sympathy gave me comfort. She said, "My father will protect you, and be a father to us both."

Mr. Smith came in and told us that on account of the storm, which was increasing, we should not be able to go on that afternoon. This appeared a special misfortune to me. To be shut up by gloomy weather, with my own gloomy soul, to brood upon a woe already too great to bear, seemed beyond the limit of my soul's patience. Such an accumulation of disagreeable elements, from its very intensity, had the effect, as it often will, of inducing sleep, and when I awoke near night, I was much improved, and was able to take some supper.

Abbe and I had a comfortable bed, and we slept well. The next morning was fair and pleasant, and I began to feel the joyous spring of life stir within my soul once more. I was very much interested during our day's drive, with the history the two wives of William Smith gave of themselves. Their names were Lucinda Curtis and Anna Rollins. They were still Mormons, and with the utmost simplicity graphically described the arts and deceptions Brother William had used to bring them to submit to spiritual wifeism, and to keep it secret, as at that time at Nauvoo it was not publicly acknowledged, or practised even, except by the heads of the Church. They were both young girls, and their story was heart-rending, as every Mormon woman's would be if known.

We had a pleasant dinner by the way-side, under a large tree, which spread its branches over us, as it had often before protected weary travellers by its shade, and that night put up at a small log cabin, the only accommodation within our reach. We found here but one bed for us all, which by common consent Abbe and I occupied.

The next day we pushed on without accident until we arrived about sundown at the river Tarkio. Contrary to our expectations, we found the water very high by reason of the late rains. This was not a wide nor swift stream, but was deep, and was crossed at this point by a wooden bridge The banks being low, they were now overflown to such a degree that the river was more than a mile wide, and had the appearance of a vast lake, covering the bridge entirely, thus rendering its exact locality uncertain. Our stopping-place for the night was on the other side of the river, and it became very important that we should cross at some rate, for if we remained on the side we then were till morning, it would help us but little, as the stream being sluggish, it rose and fell but slowly, and we might be detained for several days, for which we were by no means prepared.

Woodard, the driver, was a rough, daring man, well acquainted with the locality, and well used to adventures— for which he had more taste than for the refinements of civilized life. His team consisted of three horses—two abreast, " and one on the lead," as he called it. It was already near dark, and no time was to be lost. We could see plainly a large tree, which was known to stand upon the bank of the river, at the end of the bridge, and just below it. The problem therefore was, to guide the team just to the right of that tree, and we should probably hit the bridge, *if the water had not swept it away*, which was not likely, as the stream was not swift. A council was called, and after a hurried discussion it was agreed to put it to the vote, and let the majority rule. By counting noses, it was found we stood as follows: of the two men, Woodard was for going on, and Smith was opposed. Among the women, but one was opposed. Then we stood five out of seven for going forward, and this decided the matter, and now there was no time for delay. Elizabeth Pratt voted for the adventure, but said she knew we should all be drowned: and Lucinda Curtis said she would not go to the trouble of saving herself, if she knew she was to go to the bottom, as she was sure of being the gainer by drowning; and I think the poor girl was nearly right, with regard to herself, and not far wrong as to others of us.

Woodard mounted the leading horse, and directed me to take the lines as I knew the way, having crossed the river here repeatedly. He asked Smith to be ready to lend a hand in case of accident, as occasion might require. We put the horses under way, heading for the supposed locality of the submerged bridge. We all felt that to miss the bridge was to meet our fate at once—that it was simply a question of good guessing, or sure drowning.

As we advanced, the water grew deeper and the daylight less. Smith, who sat at my side upon a chest watching the chances, asked me if I could swim. I told him I thought not, at least I had never tried. He said he thought in case of accident he could save three of the women if they would trust to him, and probably Woodard would be able to save the others; hence he thought there was no danger. He told me to depend upon him. He evidently had no faith in finding the bridge; and his cool acquiescence in the will of the majority, and that majority made up of women, and all against his own judgment, proved not only his generosity, but that he was a man of courage. I think when we were once embarked he was really the only self-possessed person in the company, and he rose in our good opinion in the end as much as he had fallen by his opposition to the rash attempt.

As we neared the tree not a word was spoken. Each heart kept its own watch. Just as the leader came nearly opposite to the tree, Woodard halted evidently in doubt The water was then running over the wagon-box, and there was danger of its floating off with the trunks, which were swimming loose inside of it; and among them the women were floundering in the greatest confusion, and then set up the wildest screams. They all rushed to the front end of the stage, in a huddle; and Smith had much difficulty in preventing some of them from leaping into the river outright.

Smith, in no very choice terms, asked Woodard why he had halted; but before he could reply, the leading horse answered the question, by going down; and Woodard, coming to his feet, landed, as he fell, upon the upper end of the bridge, to which he clung. He had missed the bridge, by going a very little too high; but the wheel horses stood firm, as if aware of what was required of them. I had given the lines to Smith, not knowing in my fright what else to do. Woodard hurriedly, but coolly, directed Smith to give me the lines again, and assist him in cutting the leading horse loose; which he did. When the horse was freed from the others it was drawn by the force of the water under the bridge, which was the last we saw of it. It was supposed the harness by some means became entangled with the underside of the bridge, and it was held there until drowned.

Woodard now waded on to the end of the bridge, showing where to drive. Smith took the lines, drew the team smartly back, and then suddenly to the left, cheering them with a yell. The generous animals bounded on to the bridge, and we were safe, hardly realizing that we were not drowned.

The water was nearly a foot deep the entire way over; and had the current been swift, or anything like it, this light wood structure must have been taken off with it. Once on the bridge, there was no difficulty in following it over, though it was quite dark when we reached the dry ground on the other side.

We soon arrived at the house of an old man near by, very much impressed with the belief that we had been within feeling distance of a watery grave. The excellent wife of our host took good care of us for the night. We built a good fire, by which we dried our clothing, not only what we had on, but that in the trunks also—for they were full of water, and everything was wet.

I think this was the most foolhardy adventure I have ever been identified with, before or since; though more than once afterwards I was forced by necessity to look danger in the face. But in this case there was really no such necessity: and had we been in possession of thirty minutes for reflection, we should have slept over it, and saved a horse at least.

Those of my readers who lead the quiet and even lives of the settlements, can form but an imperfect estimate of a life spent among the continual dangers and exposures of the frontiers. Whatever charms such a life may have for rude and half civilized men, or even for those who frequent the prairies and mountains for the gratification of that love of the chase, which even in civilized society may not be considered unmanly or out of place; yet I have to say, that as far as my own sex is concerned, such adventures are much pleasanter in books, than when made by necessity the every-day business of a life. At least this has been my experience. Born with a strong love of home and family, my existence thus far has been a quick succession of changes from one danger to another; and from one wild scene upon the prairie, to a wilder adventure by flood; or among rude and unreliable men, until I fain would know the calm joy of a home in a quiet land—one where the curse of Mormonism has never rested.

Without further mishap worthy of note, we arrived at Kanesville in good time. I found, much to my regret, that my mother and brothers had gone on to New Fort Kearney.

We were received by my father-in-law with a cordial welcome, and in consideration of the assistance rendered us by Mr. Smith, the latter was made equally at home, notwithstanding he was not a Mormon.

My father-in-law looked very grave when he found Smith did not belong to the Church, and asked by whose direction we were put under the care of a Gentile.

We told him it was arranged by Wallace, and related to him how we were probably indebted to Smith for our safety in crossing the Tarkio.

He listened to the story with great interest and seriousness, and then said, "I understand how it is. You are under obligations to this Gentile, and hence he must be well treated; but I wish Abbe to know, once for all, I do not wish her to marry or associate with a Gentile; for, my children, you little know what influence the evil one has over our frail bodies." Abbe was greatly amused at this, as she had not supposed herself in any degree the object of Smith's attention.

Her father, though a bigoted Mormon, was an honest, kindly man; and we replied to him, that "Smith knew nothing of Mormonism, and that by setting the doctrines fairly before him, it was not impossible but he might be converted." And Abbe said, "Father were you not a Gentile once?" This ended the discussion, and when Smith came in a short time afterwards, he was received cordially.

In the evening, father asked us about Wallace, and we told him all we knew about him, in the presence of Smith. I told him I could never live with him again, and that if I could avoid it, I did not wish to see him. That I should go to my brother's, as soon as I could get to them. That in no case would I consent to live with Wallace. I was kindly treated by my father's family, and they invited me to make their house my home, if I could be contented.

They did not intend to go to the valley until the following year, and wished me to wait and go with them. I was very well contented, until one day, standing in the door, I saw some one coming, and I soon discovered it to be Wallace. I was very much excited, but was determined not to see him. I therefore went out at the back door, as he came in at the front, and went to one of our neighbor's by the name of

Derby, who was related by marriage to my brother Howard. I soon learned what Wallace wanted. His father treated him very severely, and told him he was not worthy of any woman, much less of a young girl, whom he had treated as inhumanly as he had me. That it was enough to ruin any woman, and that he was ashamed to own him as a son.

Wallace then left his father's and went to Harriet's, who lived near by, and where he remained for several days. He then went to Orson Hyde, and stated that I had left him because he had married Harriet, and that I would not submit to the spiritual wife doctrine. That I had said it was from the devil. Brother Orson told him, that according to the Gentile laws, I was at liberty to do so, and that I was free from him, and he had no remedy. That I was even at liberty to marry again, if I wished. I was then sent for to come to Orson's house, and I went. When I arrived there I found him at home. He received me very kindly, and said, "Sister Ettie, why do you object to living with your husband?" I told him I had not time to go into all the circumstances of the case. That I had a great many objections That what most interfered with my notions of propriety was the way he courted some of the "sisters," especially the Indians, by the Mormons known as the Lamanites. That Wallace was very anxious to assist in the fulfilment of that prophesy of our Prophet, which foretold that these Lamanites "should become a white and delightsome people," and that he had already commenced the work among them. I told him further, that I had other grounds of complaint which I did not propose to state then, but that when I arrived at the valley, I should lay them before Brigham Young. Orson Hyde said, "The reasons you have given do not constitute a lawful excuse for leaving your husband, according to the laws of the Church of Jesus Christ of Latter Day Saints."

I then rose up to go, as I did not propose to discuss the matter with him. But he stopped me, and said, "You may, if you wish, be 'sealed'* to me, and then you know there would be no risk to run, in case you should die. Otherwise, if by chance you should drop away, having no husband to raise you at the last day, you could not be 'resurrected' as a saint, and would only be raised like any Gentile, as a servant for the Saints, *i. e.*, for the Mormons."

I was so much disgusted with this proposition, that I left him in the most unceremonious manner, in the midst of his disinterested effort for my salvation. Orson Hyde was, at this time, forty years of age, and had at least three wives, and one daughter about my own age. I was then nineteen years old.

I went home to my father-in-law's, and told him what Orson Hyde had proposed, and that I had made him angry. He made me no reply, evidently thinking the least said about a quarrel with one of the Heads of the Church was soonest mended.

Wallace remained some time at Kanesville, and while there he lived with Harriet. I did not meet him during the time. He at length returned to St. Joseph, and soon after died, as we heard, with the cholera, which was raging fiercely at the time.

* *i. e.* Married.

Although I was sorry to hear of his death, and fully pardoned him then for the wrongs he had done me, yet I did not, I am willing to confess, mourn for him as one without hope. I should have been glad to know he died a better man than he had lived. Harriet, I understood, mourned him with the greatest bitterness.

I was alone one day in the house, the rest of the family being out at the moment, when Mr. Smith called; I was very glad to see him. He had not been in since the day after our arrival, and it was like meeting an old friend. He had so often given such unmistakable proof of his fair intentions, and always so generous and disinterested, that I valued him very much. I thought then, and still think him one of the noblest of men. He appeared to be somewhat embarrassed; and after a little, mentioned the death of Wallace, and finally fell to complimenting me, after a style to which I was altogether unaccustomed. I recollect among other things, he said he had formed a high opinion of me; and that I would be religious if I knew what it was, of course meaning that Mormonism was not religion. It is true I felt I ought not to listen to anything against Mormonism in my father-in-law's house, against his express warning, yet I was sure a man of so much honesty of purpose could not wish to do me harm, and that it could not be wrong to listen to one whose noble bearing, clear intellect, and excellent heart, alike recommended him to my confidence. He finally astonished me by saying, with a good degree of feeling, "I wish, Mrs. Henderson, your happiness was as much dependent upon me as mine is upon you."

At that moment, I saw my father-in-law coming to the house, and I mentioned the circumstance to Mr. Smith, and when he came in, Smith said to him, after passing the usual compliments, "Your daughter, Mrs. Alred, wished Mrs. Henderson, to come over, and make her a visit. I am boarding with one of her near neighbors, and shall return to-morrow, when, if she wishes, I will take her over." Father replied, that the girls had been teasing him to go over with them, and if Mr. Smith could take them, it would save him the trouble.

I noticed, with a pleasure that was altogether a mystery to myself, that Smith did not appreciate the additional number implied by "*them*," but he said he would call for us in the morning.

Father asked him if he had become a Mormon yet. Smith replied, "I know but little about your religion, but there are some things in your doctrine that have a show of reason."

"Perhaps, then," said father, "I may be able to conver you."

After some conversation of a friendly and conciliatory nature, Smith took his leave, evidently having made a favorable impression upon more than one of our household; but waking within my own breast sad memories, and a troubled and anxious foreboding for the future. I was free to marry again if I chose to do so, that was clear, but I would never marry a Mormon, and it was certain I should never be allowed to marry a Gentile. The idea was entirely new to me, but I felt from this day that my future was in some way intimately connected with Smith's. I knew we could not marry, at least not then, and I was not fully satisfied that I wished to do so under the circumstances

There was no mistaking his intentions; and I could not deny to myself that, were I free to act untrammelled, it would have been my highest pleasure to unite my fortunes with his; yet his was too noble a nature to be sacrificed to Mormonism.

Although I believed in our Church implicitly, for I knew no other religion, yet my woman's instinct told me that all a woman holds most dear in life was to be sacrificed to a certain community of interests, which, though I could not fully understand why, had thus far characterized every act and feature of the Church; if I could do no more, I could at least save Smith from the blighting evil; and my soul felt itself charged with a high commission when I undertook to guard him against Mormonism.

My conduct may, perhaps, involve a contradiction in this, that, while I would not listen to the claims of his religion, nor allow him to teach me its principles, I yet warned him against the adoption of mine. The fact was, that I believed my religion to be true; but regretted that it *was* true; a moral and necessary evil to be borne by me, but from which I fain would guard any friend. This subject assumed a higher importance in my mind, when I judged that the strength of the attachment he had exhibited for me, a point on which a woman is seldom mistaken, clearly indicated that it was even possible for him to accept Mormonism, for the purpose of removing all impediments to our union. Thus I found it was likely to happen that, while he supposed his intellect was approving the claims of our Church, his heart would be the real prompter to his belief in our Prophet, and this would have been an effectual bar to our marriage, as well as a real misfortune to him, for I had noticed that the spiritual wife doctrine had the mysterious power of corrupting the purest men of our Church.

CHAPTER XIII.

OFFER OF MARRIAGE—SETTING OUT FOR "ZION."

Mr. Smith came in due time the next morning, and found us waiting for him. It was a gloomy day in midwinter; the weather was cold, but no snow upon the ground, and the road lay mostly through the woods, and was very rough. We had about ten miles to drive; Smith appeared to be cheerful and happy, and by various means which Abbe did not understand, indicated how much he desired to be alone with me, in order to have a full understanding. He asked me if I recollected the command, "If your neighbor ask your cloak, ye shall give him your coat also?" by which I understood that my father-in-law had granted more than he had asked, in sending Abbe with us. But I took occasion to say, that it would be more than a Mormon girl's life was worth to be seen riding with a Gentile alone.

We arrived at my sister-in-law's in safety. She was glad to see us. She had been living alone with her associate wives for some time, as her husband was absent on a mission. We had a very cheerful and pleasant visit that evening.

The next morning I went down to the spring, not far from the house, which was snugly nestled among the trees, and approached by a narrow path winding between smooth rocks

It was a secluded little fountain of pure water, bubbling from beneath the roots of a large tree, with rocks and trees clustering all about it; a place where one could hide away and be content.

I had been there some time, drinking in the quiet beauty of the place, and was just leaving for the house, when I met Smith coming to the spring. He said he wished to say one word to me alone. I was very much alarmed, and asked him if he had never heard the story of the Gentile Brown? He said he had not. I told him I dare not remain with him there one moment, not even to tell him the story, as, if we were discovered in private conversation, it would be at the cost of his life and, perhaps, of mine. I therefore left him looking after me in astonishment, and ran to the house, where I found breakfast was waiting for me.

The story of Brown, which I afterwards told him, was as follows: the year previous, Orson Hyde was courting another wife, by the name of Eleanor Manheart, a very young and pretty girl. This Brown, an emigrant, on his way to California, chanced to get acquainted with Eleanor, and cut the "Apostle" out, and proposed to take her with him over the plains. But the "Danites" interfered with the arrangement, and he was murdered; and Wallace acknowledged he assisted in burying him under the schoolhouse. Hyde then reported the story that Brown had absconded. Of course he was murdered by direction of Orson Hyde, who very soon after married Eleanor, and still has her as one of his wives. I know these to be facts, which I learned from Wallace at the time.

After breakfast, Mr. Smith called to take us home. We had a long and tedious journey, as it was cold, and one of the wagon tires came off repeatedly, and gave Smith a great amount of trouble. He was not in good health, and was unaccustomed to hardships, until our trip from St. Joseph. His object in going to California was mostly to improve his health.

When we arrived at home he was very much fatigued, and was covered with mud, and it was with some degree of discontent he said, while washing the mud from his hands and face, "I think Mormonism a very uncomfortable religion in this world, whatever it may be in the next."

When he was ready to take his leave, he handed me a note, while bidding me adieu, which I read after he was gone, as follows:

"DEAR ETTIE:

I find it very hard to part with you; but, unless you could abandon your religion, I could not expect to live happily with you. But, as I still indulge the hope that you may, I shall endeavor to see you again in Utah. I shall, on your account, go that way when I go to the mines; and I expect to leave St. Joseph about the 1st of March next. Some business of importance calls me back to that place before I cross the plains.

"I remain, as ever, your faithful friend,

"R. P. SMITH."

I read this note with the keenest emotions of pleasure and pain. I was glad to hear he was not disposed to become a

Mormon, and glad that there was even a distant prospect of seeing him again; and pained, beyond measure, that the obstacles to our union now appeared insurmountable, as well as at the prospect of parting with him, perhaps forever; at least, for a very long time. Not until he was gone did I fully understand my true position, or half the interest I had in him.

Mormonism taught me that, to love a "Gentile" was illicit; but I looked into my own heart, and while I did not discredit my religion, I felt it could not be wrong to remember with gratitude the generous and noble conduct of one whose motives were above reproach.

I very soon heard Mr. Smith had left St. Joseph for the mines. I was anxious to go on to New Fort Kearney where my mother and brothers were. Joseph Young, the brother of the Prophet, was now about to leave, with his family, for Utah, and his first wife, that is, the one he first married—his lawful wife—was very anxious I should travel with them; and I therefore went to her house to prepare for the journey. We were about ready to set out. I happened to look out one day, and saw some one coming, accompanied by two women; and, as they approached the house, I was astonished to see Wallace, whom I had supposed to be dead. It proved that he had not died as reported; so far from that, he had married another wife, Ellen Cutter, in addition to Harriet. He had now two wives, and both were with him.

Mrs. Young wondered if they could be coming to see me, and I told her I thought they were, but that I should not run from them.

Sure enough, they came to the door, and Wallace knocked,

OFFER OF MARRIAGE—LEAVING FOR ZION.   141

and I opened the door to him. Wallace offered me his hand, which I could not well refuse, and I shook it with more reluctance than anything I had ever done in my life; but I could not take the hand of Ellen or Harriet. Wallace said, "We called to invite you to go on to the valley with us, if you wish, you shall be as one of the party."

I replied that I was provided for, as I was going with Mrs. Young. That I did not think he had any claim upon me, and pointed to his two wives, and said, "I supposed you knew me better: good bye," and left the room. I saw no more of Wallace until I arrived at Utah Valley.

Everything was now ready, and in June, 1849, we commenced a journey that was to last for months, over a wild stretch of prairie and desert, and among bleak and snow-capped mountains—a journey memorable for its hardships, from fatigue, hunger and sickness. The cholera raged that season with uncommon fury on the plains, among all classes of emigrants, and the entire route was almost an unbroken succession of burying-grounds. Newly made graves met the eye at every step; and there, amidst these, and the loneliness and solitude of the great desert, we struggled on. Alone with the one great God, of whose mysterious existence we knew but little, and between whom and us stood our own Prophet, as our guide over the wide plains, sublime in their vastness.

When we arrived at New Fort Kearney, I was again disappointed at finding my mother and brothers had gone on to the valley, and I was under the necessity of making the entire journey with the family of Joseph Young. The company in which we travelled, were uncommonly fortunate in losing but few of its members by cholera, while other parties were in some cases nearly cut off by it.

But the Gentile emigrants were still more unfortunate. Whole companies were swept off, and their cattle and other effects fell into the hands of the Mormons. Their teams, too, were liable to become worn down, and would often die; and then, the emigrant who had loaded his wagon with such articles of furniture and tools as he had deemed indispensable to him, would be under the necessity of leaving them on the way. Of course they could not be sold, as no one would buy, when the chances were, that sooner or later he could find more than he could carry, abandoned on the way. The Mormons were generally well provided with teams, and owing to their experience in the hardships of such migrations, and the better discipline introduced by the Prophet, among their various companies of ten wagons each, their cattle seldom gave out, and they were thus always prepared to appropriate anything valuable to be found on the route.

This state of things was soon understood among the Gentiles, and they adopted the plan of privately burying their most valuable property when obliged to leave it, among the graves of the dead, and erecting over it a headstone, and marking thereon some name to indicate the locality of a stranger's grave—so that one unversed in the secret, might unwittingly walk among real graves, mingled with valuable property "cached" among them, and if sentimentally inclined, might drop a silent tear of sympathy over a valuable stove, or plow, or the like, purporting to be the grave of Amos Brown, or Hackaliah Thompson, of Connecticut or Kentucky

But nothing escaped the ever-watchful Mormon. They soon discovered the cheat among the cholera graves, and many of these "cachés" were opened by them, and the property carefully removed, while the earth was replaced, and the headstone again erected. Months afterwards, when those owning the property returned for it, they would find it gone the way of all Gentile property within the reach of Mormon hands.

I recollect one night, while on the Platt River, before we reached the North Fork, we had encamped in the midst of almost numberless graves. The cholera had swept off hundreds at this point, and the graves were far and near, clustered in every conceivable irregularity about the camping ground.

We went in to camp a little before night, and there was ample time for our caché robbers to look about for valuable prizes, which from the number of new graves, promised well.

Two of our wagon-drivers had, as they told the story, the next morning, discovered before dark, in a secluded place, a very large grave, which was, as they imagined, entirely too long for the ordinary purposes of human burial. They therefore marked the locality, and when the camp was still, late in the night, took a lantern, and went alone to secure the booty; not wishing to share it with any of their comrades. It was a dark disagreeable night. A night when spooks and hobgoblins would be abroad if they ever were. The rain fell in torrents. They found the "caché" they were looking for, and went to work; one with the spade, and the other holding the light. The prospect of gain gave them nerve. A strong thrust upon the spade, sent it full length into the bottom of the grave, and upon examination, they found the spade had laid bare the face of a dead body, apparently a very large man. The face covered with whiskers, was half torn off by the spade. The body had no coffin. The effect was terrible upon them. To open alone at such an hour, the grave of a cholera victim, surrounded by the thick and inky atmosphere of night, so lately vocal with the wail of death, was horrible.

They were at first disposed to run, but they mustered sufficient courage to refill the grave, and then went cowering back to camp—satisfied for the balance of the route with that night's experience in robbing "Gentile" cachés.

I do not propose to give a detailed account of our journey to Salt Lake, as I kept no journal of it. It was long and tiresome, occupying four months for its accomplishment, every day bringing with it a new adventure. Now harrassed with the fear of an attack from the Indian bands, that roam the boundless plains through which our route lay, who are governed by no law save that of a strongest arm; parched one day by thirst under a scorching sun, and the next, drenched by soaking rains. Suffocated by the hot airs of the plains during the day, and at night, chilled by the cold breath of the mountains: in short, suffering all the chances and mischances of a wandering life in the open air. Joyous and glad when the sun and the heavens were propitious, and sternly resolute to protect the aged, and the frail women and little children, when the face of nature frowned upon us, we struggled through to the end, and about the middle of September, 1849, arrived at Great Salt Lake City.

This had been regarded by all good Mormons, as the end of all earthly suffering and hardship. Once at this, "our Zion," all wrongs were to be redressed, and all doubtful points settled by the Prophet of God, upon a basis so simple, and easily understood, that all ground of complaint should cease, and the Church should find rest, and rule the earth in peace. No one more than myself looked forward with hope, mingled with fear and trembling, for the fulfillment of these glowing expectations. But I think I was not the only woman who was bitterly disappointed in the realization.

I had, by mingling with Gentiles in Missouri, by chance picked up here and there a hint, that Mormonism was not true; and Smith had more than once hinted the same, and now I had come to the last step in the proof. I knew that robbery and murder could not be right in the abstract; and certainly, when not required by necessity to protect the Church, upon the principle of self-defence, it would not be justified by the Prophet. I said to myself, "has he not led his people to a far-off land, to avoid the crime, and bitter strife, and bloodshed which had thus far followed the intercourse of the Church with the world; and will not these irregularities be condemned, now that the necessity for them has been removed?"

How bitterly I realized my mistake, and how heartily I repudiated Mormonism, and what ample reasons I found for doing so, will be found in the following chapters."

CHAPTER XIV.

GREAT SALT LAKE CITY, UTAH.

BRIGHAM YOUNG, with the main body of Mormons, had been at the valley about two years. The anniversary of the day on which the Prophet, with the Heads of the Church, arrived there, is still observed, and is celebrated with great pomp and ceremony. This event occurred July 24th, 1847, hence July 24th, instead of July 4th, is the great national day among the Mormons, for they already familiarize themselves with the idea of a Mormon nationality.

The Prophet had selected a site for a city, which was to become the centre of the Mormon world; and Great Salt City, the name by which it was christened, was founded on the east bank of the Jordan River. The Jordan connects Lake Utah with the Great Salt Lake, and is a beautiful stream. The city occupies a bench which rises gradually from the river, and is one of the most eligible and lovely localities imaginable. The streets are regularly laid out in squares. The main street, which is now built up with valuable buildings for the distance of two and a half or three miles, runs parallel to the Jordan, and is intersected by other streets at right angles. Streams of pure soft water are brought from the mountains behind the city, for the purpose of irrigation, and are conducted through the city, and allowed to gurgle down the gutters of each side of the principal streets, singing amid the busy hum of trade and strife wonderful tales of the mountain homes they have left behind, while the streets are ornamented by long rows of trees of different kinds, the thick and delightful shade of which, joined with the refreshing murmur of the rills ever rippling beneath them, give the city an air of rural, and even sylvan beauty, perhaps never before realized in so large a town. The buildings are mostly " adobé " (*i. e.*), built of sun-dried brick, moulded from blue clay. The land is very fertile when irrigated by the streams just mentioned. These streams are in charge of the police, whose duty it is to see that each person having land has the use of the water, generally two hours each week or as he has need according to the number of acres he has under cultivation; and when not thus diverted, it runs through the city as before described. The climate is perhaps the most healthy and enchanting in the world. The atmosphere is very dry and clear. Rain seldom falls. There will be perhaps one shower or so during the summer—sometimes two, but seldom more. The snow upon the mountains, which is always in sight, serves to keep the air delightfully cool and pure. Sickness is almost unknown there. The nights are apt to be somewhat cool.

During the first three winters after the arrival of the Mormons at Utah, there was no snow, and no cold weather to prevent the cattle from feeding in the open fields, along the Jordan bottoms; and then they required no extra attention. Since that time there have been some very severe winters, with more or less snow, and the first occurrence of this increased severity of the climate, which has since for the most part continued, caused much suffering among the cattle, great numbers of which died, as experience had not shown the necessity of barns and sheds for their protection against such emergencies. The cattle are pastured in summer on the rich bottoms, along the banks of the gently flowing Jordan, which are too low for cultivation, but furnishing abundance of excellent pasturage. The country is well adapted to raising cattle, and by irrigation, which will always be necessary, as there is no rain, it is equally so for all kinds of grain, if the water does not fail. It is, in short, one of the most desirable countries, both as regards climate and agricultural products, as a residence for man, and once fully developed, and freed from the curse of Mormonism, with a good government to which the peaceable citizen can look for protection, it is capable of sustaining a large population, and of producing the highest type of physical development of which the human race is capable.

As for myself I speak from the convictions of my best judgment, and from the results of my own experience, when I say, that could I see Utah freed from Mormonism, I would prefer by all odds to live there, in preference to any other part of the globe of which I have any knowledge; and that great Salt Lake City would be the particular spot at which I would pitch my tent, "*forever.*"

The foundation of a most magnificent temple has been laid in the city, and the inclosure, an adobé wall, is already finished. This wall, which is about twelve feet high, incloses ten acres of ground, in the centre of which are rising the walls of the temple. The whole energy of the Church is now directed towards its completion. The plan of the temple was a special revelation to Brigham Young. Many other public buildings have been erected, and large and expensive blocks have risen in the business quarter, the result of private enterprise.

Perhaps history has seldom, if ever, recorded an instance of success so rapid and remarkable, as that which has attended the combined enterprise of the Church at Salt Lake City, and in Utah generally. The end of which success, if unchecked by Gentile interference, is not yet.

CHAPTER XV.

CHURCH POLITY.

BEFORE proceeding further with my own personal narrative, I deem it proper to give, in a brief form, some account of the Mormon Church Polity. This may be found the more necessary to a clear understanding of the following pages, as affording the key to some acts of the Heads of the Church, which otherwise might appear devoid of motive.

THE "PROPHET"—BRIGHAM YOUNG.

Brigham Young is "the President of the Church of Jesus Christ, of Latter Day Saints." The acknowledged "Prophet." He holds the "Keys of the Kingdom," that is, the keys of Heaven. Without the permission of the "Prophet" *none can be saved.* He is an acknowledged revelator. Claims, and is acknowledged by the Church, to be the supreme Pontiff of the world, with both temporal and spiritual jurisdiction, and as such, is entitled to the implicit, personal, and unquestioned obedience of all Mormons. To whose power there is in fact no limit among the faithful: and when we add to this, a knowledge of the dogma, that it is allowed and enjoined, " to smite the Gentiles to enforce obedience," we understand how dangerous the "Prophet" *might* become if he had the power.

THE FIRST PRESIDENCY.

The second great power in the Church, next to the Prophet, is the First Presidency. This is composed of the Prophet and his two counsellors. The three together form that fearful centre of all ecclesiastical and temporal power in the Church, known as the First Presidency, or simply the " Presidency."

To be a member of this august trio, is to be a right-hand man with the Prophet—his shadow, and to be authorized to act for him in his absence, or disability.

When I left the valley it was composed as follows :—Brigham Young, Hebir Chase Kimball, and Jedadiah M. Grant. The last has since died, and his place will be filled by another, probably by John Taylor.

COLLEGE OF THE "TWELVE APOSTLES."

The next "order" in the Church is that of the "Twelve Apostles," usually called the "Twelve;" among whom I may mention the names of Orson Pratt, Parley P. Pratt, Orson Hyde, John Taylor, Willford Woodruff, Samuel Richards, Amasy Lyman, Ezra T. Benson, George A. Smith, and Charles C. Rich. I cannot recollect the names of the others. Some members of this college have been called to a foreign mission, or otherwise disqualified for the performance of the duties of this office, in which cases, it has been customary to fill their places, and hence it happens, that there is in fact, at present, at least fifteen of the "Twelve;" only twelve are however, entitled to seats in this "quorum" at one time. The "Twelve" come still nearer the people, and the President of the Twelve, first, and next to him one of its members, act and "counsel" in all matters in the absence of a member of the "First Presidency." The members of this order are subject to do duty as missionaries, in which case they join the "Seventies," mentioned hereafter.

PRESIDENT OF THE SEVENTIES.

The next office in point of dignity is the President of the Seventies. This is at present filled by Joseph Young, a brother of the Prophet. The body over which he presides is made up as follows. The seventy quorums, hereafter mentioned, have each a President. These presidents form a sort of administrative council over the subject of "missions and preaching," called the Seventies, and it is over this body, the President of Seventies presides. The "Seventies," thus made up, have the direction of all matters connected with the propagandism of the Church. From this body emanate all missionary efforts, and instructions to those connected therewith, as also the subject of preaching, and preachers in general. The President of this body is the head of all outside effort for the conversion of the world, always subject, of course, to the higher powers before mentioned.

THE QUORUM OF SEVENTIES.

Each member of the body last mentioned, numbering

seventy in all, is himself a President of another body, called a Quorum of Seventy, having also in theory, seventy members. These Quorums are not always full, in fact, they seldom are all so. They form the bone and muscle of missionary labor; and have no reference to rank in the Church, as an Apostle, or a High Priest or Elder, or Priest, may be a member of one of these Quorums. They constitute the instruments by which the measures of the "Seventies," and its President are carried into effect. They are the outside working bees of the central hive, and "go into all the world to preach the gospel," without "purse or scrip," and often come back again loaded with money, and bringing many converts with them. They are scattered over the whole earth, and are continually going and coming, leaving their many wives at Salt Lake, that they may not want an inducement to return in due time, to render an account to the President of the Seventies. Each Quorum preserves in its secret archives, a complete record of the genealogy of each of its members, as also of the official acts of each. Organized as they are, they constitute the most effective body of working men conceivable; second perhaps only to the celebrated order of Jesuits, whose fame and crimes are known to the ends of the earth. It was the apparent miracle performed by one of these, that effected the conversion of my mother to Mormonism.

THE PRIESTHOOD.

The orders referred to heretofore, as well as those hereafter described, have more particular reference to the practical

7*

administration of the temporal business of the Church. The priesthood, however, appears to be charged with the execution of its spiritual affairs exclusively—a sort of spiritual executive body, though as heretofore seen, the priesthood is possessed by all who belong to the Quorums. The High Priest is first in rank of this order, and next after the Apostles. Next in this order come the Elders; and last and lowest, we have the simple priests. But if any of these wish to preach, they must join a Quorum. The priesthood, in some form, is understood to be necessary to the salvation of a male, or at least, to his exaltation; and a female cannot be saved without being "sealed" to some male who is a Priest. Hence all true Mormons are Priests, and women really do not amount to much in themselves, as they have no souls of their own. Hence women are often "sealed," that is married to men, when they do not intend to live with them as an earthly wife, but merely that they may be saved by them: in that case they are "sealed" for eternity, as it is termed. But when they are married for the natural purposes of a wife, *i. e.* to have children, they are then said to be "sealed" for time; and they may be "sealed" for one alone, or for both. If a woman's husband is dead, she need not be sealed again, unless she chooses, and when she does marry again, she is "sealed only for time, as when she dies, her first husband will "resurrect," *i. e.* save her; and she will be his in the next world.

The difference between "exaltation" and "salvation," in the Mormon use of these terms, is this. A male Mormon without the priesthood may be saved by favor of the Prophet; as also may a Gentile to be used as a servant; but can never be exalted. This exaltation means having in the next world a kingdom, and a great many wives, and many Gentile servants, and being great in power as a sovereign. All the wives and the children of a priest in this world belong to his "kingdom" in the next, and are a part of his "exaltation" there. A woman's "exaltation" in the next world depends upon her being "sealed" to a man that is a priest in this, and who can exalt her there, by winning for himself a high exaltation. That is to say the glory of the wife, in the next world, is dependent upon the glory of her husband. Hence, among true Mormon women, it is an object to marry some of the Heads of the Church, or those of high official dignity. To marry an Apostle or a High Priest, is considered a great honor; while to be a wife of the Prophet, or of a member of the First Presidency, is the highest dignity to which a woman can aspire; and this is the reason why the Heads of the Church get so many wives. This principle is often used among the girls, as a bug-bear to force them to marry, and often old men succeed in winning young girls to their beds by it, if they occupy high positions. Coercion is seldom used to effect marriages among the women. They are indulged in the utmost freedom of choice among the men. They are only required to marry some one, "and the man of her choice," is not at liberty to refuse to marry a woman when asked to do so. Proposition for marriage comes as often, and with as good grace from the female, as from the male. An apparent hardship in this system, and it is only in appearance, is that it would be likely to leave some men without wives, while others have a great number. But a man who lacked the necessary address to win a wife or several of them, would not be likely to complain; besides the fact is, that women accumulate under the system. I think it seldom occurs, that a man wishing to marry, who is able to support a wife, cannot find at least one; although many not over good looking men, who have no high official dignity to recommend them, are obliged to content themselves with one or two. It is considered, however, in "good society," to be a want of position and rank to possess but one wife; and few men have the moral courage to appear in public with less than two; while on great occasions, when it is an object to make an impression upon the public mind, it is the custom for men of position to appear surrounded by a numerous train of wives—the more the better.

It will be seen from the above, why all the wives after the first are called "spiritual," *i. e.* because they are to be wives in the spirit world, and are now raising children for the exaltation of the spiritual kingdom of the husband. It is possible also to be the "spiritual wife" of one man, and the temporal wife of another at the same time. I have thus given a fuller account of this part of Mormon practice and belief, not because I think it a very interesting subject, but because it was necessary to a clear understanding of what follows, and as affording a key to Mormon success and discipline. It is proper that I state that it is believed and taught, that when a man dies unmarried, he has no kingdom in the next world; and hence he is not "exalted" there; and that a man can, by consent, be annexed in this world to some other man's Kingdom for the next. Also that the sons and sons-in-law, with their wives, may be in like manner annexed to the Kingdom of the father or father-in-law; thus swelling his and waiving their own claim to a Kingdom.

This system is capable of many other applications, which are amplified and pressed into service by the Heads of the Church, in order to keep their deluded victims in the line of "duty;" a full account of which would be too long and tedious for the limits and design of these pages.

I may state, however, in a general way, that all "Gentiles" are to be in the next world servants of the "Saints;" and that the second coming of Christ is soon expected, and is in fact now waited for. And then that Christ will reign upon the earth, a thousand years, and then Mormons will "possess the earth," and all the Gentiles living at that second coming will give up their property to the Church, and serve the "Saints" in whatever menial capacity the latter may direct.

Brigham Young says he knows some persons in the States that would make excellent servants; and instanced Franklin Pierce, President of the United States, and other men of position in the country connected with the Government. This remark of the Prophet has been deemed by some an ungrateful return to President Pierce, for the appointment by the latter of Brigham Young to the office of Civil Governor of the territory of Utah.

THE PATRIARCH.

The office of Patriarch is one of great sanctity and honor,

although not one of much power, as it is confined to granting "blessings,"* usually written out after an approved form

* The following is an exact copy of a "blessing," pronounced by Hiram, who was afterwards killed with his brother, the Prophet Joseph Smith. The authority to pronounce these blessings, is possessed by all the Heads of the Church, in common with the Patriarch, but it is the special duty of the latter.

"PATRIARCHAL BLESSING OF MARY ETTIE CORAY, DAUGHTER OF SILAS AND MARY CORAY.

'Born in the Township of Providence, Luzern County, and State of Pennsylvania, 31st of Jan., 1829.

"Sister Mary Ettie, I lay my hands upon your head in the name of Jesus of Nazareth, to place and seal a blessing unto you, even a Father's blessing, which blessing is Patriarchal as from under the hands of your father or any one of the Patriarchs of old, that a blessing should be placed upon your head, according to the covenants with your fathers Abraham, Isaac, and Jacob, and in future time, receive a fullness of those blessings, according to the promises as touching your inheritance and the glory of your father, and the honor and immortality and felicity of your Mansion in the resurrection of the Just, therefore there is a blessing for you and a reward laid up for your obedience, for the integrity of your heart, in the days of your youth; remember that you are now in your youthful days, and this life at times and seasons in the intermediate spaces of your existence, will be attended with tribulations, but in the world to come, you shall have immortality and eternal life. This is your reward because of the integrity of your heart. And again you shall be blessed temporally and spiritually in your house and habitation, in your field and in your flocks, in your basket and in your store, as also in your posterity, and your name shall be perpetuated from generation to generation, and your miracles and acts shall be written in the archives

and over the signature of the Patriarch, which are supposed to act as a sort of charm in favor of the possessor. These benedictions are made for a fee of one dollar, and their delivery constitutes the sole business of the Patriarch. The office is held during life, which is an exception to the general rule of the Church, as all other elective offices are limited to a specific term. This office has always been in the family of the Prophet Smith. Joseph Smith, father of the Prophet, was the first Patriarch, and John L. Smith is the present incumbent. He is still a young man. The Prophet Joseph was his cousin.

JUDICIAL AND EXECUTIVE OFFICES.

There are a few minor officers on whom devolve the execution of all the municipal regulations of the Church—a set of men who stand directly between the governed and the governing class; at once officers of the Church, and of the civil executive. Among these the most important, though not highest in rank, is that of Bishop. The city at Salt Lake is divided into twenty-four wards, each of which has a

---

and chronicles of your brethren. And your days and years are numbered and shall be many. These blessings I seal upon your head. Even so, Amen.

"Given by HIRAM SMITH, at Nauvoo, Ill., Sept. 24th, 1840."

"Howard Coray, Clerk.

Endorsed on the back as follows:

"Entered in Record-book, page 181.

"H. CORAY, Clerk."

Bishop. In other settlements of the territory similar divisions of convenient size are made and placed under a like officer. The duties of their offices are partly judicial but mainly that of an *informer*. They "hear and determine" complaints, either civil or religious, upon which they act subject to appeal to the "High Council." They make domiciliary visits each week, to inquire into the temporal and spiritual condition of each person of their ward; and all persons disaffected, as to word or doctrine, are reported to the First Presidency. They are, in short, the general informers, as between the Prophet and the people, and all "Gentiles" within the wards are watched and reported upon in like manner. They also collect the tithing.

The intermediate tribunal, to whom appeals may be made from the award of the Bishop, known as the "High Council," is composed of fifteen men, chosen from among the High Priests, twelve of whom act as jurors, and a majority of these decide the case by vote; the remaining three acting as judges, passing sentence, and fixing damages and costs and the like. An appeal can be had from this tribunal to the First Presidency, from which there is no appeal. A Mormon cannot appeal for redress as between himself and another Mormon to the civil courts; but must in the first instance carry the case to his Bishop, unless he gets the permission of the "High Council."

The Bishop is assisted by another officer, called a Teacher; and he has sometimes two of these, as occasion may require. The duty of the Teacher is to assist the Bishop, more particularly in the religious part of his duty. He makes domiciliarly visits, and catechises the people and children, and reports to the Bishop all heresies or other irregularities among them. Al. offices of the Church expire by limitation, once in six months, except that of Patriarch, which is held during life. The different orders of the Priesthood and the Quorum of the Seventies, of course, are not now referred to, as they are not elective offices, but permanent orders in the Church; but every elective office, from the Prophet down to the Bishop and his teachers, go out of office twice in each year; and this occurs on the 6th of April and October, at which time the semi-annual conference is held. This conference is made up of the whole people, assembled in one body, and presided over by the President and Prophet, Brigham Young. When all are assembled, then each officer is called to an account, and any one is at liberty to prefer charges, beginning with the Prophet.

It speaks well for the shrewdness of Brigham Young, that no opposition has ever been made to his administration, and that he has been reëlected twice every year since he succeeded Joseph Smith at Nauvoo. Thus each officer, after the Prophet, comes before the people for reëlection, and however absolute may be the power of his office, he is still accountable to the great body of the people, as the original source of power. The supposed power of the Prophet, as such, and the timely revelation of which he avails himself when too closely pressed, are the true secrets of his power. This detracts very much from the merit, which would otherwise attach to the *apparent* democracy of the Mormon Church Government. Besides the officers before mentioned, there is one known as the Captain of the Police, who has under his command a necessary number of policemen to enable him to keep up a night guard in all parts of the city, and around the public works. There are other organized bodies within the Church, of a secret character, which may be regarded as being a part of her recognized institutions, such as the band of the "Danites," and the various and mostly unknown ramifications of the institution connected with the "Endowment" rooms. It is here, in what is termed the "second anointing," where none but the most approved Mormon enters—none but those who have been tested by years of trial, and then bound by the most solemn oaths, which involve life and limb as a forfeit, that are hid the real secrets of the Church. Here her true aims are fully developed, and the plans by which she proposes to accomplish her final mission conceived and put in motion. The Danites are supposed to be merely a secret police, for the execution of the commands issued from behind the veil of these dark mysteries; and judging from what we know of their acts, we are justified in believing the aims of this secret power are by no means modest. Enough has escaped the lips of the Heads of the Church, in moments of excitement and anger, to indicate that the propogation of the principles of the Church, and the spread of the Prophet's sway, are not to rest entirely upon the slow and uncertain process of moral suasion. One thing is certain. They are well organized to-day in a military point of view; and the habits of undying watchfulness, and hardy enterprise, acquired by a long experience of continued conflict with the "Gentiles" in Missouri and Illinois, and during their migration through the wilderness among the wild Indian tribes, and wild beasts, over the wide prairies to their new "Zion," render them to-day the best disciplined people in the world. Ever on their guard; skilled in all the learning of wood craft; able to read as upon the printed page, upon the great desert by which their isolated homes are surrounded, those signs, which to inexperienced eyes, would pass unnoticed; familiar with the laws of life and climate, which characterize their country; and thus enabled to turn all these to their own advantage, as against strangers; and lastly, familiar with the wild mountain passes and deep cañons, through which all approach to them must be made; they would certainly seem to be in possession of some elements of strength, in case they found it necessary to use them for self-defence. Added to which, it is well understood, that measures are being taken by them to locate defences among these passes of the mountains. And where they do not actually erect defence, examinations are made, and plans matured, which can be easily put into execution when they are needed. Many, and most of these passes in fact, need no works of defence. A few determined men in the right position, well acquainted with the locality, is all that will be needed to prevent the passage of a much larger body of armed men.*

The policy of the Church in regard to the Indians is very peculiar. Every tribe is visited by missionary Elders, who instruct them in the Mormon faith; and by intermarriage, and by every other means, efforts are made to bring them under

* Among other means of defence against Gentile interference, often mentioned at the valley, may be included that of poisoning the wells and fountains, as a last resort.

the Mormon control, by which means they are gaining countenance among them. This influence they are using to prejudice the Indians against the people of the United States, and against the American Government. This is now the settled policy of the Church, and if it has no other influence, it *will* have the effect, if it has not already, to stir up the tribes to open hostilities against the undefended settlements of the Far West. And in case of collision between the Mormons and the United States Government, which must come sooner or later, this control over the Indian tribes would give the former a great advantage over the latter.

I deem it proper to state in connection, that the mysteries of the Second Anointing of the Endowments, among other inhuman ceremonies, are supposed to be defiled by the monstrous rite of offering human sacrifices, or at least, that the doctrine is fully taught and developed there. Enough has already transpired among the women to justify this conclusion. Those who have not taken this anointing, and but a comparatively small number of them have taken it, are very much alarmed about this, as they know not what to expect. They are always upon the rack, as they are liable to be called upon at any time to go to the Endowment rooms for that purpose.

THE CONSECRATION OF PROPERTY.

Another effect of the mysteries of the Endowments, is the consecration of the entire property to the Church by placing it in the hands of the Prophet. This is a high test of faith, but one at which the true Mormon, if he has penetrated those inner mysteries, never falters. The consecration itself is not a secret, but is made in a public manner. By proper and legal modes, the whole earthly property of the person making the consecration is conveyed to the Prophet, who holds the same not in trust, but in his own right. The consecrator in the main is allowed to keep possession until called for by the Prophet, who takes it only as he has need, and exercises great discretion and kindness in the assumption of his legal rights over it. If the Prophet is in want of a yoke of oxen and *he judges* a man who has consecrated his property can spare them, he sends one of his servants to drive them away, but he is careful never to do it in such a manner, that it shall be considered a hardship by the one in possession; for the latter is always considered the owner, until it is called for by the Prophet, and he is at liberty to use, and even to dispose of it for his own support, and for that of his family, but for no other purpose.

When we consider the enterprise and energy which characterize the Mormon people, and their increasing wealth at Utah, we must acknowledge that Brigham Young is at this moment not only in theory, but in fact, an untrammelled sovereign of great wealth, and to say the least, is one of growing power, if not *already powerful.*

TITHING.

Every male member of the Church is required to devote every tenth day of his time in labor upon the Temple, or other public works, or pay a sum of money equal to the hire of a substitute: and the Church is also entitled to, and scrupuluosly exacts from, all property holders a tenth of their income, and a tenth of the produce of all lands. No one's property is exempt from this ta,x as it goes into the general treasury for the propagation of the gospel, for bringing converts to Utah, and defraying the expenses of the public works; and after these, for the erection of the Temple. The cheerful payment of this tithing is regarded as a test of orthodoxy.

CHAPTER XVI.

**REUBEN P. SMITH'S ARRIVAL—NARROW ESCAPE FROM BE-
COMING A "SPIRITUAL."**

ONCE at the end of the tedious journey over the plains, and safely reunited with my family, and above all, in my own mother's house, I was happy again. My mother had bought a house and lot in a pleasant part of the city, and was already settled, with Lizzie and Uriah with her. She had an acre and a quarter of ground, the size of all the city lots designed for dwellings. My brother Howard was also there with his family, so we were all settled near each other. My brother William's wife was also there. It will be recollected that William had joined the Mormon battalion for the Mexican war, and we had just received intelligence of his death. All our family that were Mormons, and yet living, were now at Salt Lake City, and I was more disposed, and apparently had it more in my power than ever before, to settle down contentedly and lead a quiet life. Thus far the sea of my life had been troubled and stormy, and if I did not find myself disappointed in my expectations as to what I still supposed Mormonism to be, I saw no reason why my tempest-tossed bark should not rest secure within the calm haven of our new Zion. Yet all depended upon what the Prophet had to say to the wrong I had suffered. If he justified all the Mormons had done in his absence, and if he approved their crimes, and that was Mormonism, then I was not a Mormon, and I should regret having left the States. But I was soon to know.

My brother Howard, now a High Priest, was one of the Prophet's secretaries, and one day I went to the office to see him, and while there the Prophet came in, and recognized me, although we had not met since the cold and dreary march through Iowa, at which time we were in the same company with him for a few days.

The Prophet, who is acknowledged to be one of the finest looking men in the Church, and possessed of a remarkably easy and winning address, received me very cordially, and said, "Well, Nettie, how do you like Mormonism by this time?" I replied to him at some length, that if Mormonism was the same at Salt Lake that it was in the States, I did not think I was a Mormon. I told him the whole story as to Wallace, and how he had treated me. I felt the utmost freedom in unburthening my heart's secret to him even as to a parent. I referred to the hardship and crime of the double wife doctrine, and to the crimes of the Heads of the Church, and the "Danites."

He listened to me with great patience and kindness of manner, and I waited his reply with untold interest. My faith in Mormonism hung upon his reply. He evidently understood the difficulty of my case, for at times he looked troubled and anxious. When he replied, he made no mention of any matters but those which personally interested me. He said, "I will tell you, Nett, how it is. There *is* a right in the matter. It is perfectly right, as well as a privilege, and has now become a duty, for every man in the Church to have a plurality of wives. But if a man's wife tries to do what is right about it, her husband should be reasonable. There are some shrewd women in the Church who cannot stand that doctrine. They were intended from the foundation of the world for another purpose. We are all calculated to be beneficial in the hands of our Heavenly Father, in rolling forth this great work. But if all our women were like you, our Mormonism would soon come to naught."

I said, "Brother Brigham, I do not understand what a mere woman can do." To which he replied, "Such a woman as you are can be very useful. I cannot explain it now, but you shall know soon enough. Make yourself contented. I do not uphold Wallace. I think he has done very wrong. *He must be rebaptized*, or I cannot fellowship him."

At this point, his daughter Luna came in, and called him to supper. He said, "Tell your ma I will take tea with Augusta to-night." The Augusta referred to was Mrs. Cobb, mentioned in another part of this book, and now one of his wives. I then told him I was disappointed, and was sorry I was there, but that I must make the best of it. To which he replied, "That is the right spirit. Be 'sealed' to some man that has a wife, and then you will not feel so bad." Here the interview ended, and I went home to my mother, and told her how matters stood, and what the Prophet had said. It was then too late in the fall to return to the States; but I would gladly have done so, had it been within my power.

My mother until then had believed with me, that the Prophet would condemn the spiritual wife doctrine; and we were both greatly distressed; but we soon had greater cause for alarm. I have neglected to mention, that almost the first person I had met upon my arrival at the city was Wallace. I met him in the street, and he told me that he was going to South California, and perhaps to South America. He said his health was very poor; and he seemed to be in low spirits. I wished him well as we parted; and this was the last time we ever met. He went, and soon after died. The news of his death was published in the city paper,* which mentioned his disease as having been some difficulty of the

---

* Although I have never heard of Wallace since I saw the notice of his death, it now occurs to me, that this of *itself* would be no evidence of the fact, if the Prophet had a motive in inducing me to believe him dead.

I recollect a circumstance of this kind, that occurred when I was at the Valley, as follows:

George A. Smith, who is a bald-headed old man, and one of the "Apostles," wished to add to the wives he already had, a young girl; but she preferred a younger man. Soon after she was married her husband was sent away from his home, and from his young wife, upon a mission by the influence of Smith, and the story was afterwards circulated of his death; and the wife was "counselled," and at length induced to marry the "Apostle" Smith, before rejected. But the husband returned, and claimed his wife. Smith refused to give her up, or to allow her to be seen by him, who thereupon apostatized, and left for California, and nothing more was heard from him.

Entering into competition with an "Apostle," for the possession of a "spiritual" at the Valley, is not thought to be a safe or equal contest

throat. Notwithstanding his life was now no more to me than to a stranger, as I had no intention of living with him again, yet I received the news of his death the second time with feelings of sadness, the more so as I now felt we had both been the victims of a cruel religious delusion.

The following winter was one of uncommon gaiety in the the city. The Mormons exceeded themselves in the number of the balls and parties, and amateur theatres, by which nearly every night was enlivened. These amusements are reduced to a system among them, and all classes and ages join in the wild and sometimes boisterous round of amusements, which here succeed each other. I have often danced at these places with the Prophet and other heads of the Church. Appointments are made by the Church authorities, for the balls for each week, in such and such wards, and there are sometimes several in the city on the same night. Such arrangements are made, that every person in the Church can attend once or twice each week, or oftener if they choose. I made it a point to attend these parties during most of the winter, as this was the only relief I had against the presentiment of evil which oppressed me. I felt at this time that I could no more endure double wifeism now than before, and if I had understood the Prophet rightly, there was no escape from it if I remained in the valley. I cannot deny that I sometimes thought of Smith. But I could hardly flatter myself I should see him again, as he had started over the plains before our party, and since he had not yet arrived, I concluded some misfortune had overtaken him or he had forgotten me. I found upon a close self-examination, that the possibility of either being true gave me great uneasiness, and yet I could not bring myself, even to wish, to expose him to the evils of Mormonism. And if he came how could he escape? If he did not become a Mormon, he could be nothing to me, and rather than have him become one, I would forego forever the pleasure of seeing him again.

I spent, during the winter, much of my time in the family of Heber C. Kimball, who had over thirty wives; not all of whom were at home, however, as they lived in different houses.

I had no lack of offers, for it was a very common thing for me to make a *conquest* of some one almost daily. I was yet young, and for the first time began to think myself attractive, if the number of my suitors could be taken as an evidence of it. Among them were numbered men of all ranks and conditions in life. Heads of the Church, and undistinguished priests, and men of all ages, from the old man of seventy-five, with a stately train of wives at his heels, with babies to match, to the mere boy of eighteen; who looked forward with pride to the day when he should have as many. If I did not think best to avail myself of any of these tempting and flattering offers, it does not follow that they did not afford me a great amount of amusement, and yet the reflection oppressed me, that many of these men were acting under instructions from the Prophet, and that a continued obstinacy on my part might bring with it serious consequences.

Oppressed with a vague fear of something which I could not well define, I went home one day, and when at the door, my sister Lizzie met me, and with a face full of quizzical fun, said, "Oh you can't guess who has been here, nor can I tell you. But I expect you will know well enough." "Who is it," said I, and Smith came to my mind at once. "Did his hair curl?" "Oh yes," said Lizzie, "I knew you were waiting for some one, but you sha'n't have him; we will some of us cut you out."

"Now I understand something," said Brother Kimball, who had brought me home in his carriage. He referred to my refusal of so many offers of marriage during the winter, which was, he said, very extraordinary among the Mormons. There was no need for Lizzie to tell me, as she did, that the stranger was one of our boarders at St. Joseph, or that he had mentioned our passage of the Taukio in company. I knew it was Smith, and I was nearly wild with excitement. He had left word that he would call the next day, and I had ample time to look over the ground, and fully realize my position. I now felt I loved him too well to give him up, and that this would probably be the only chance I was likely to have of marrying a man, not a Mormon. I thought by marrying him I could get away from Mormonism, and otherwise I had no means nor excuse for going. The only embarrassment that presented itself was the thought of leaving my mother again.

The next morning he came, and I was astonished to find him so much improved in health and appearance. He had allowed his beard to grow, which added very much to his manly beauty. I was happy in meeting him once more. He told me he thought the journey over the plains must have agreed with us both, judging from appearances. He said, "I thought I would call, as by agreement, and see you."

I replied, "has no other motive impelled you?" Smith looked at me earnestly, and said,

"I think I can say in good faith, other motives have brought me here. I wish to have a few words with you alone, if convenient. Can I?"

I gladly consented to listen to him, and indicated to mother what we wanted. As we had but one room in our house, my mother made an errand to one of the neighbors, and left us alone. I cannot well describe in detail this interview. Smith said, "It is now about two years since I have been looking forward to this moment, and during all that time, I have fondly indulged the hope that you would yet be mine; and I trust I am not to be disappointed now—am I?"

Of course I told him what my heart so gladly prompted, or at least he took it for granted.

I fully realized the difference between an undivided attachment like his, and that of which I had been the victim, when the wife of Wallace Henderson. I had married Wallace to escape the terrible fate of being obliged to marry some old man, who had already more wives than he should have. It is true I had learned afterwards to love him, and if he had treated me fairly, I should have been contented and happy.

But my attachment to Smith was of a different and more absorbing character; and yet I felt the embarrassment of our position. I told Smith I could not marry him without Brigham Young's consent, and that I would do it on no account, it I believed he could ever become a Mormon; and yet, if we were married in Utah, he must at least assume the appearance of being one.

He said, "In the spring we will go to California, and in the mean time, I will say nothing about being a 'Gentile;' and I will also pay my tithing regularly, and if they do not press me too closely, I can pass for a good enough Mormon to keep them quiet until we get away."

The balance of the winter passed very pleasantly. We were very careful not to make our new relation, now fully understood by none but ourselves, conspicuous before the public, as Smith wished time to establish in the Church a character for orthodox Mormonism, in an easy and quiet manner, without exciting much inquiry upon the subject. With regard to myself, I was still the object of great anxiety in a matrimonial point of view, as the following story will show:

Captain James Brown, who I have mentioned in the first part of this narrative, had married my aunt. Not content with that, he had also among other wives married her daughter, my young cousin, a very pretty girl. Captain Brown came to my mother's, to make a visit, and stayed all night with my aunt; and the next night he returned, with my cousin, and they also remained all night. The next morning he said to me, in a manner, and with a levity that perfectly disgusted me, "Nettie, night before last, I lodged with your aunt, and last night with your cousin, as you have seen; and to night, I am going to get your consent, and Brother Brigham will seal us, and I will lodge with you." The hero of this exploit was an old grey-headed man and was the true and lawful (as the "Saints" reckon law) husband of eight wives. I acknowledge I was somewhat ruffled in temper by this proposition, especially thus backed up, as it had been, by an ocular display of the working of the system. My aunt soon came into the room, and I said to her, "I really hope when the 'Gentiles' come to shoot down the Mormons (an event considered by the Church as not unlikely to happen some day), that you will be the first one aimed at, for I believe you will well deserve it. I think you are a most ridiculous woman; you have brought up your daughter to believe that it is right and necessary for her salvation to marry an old white-headed man, her father-in-law." My aunt replied very quietly. "I think your mother has not instilled quite Mormonism enough into your mind for your good, my girl." "My mother?" said I. "Do you not think I have some idea of what is reasonable and honorable myself?" Captain Brown, after hearing so much of our conversation, took his hat, and went to the Prophet: and told him I was speaking disrespectfully of the Celestial Law. Brother Brigham directed him to bring me with my aunt to his house that evening, and they would talk to me of the consequences of such sentiments. When Captain Brown returned he was quite cheerful, and said very pleasantly to me, "Brother Brigham has sent you an invitation to visit him this evening, with us. I think we shall have a pleasant time, will you go?" I knew better than to decline, and I accordingly went. We found Brigham with his first wife, Eliza Snow, and another of his wives. We had been there some time, and the Prophet had exerted himself to make the visi easy and agreeable, when he at length turned to me and said, " Well, Nett, what do you think about men who marry their step-daughters ?" "And half sisters," said I. " That is not the question I asked you," said the Prophet with severity. " I know it is not" replied I; " but the first wife of George Watt has occasion to ask this question very often, as his second wife claims it as her right, to take the lead in the management of home affairs on the ground that she is the half-sister of her husband, they having a common mother. The spirits of a half brother and sister, husband and wife, would be likely to be the most congenial."

The Prophet appeared somewhat nettled at this, and said, "I discover you are in the habit of making light of sacred matters. Have you never received the gift, and felt the power of the Holy Ghost, which it is the privilege of every one to feel who has been confirmed under the hands of one of the Apostles of Jesus Christ?"* "I was confirmed" I replied," by John C. Page, at that time one of the Apostles, but he has since apostatized, which may account for my not having experienced the change of which you speak. And yet I must admit that I was at one time healed by old father Bawsley, under peculiar circumstances. I had the rheumatism in my right arm, for several months, and at length it was so disabled that I could scarcely straighten it. The old man came, and anointed it with consecrated oil, and prayed, and rubbed the arm a long while, and I was then able to straighten it with ease, and that was the last of the rheumatism, which

* Sometimes represented to be " Apostles " of Joseph Smith. There is a difference of opinion in the Church upon this point.

resulted I suppose from some virtue of the oil, or perhaps from the friction."

"By virtue of the Priesthood," said the Prophet. "I see you must have a husband to strengthen your faith. Perhaps brother Brown would suit you. I know he is somewhat old, but then you will be less likely to be jealous of him, than you would of a younger husband."

"Uncle," said I, "necessity may compel me to marry you, but nothing else will. As far as Mormonism is concerned, as it existed eight years ago, I believe it. I am a Mormon as Mormonism was then understood: and it may be right now; but I do not understand it. I do not see through this new order of things." "But no doubt you will yet," said Mrs. Cobb, another of Brigham's wives, who had just come into the room.

The Prophet had watched me closely during this conversation, as if expecting to hear some damnable heresy, and I knew Captain Brown had represented my case in no very favorable light to him, and I was determined he should get no advantage of me. He turned to the redoubtable captain, whose prospect of being sealed to me that night was now growing less and less, and said:

"Captain Brown, I cannot see that Nett is altogether beside herself, she can get along yet without a husband. Her case is not desperate by any means. Plenty of our women believe as she does. All she needs is a little time."

I knew by this what the intention of Capt. Brown had been. He had expected the Prophet would have "counselled" me to be sealed to him then and at once, which would have been equal to a command to do so; and a refusal would have involved me in serious difficulty. I therefore took occasion to say to him what I understood to be his aim in citing me before the Prophet.

The latter said to me." No matter as to that. All you have to do is to obey 'counsel,' and if you do not do that, you know the consequences as well as Captain Brown."

The Prophet possesses the faculty of settling such differences, and harmonizing discordant elements, without compromising his dignity or authority to a remarkable degree. The constant recurrence of similar cases has made him an adept in reading human nature, and enables him to divine at once, if there should chance to be a selfish, or personal motive at the bottom, and by his skillful use of the cant phrases in common vogue among them, in which are embodied the ever present, and ever acknowledged idea of his divine commission, he is in general enabled to make a favorable impression upon both parties, and, to use his own words, " to strengthen the stakes of Zion."

As for myself, this interview admonished me of the delicacy of my position, and especially that it behoved me to avoid, rather than disobey, the counsel of the Prophet. As for the captain he considered himself a disappointed lover, and found it hard to bear up against the fate of single blessedness to which he had been doomed, with but eight wives to solace him. It is due to Captain Brown that I state, that he had served with some distinction in the Mormon battalion in the Mexican war.

CHAPTER XVII.

"SEALED" TO THE BUTCHER FOR ETERNITY—A FEARFUL DISCOVERY.

I WAS left in the undisturbed enjoyment of personal freedom for some time after this; and my life passed pleasantly enough, in the exercise of due care not to speak openly against the general principles of Mormonism.

Nothing had occurred to disturb my quiet, until one day a message came in some haste from the Prophet directing me to come to his office immediately. I had never for a moment hesitated in obeying his commands, and always, I believe, without thinking it a hardship, for I still believed in him as the Head of the Church.

My readers can form but an imperfect estimate of the absoluteness of the Prophet's rule, or the cheerfulness with which obedience to him is rendered. The performance of this duty is counted a pleasure among the faithful, and it is evidently the intention of the Prophet to make it attractive. For instance, when he issues a command, he does it under the pleasing fiction of administering "counsel," although it is well understood, that to disobey such "counsel," would be to incur the greatest peril, as well for this world as the next.

Upon going to his office, I found the Prophet alone. He said to me kindly: "Nett, you are determined, I see, to uphold Mormonism, notwithstanding it goes against your natural feelings. Being in something of a hurry, I must be brief with you. I suppose you understand that I have selected the Bishop of your ward for your 'spiritual' husband for eternity. I have done this in order to effect some things about which I cannot be very explicit to-day, as I have not time But he is a good man, such as would suit me if I were a woman. You need not live with him on earth unless you wish. But it is necessary to have a husband to 'resurrect' you. And more than that, it has become your duty to have children; but I do not now feel at liberty to insist upon such a thing. Brother Jones has spoken to me several times about you, and I think myself, it is a good plan to have you 'sealed' before you get an opportunity of marrying a 'Gentile.' The place is filling up with them, but I'll put a stop to their career before long."

I was at first somewhat alarmed; but before he had finished I regained my self possession. I told him about Smith, hoping he would give his consent to my being 'sealed' to him, as Smith passed now for a Mormon.

To this the Prophet objected, saying, "he is a stranger, and had better stay and be tried before he marries a Mormon girl. He should go upon a mission and return honorably, pay his tithing, work on the Temple, and the like, before he thinks of being 'sealed' to any of us."

To which I replied, "Brother Brigham, I very much fear I shall not want Nathaniel Jones in heaven, as I have so great an aversion to him on earth. But as far as marrying for eternity is concerned, one would be the same as another. You may therefore perform the ceremony with whatever unction and virtue may belong to your office; but it will not do for time. I trust you will remember that I would rather die; and I shall pay no attention to it until after death. That is the way I understand it." Brother Brigham replied, "Just as you and brother Jones can agree about that."

I had before this seen the danger of disobeying the Prophet's "counsel;" but it was a great mystery why he wished me to be sealed to brother Jones. At all events, I dare not disobey, and to falter, was an implied disobedience.

Nathaniel V. Jones was a very fine looking man, about thirty years of age. He was over six feet in height, and in appearance was interesting and noble; but he was well known to be a hard, cruel man, as the sequel of his story will show. He was the bishop of our ward, and by trade a butcher. He soon came into the office, and sat down by my side, looking very sedate, and after a moment he said, "Brother Brigham, I think upon the whole we have made a very good selection." Then looking at me, he said, "Mary Ettie, do you feel competent to fill the mission that has been appointed you?" I replied, "Sir, I do not fully understand your meaning, but I can try to do almost anything."

Hereupon the Prophet rose up, and said, "We will now proceed, with your own free will and consent, Nett."

I was so much excited, that it was with difficulty I could stand. I trembled from head to foot; but I managed to reply, "Not with my free will. My consent is given with reluctance." I supposed this reply would induce Jones to make some inquiry as to the state of my feelings concerning the matter; but he paid no attention to what I had said.

Brigham Young then read over the Celestial Law concern the matter of "sealing" for eternity. I cannot recall the ceremony in form; but I recollect we were "sealed" against all sins excepting the shedding, or consenting to the shedding of innocent blood. The shedding of innocent blood being understood to mean, taking the life of a Mormon, or of the Lord's Anointed. Brother Brigham told me I must expect to obey all "counsel" brother Jones might see fit to give me upon all matters of importance. I made no reply, but put on my bonnet, and went to brother Kimball's, greatly distressed, and asked his first wife, if she knew what to think of such proceedings. She told me, with an air of sadness, she was not at liberty to disclose it to me, if she knew all they intended me to do. Not so much from what she said, as from what she declined to say, I saw myself in the hands of those who had some views in regard to my future, of which I was not informed, and upon which I had not been consulted. I felt myself beset by a mysterious power, not beyond my control only, but beyond my knowledge. Mormonism was assuming a new and fearful form. From regarding it with feelings of reverence and love, which from childhood had been my wont, I began to quake and tremble at its encroachments, and now I shuddered outright under the vague sense of an approaching evil, too hidden for my detection, and too powerful for my resistance.

Oppressed with this conviction, I went home, hoping to meet

Smith there, that I might inform him of the new turn affairs had taken with me; and indulging the wish that he might find some way by which we could escape from the dangers that thickened around us. But before I saw him, Jones came to our house, and said, "Mary Ettie, I wish you to board at my house, and teach the ward school."

I told him I could not come then, and gave him some excuse which satisfied him for the time. Jones had but one wife, whose name was Rebecca. She was a sickly woman, apparently just gone with the consumption, but she afterwards recovered, when Jones left home for a year or two upon a mission, as he did soon after this.

Within a few days, Smith came in, and I told him what Brigham had done, and what I had reason to expect. He was very much disturbed at hearing my story, and after listening seriously to the whole of it, he said, "Nettie, if you can, you had better avoid going to Jones's; but if he insists upon it, you must go. But never yield to what he no doubt intends to extort from you, *i. e.* to become his wife in fact." As he said this, his voice fairly trembled with rage and manly resolution. I begged him to calm himself, as I saw the idea of open resistance was in his mind. After the reflection of a moment, he did so; and then we calmly discussed our position, and coolly looked the danger in the face.

He at length said, "Trust not in the arm of flesh, Nettie; but pray to your Heavenly Father for deliverance—to the God of the Bible—to the Christian's hope—not to this Mormon ideality. I can see no way by which I can get away from here with you at present. I would to God I could. I have taken a farm about fifty miles from here, and I have given currency to the idea that I am a Mormon, and if I am not betrayed, I shall yet accomplish what has been so long the wish of my heart. I shall pay my tithing, and do everything that Mormonism can require of me that is not positively wrong, until I can get the recommendation of my bishop, and then we can marry under the provisions of their own creed."

Smith's hopeful view of the future somewhat cheered me, but when he left, I still had serious forebodings. He had scarcely gone from the house, when brother Jones came in, and said to me, "I wish you to come up, and stay with Rebecca a few days. I am going away. Will you come?" I replied, "I *can* do anything from which there is no escape." To which he said, "You always make that reply. After a while, I will see if you *will* do anything. People who appear so submissive, are generally the hardest to manage in the end."

"I should suppose," said I, "you would by this time regard me as easily managed."

"If you are, I have misunderstood your character."

He then required me to promise that I would come up immediately, and left. As I had promised, I soon went to brother Jones's house, and found he was going away as he had said. When he was gone I had a long talk with his wife, from whom I soon learned that Mormonism was killing her by inches. Poor thing, she was not the only victim to this cruel delusion among the trusting women, who had come to the valley believing in the Prophet, and in a faithful husband who afterwards deserted them for some "spiritual," with a younger face, whose spirit was less careworn and broken by harsh neglect. Her agonized soul was crushed under a system against which she dare not rebel. Of its terrible bitterness she had never before uttered a whisper.

Mormon women dare not disclose, even to each other, the story of their wrongs; but if not "read of all men," they are at least understood by an intuition, sharpened by a personal experience among their own sex. Words are unnecessary. A common fate oppresses them. The forlorn look, and wild abandon of some, and vacant acquiescence of others, and the common sadness of all, tells its own story. It is true that many Mormon women find themselves capable of acquiescing cheerfully in this arrangement, and many more do so in appearance; but I have no hesitation in expressing the opinion, founded upon actual observation made during a life spent among them, that at least two-thirds of them, if they were at liberty to act freely, would to-day repudiate Mormonism, and avail themselves of Gentile protection, if it were once proffered in a safe and reliable form.

It was quite late at night when Jones came home, and he went to bed immediately, telling us to be very particular and wake him, and get breakfast before daylight the next morning.

He repeated the direction so many times, that it excited my curiosity, and I asked Rebecca what it meant.

After Jones was asleep, she told me something was wrong. She said brother Jedadiah M. Grant, and others, had been at her husband's meat-market several times that day; and that Nathaniel, meaning her husband, had borrowed my mother's dog, and taken it to the market, and had chained it by the door. Our curiosity was greatly excited by these extraordinary movements about the meat-market. Rebecca then said, she had no meat in the house for breakfast. I told her not to wake Jones, as I knew where he had put the keys of the market, and that I would go after the meat myself. I could do this with safety so far as the dog was concerned, as the animal knew me well, being my mother's watch-dog, Pete, and a great favorite with us.

My curiosity was aroused, and, if possible, I was bent upon solving the mystery connected with the market. I went to bed and soon fell asleep, but awoke again long before morning, and getting up, I dressed myself, and going carefully to their bed, took his pantaloons from under his pillow, and in one of the pockets found the keys after a little, and succeeded in getting away from the bed without disturbing him.

It had been a dark night, and was none the less so when I left the house. The market was nearly half a mile off. Taking a lantern with me, I arrived there safely, and found John Norton on guard before it. He was one of our nearest neighbors, and also one of the regular police. He knew me well, and also knew of my going to Jones's to stay with Rebecca, the day before, as well as that I had been, with the rest of my family, upon friendly terms with the Prophet. My brother Howard being one of his clerks or secretaries, he had always made it a point to treat us with consideration. The Prophet had called but a few evenings previous, and taken me to the theatre, which was noticed by John Norton, as he happened to be in our house at the time. These facts threw him off his guard, otherwise my further progress would have been arrested.

As I approached him, he appeared astonished at seeing me, and asked where I was going; and I told him, with an air of indifference.

"Have you the key?" said he.

"Certainly: how could brother Jones expect me to go in without that?"

He then said encouragingly, "won't you be frightened? Either of my wives would go into hysterics."

I replied, that I feared the living more than the dead. Why I said this I know not; for if I had known what I was about to encounter, I should have fled at once; and yet, as the sequel will show, my answer could scarcely have been more in accordance with the facts. He questioned me no further, and I unlocked the door, while he continued his patrols up the street. I found the meat hanging around the walls as usual. I had often been there before in the daytime for meat. I held up the light, and was about stepping forward to find a suitable piece for breakfast, when I stumbled and nearly fell over the body of a man, lying at full length, just inside the door, stretched upon the earth, for there was no floor to the shop. I lowered the light quickly, and was alarmed to discover that it had the appearance of being a dead body. I could hear no breathing. I stood for a moment paralyzed. A quilt was thrown over all except the feet. It then occurred to me that the man had been intoxicated, and possibly was not dead, and might have been arrested by the night-guard, and laid there to sleep off the fumes of drunkenness.

This gave me courage, and my woman's curiosity prompted me to make further investigation. Stepping nearer, I spoke to him, but he made no reply. Determined not to be foiled, I stooped down, and with some difficulty, pulled the blanket from his head, which seemed to be fastened in some manner around it. I was delayed for a moment in undoing the obstinate fastenings, but when they gave way, a sight was revealed that sickened and horrified me. The head fell away nearly severed from the body. It was indeed a corpse, just murdered as I believed by the Mormons, and by direction and full knowledge of the Heads of the Church.

The blood yet lay in clots upon the ground. He was not murdered at that place, as there would have been a greater show of blood, but had probably been brought to the market after the act, for concealment until he could be buried. As brother Grant and others had been at the market during the day and evening, they must have known all about it. The neck had the appearance of having been nearly severed by a strong blow of something like an axe.

He was a very tall, stout man; and I think had black hair. Upon his boots he wore a pair of Spanish spurs. I did not notice his dress otherwise, as he was mostly covered by the blanket, and cannot give a description of his features, as I was too much shocked to observe anything closely.

I was never able to get a clue to the history of this murdered man, or the causes which led to it. He was probably a "Gentile," on the way to or from the gold mines, and may have left his company to make purchases at the city, or something of the kind, and probably had made an imprudent show of money; and thus had fallen a victim to Mormon cupidity. For I afterwards had reason to believe that a mere money consideration, was sufficient inducement for the sacrifice of human life by the Mormons, when it was only the life f a "Gentile" that stood in the way. This was the first proof positive that had fallen under my own personal observation, and set at rest forever, in my own mind, the long-mooted question, as to the real character of our Church. The taking of human life was countenanced by the Heads of the Church. And certainly nothing of that kind had been done without the "counsel" of the Prophet. It was then a Church dogma, that the hand of the Mormon was to be against the "Gentile" forever, and in all things. I knew this could not be right.

Hastily cutting some meat, and crushed by the responsibility of my new discovery, I re-locked the door, and wended my way back, deeply regretting the rash curiosity that had put me in possession of a fearful secret. The image of the headless man, all booted and spurred, still clouded my imagination, with the thought that may be some loving wife, a stranger in a strange land, was at that moment listening, with an anxiety that would not sleep, for a footstep she should hear no more, or for the well-known whinny of his steed, while both were lost to her forever.

When I arrived at the house, Jones was just getting up I went directly to the kitchen, where he soon followed me, saying, in an excited manner, "Mary Ettie, where have you been?"

I told him very calmly that I had been after some meat.

"What possessed you to go?" said he.

"What do you think? The evil one perhaps."

He replied, "I intended to have gone for the meat myself."

I called his attention to what I had told him the day before, to the effect that "I could try to do almost anything."

"I recollect it," said he, "and I will try you. To-night you must sleep in my bed. It will not do to allow a woman who knows what you have discovered this morning by intrigue, to live without a husband to control her. You must remain here to-day, and to-night you must yield to the decree of fate."

"And before night, perhaps," said I.

He took my hand, and said reverently, "May the Lord bless you, Mary Ettie."

He then left immediately, saying he might not be at home that evening, but expected to.

I have no words at command by which to express my state of mind when left alone. I saw a crisis in my affairs was approaching. I had suffered so much already that it appeared impossible for humanity to bear more. I went to my chamber, and kneeled down, and prayed my Heavenly Father for protection from this new danger that threatened me; but when I had laid my soul's agony before Him, with the full conviction that I had no other hope, it there occurred to me to doubt whether I had any hope even there; and that I had often prayed to be delivered from the oppression of cruel men, and that I was unprotected still. Then a terrible thought came into my mind. The cold hard reality of my earthly lot froze my soul with horror The iron of despair went to my heart, and I cowered shivering upon the floor. When I rose again, my soul had taken measures for its own protection. During the day, I went to the office of Dr. Hodgekiss and procured a phial of laudanum, which I secreted safely about my person, and returned to Jones's house.

SALT LAKE CITY.

THE ESCAPE.

CHAPTER XVIII

THE ESCAPE.

THE day was passed in a state of mind bordering upon insanity. Not once did my soul relent its high purpose. I thought often of Smith. It was hard to part; but either alternative was the same as far as he was concerned. If I submitted to Jones, Smith was lost to me, and if dead, I was lost to him. It was all the same; I chose to die rather than submit to vileness or violation.

Jones did not return that evening, and I went to bed to pass a sleepless night of agony. I fell at times into an unsound sleep only to start affrighted by horrid dreams, and I was glad to see the light again. But early enough in the morning he returned. I knew when he came in his hands were polluted by the stain of innocent blood, and that the object of his absence had been to put aside all traces of his victim. But why should I hate him alone for that? Was he not acting in concert, and even under the direct orders of the Prophet and the Heads of the Church? Jones went to his room, and dressed himself very finely, and after breakfast called me in, saying he would like to have some conversation with me. As I went in, I found him sitting in a large rocking-chair. His room was pleasantly furnished. He said, "Sit down upon my lap, Mary Ettie; you can do it now as well as a month from now."

I did not move, but stood perfectly amazed, and yet this was what I had expected. He said at length, "Have you forgotten what brother Brigham told you?"

"I have not; but have you no more principle than to take advantage of a submission extorted from me when I was not free, but under the compulsion of the Prophet's 'counsel?' Where is your manhood?"

"That," said he, "was done for your good, and must be explained to you hereafter."

"Brother Jones, I will not ask for an explanation," said I, "if you will permit me to go to my mother's house. May I go."

The fiend, laughing, arose from his chair as if to come to me.

"Stay where you are, for I would rather feel the cold and slimy touch of a serpent than be near you."

He laughed outright, and moved towards me again, saying, as he came, with a show of resolution, "the bishop is not to be trifled with."

"Neither is his prisoner," said I.

There was not a moment to lose. Taking the phial of laudanum, and drawing the cork, I swallowed the contents before he reached me or half comprehended my intention; and then throwing the empty phial to him, asked if he was atisfied, and if he would send for my mother. He caught me in his arms, and rushed into the other room, saying, "Rebecca, here, Mary Ettie has killed herself."

Rebecca, who fully understood how the facts were, replied with a spirit I had never before seen her exhibit, "and you are her murderer, and I think you will find you must answer for it in the end."

Jones then left me on the bed, and went for Dr. Hodgekiss, and soon my mother and sister Lizzie came. They gave me some strong coffee and an emetic, and when the physician arrived, he said I was out of danger, and that the quantity I had taken had saved me. In my inexperience I had taken too much, which had the effect to throw the drug from the stomach before it had time to poison fatally. My mother did not leave me that night, and in the morning I went home with her, without let or hindrance from Jones. The latter was under the necessity of acknowledging himself defeated, and for some reason he was soon after sent away upon a foreign mission. He went to Hindoostan, where he remained until the fall before we left the valley.

Mr. Smith was at this time on his farm fifty miles away, but it so happened that he had sent a hired man to the city for meat, who arrived the morning on which I had taken the poison. The climate of Utah is so remarkably pure, that fresh meat, if hung ten feet or more from the ground, will keep perfectly well for a long while; and hence the farmers who kept but few cattle, or the beginners in the new settlement, came from great distances to supply their wants in this line at the city markets. Smith's man was getting his supply ot the moment I had taken the poison, and as the news soon flew, he heard of it, and came to my mother's to learn the facts, and then he hurried home. When Smith heard what had happened, he mounted a horse, and came to me in all haste.

The next day I was standing at the window, and saw a gentleman dismount at our door, from a noble, but apparently over-ridden horse.

I think it will be deemed a pardonable vanity in me if I give a short description of the rider. He was a tall, young, and, to my eyes, a fine looking-man; and feeling as I did just then, after my narrow and perilous escape, it was the happiest meeting of my life. In accordance with the custom of the country, he wore a broad Panama hat, white linen pantaloons, and a black satin vest, while a sash encircled his waist, with buckskin gauntlets that reached to his elbows, and leggings of the same, with spurs at the heels. He was so covered with dust, that one not well acquainted would scarce have recognized him. This was Reuben P. Smith, and I received him with joy, which I flattered myself was mutual between us. Smith was impatient to hear all the facts of my late peril. I told him the whole story, to which he listened with great eagerness, and his heavy breathing during the recital told how deeply he felt.

When I had finished he said, his whole soul swelling with rage: "If I ever find that precious scamp out of this territory, he shall know the pleasure of having a lariat around his neck." "Oh, I suppose," said I, wishing to appease his useless excitement, "he would prefer to remain, and have a Mary Ettie around his neck." This had the effect I had expected, and he said, laughing: "Well, I hardly think I could blame him for wishing that, although it would very much interfere with my arrangements." We then went into an earnest and serious review of our present position. Judging from what had happened since we last met, the prospect before us was not very flattering. Smith concluded the best thing for us both was, for me to remain with my mother, as quietly as possible until spring, and to obey the "counsel" of Brigham Young, in everything. By that time he could succeed in establishing a character as a faithful Mormon, when he would get the recommendation of his Bishop, and we could be married. In the meantime, he thought it best to say nothing about going to California"

He did not wish to excite remark by making a long visit, and therefore he soon left me, to return to his farm, saying, we should not meet again perhaps till spring.

When he was gone, I was very lonely. Soon after this my brother Uriah was sent to California to transact some business, and we were still more alone.

CHAPTER XIX.

MY FATHER'S FRIEND—DR. ROBERTS.

I was not long idle, but soon fell under the notice of the Prophet. I was made an unwilling instrument in his hands, for the service of the Church, in a manner I had little expected. Since the terrible discovery I had made at the market, I was not only prepared to believe his followers were capable of the perpetration of any crime, but I fully comprehended how utterly powerless I was, alone in the midst of such a swarm of his devoted creatures.

Towards spring a circumstance unfortunately happened which well illustrated the state of things at this time existing among us. It would appear that an old man, a Dr. Roberts, who had lived in Illinois, and was acquainted with my father, there, was on his way to California from the States, intending to get through before winter set in. He succeeded, however, in getting only to Utah, late in the fall, and was obliged to lay over, for the winter, near Salt Lake City. He had heard before he left Illinois, that my father's widow and some of her children were with the Mormons; and after his arrival at Utah, from what he saw and learned concerning the Church, and the position occupied by women in it, he conceived it possible that we might wish to return to the States. By inquiry he had heard that I was living with my brother Howard Coray.

Dr. Roberts was at this time stopping at Utah, a settlement at Utah Lake, about forty miles south of the city, from which place he addressed me a letter, and sent it by a brother Redfield, who was a Mormon; telling him at the same time, that I was at Howard's.

Brother Redfield therefore left the letter according to direction, and handed it to Martha, Howard's wife, who, supposing the letter was for herself, opened and read it, without noticing it was directed to me, although I happened to be present. The contents of the letter, as near as I can recollect, were as follows. The writer said he knew my father, who was his personal friend in his lifetime, in Illinois; and that they were both masons. That my father had as a friend and a mason, on one occasion, rendered him an essential service, which he had never been able to reciprocate before he died; but that he should esteem it a pleasure if he could repay it in a measure now by doing his children a service; and that he knew of no way by which he could do this so well, as by making an effort to restore my father's family to a land of Christian freedom. That unless he had mistaken the state of things at Utah, the females of our family would be likely to avail themselves of the first opportunity to escape, and that he would undertake to effect this for us, if we wished it. He was prepared, he said, to take us along with his company to California in the spring. This was a mystery to Martha, and without reflection, she read the letter to the company that happened to be present; and upon further examination, it was found to be addressed to me. Robert Berton, who was connected with our family by marriage, was there, and he took the letter directly to brother Brigham; and it was not long before they both came back to see me, bringing the letter with them.

The Prophet said, as he came in, "Well, Nett, how do you do? I understand you have a very good friend in the Territory." I replied that I knew nothing about it; but it appeared that some one had taken some interest in us, but I believed it was on my father's account. "Yes," said Brigham, "I did not know your father; but they say you are the exact image of him; and that he had a great many friends; but this Dr. Roberts is not going to interfere with the gathering of the Saints, nor with the building of the Temple. The imp of Satan shall be foiled this time. I am going to advise you what to do. I must acknowledge it to be a great expedition for a woman; but you can do it, and must." Taking a letter from his pocket, which he handed me, he said, "Write him a letter like this." The letter he handed me directed the doctor when and where to come and see me; and gave him encouragement as to the object he had in view, expressing a desire to go with him. I copied the letter by the direction, and in the presence of the Prophet, not thinking it safe to decline to do so. When the letter was finished, he put it in his pocket, saying, "This shall bring in the dimes before we get through with it." Then turning to me, he said, "Nett, you look as if you had lost all your friends, while I am sure you are getting more every day. I wish you could ever be contented, and obey my counsel cheerfully."

"Brother Brigham," said I, "this business does not suit my taste. I can plainly see how the duty you have imposed upon me, if fully successful, is likely to affect at least one of the parties seriously. I can see how it will be. I cannot think of doing it."

"You cannot," said the Prophet, giving me a look that at any other time would have frightened me beyond measure. "You cannot," he repeated, still bending upon me that frown, never yet met with defiance by one of the Church, and before which even the "Apostles" are wont to quail. "Nett," he said at length, in his sternest mood, "what do you mean? Can you not do what you have covenanted to do? to be firm, and unshaken, ever willing to obey the command of your guide and Saviour?"

"Brother Brigham," said I, with a firmness of resistance I had never before felt in his presence, "are you my Saviour?"

"Most assuredly I am," said he. "You cannot enter the Celestial Kingdom, except by my consent. Do you doubt it?"

"My belief," said I, "is not what it was one year ago, although I never expect to leave the Church. I am, in fact, not so much in doubt as to the leading doctrines of the Church, as I have heretofore understood them, as I am how to reconcile these doctrines, new and old, with each other."

"Leave the Church," said he, "that is impossible. You may yet become reconciled to the spiritual wife doctrine, and I really hope you may for your own good. As to that Smith, I believe he is an impostor; that he talks one thing to his bishop, and maybe another thing to you. But as he has gained the good will of his bishop, and as we can find nothing of importance against him, we are compelled to fellowship him. But now to the point. When the doctor comes, tell him you will go, if he can assure you against all liability of being left destitute on the way, at the mercy of strangers in a strange land. Tell him you have no money of your own, and that it would be too much risk to set out with him, unless he is abundantly able to take you through. Now, Nett, in this manner you will find out how much money he has, and if he has enough worth our while, you must start with him, and we will have what money or valuables he has. For 'the earth is the Lord's and the fullness thereof.' When he comes, first find when his company starts, and then tell him you cannot get ready until a day or two after they are gone, and that he must come after you alone, as otherwise your friends would mistrust, and prevent your going. Tell him you will meet him at Capt. Brown's, who lives at the last of our settlement on the road to California. You can explain to him that one of Capt. Brown's wives is your aunt, and that you can go there under the pretence of making her a visit. This letter will bring him—now, be on hand."

The Prophet, while giving me these instructions, had warmed himself into a better humor, and now addressed me in that spirit of genial frankness, so full of winning ways, which forms so important an element in his character. I saw it would be impossible to disobey him and live, and I thought it best to trust in Providence for the result. My refusal could not save the doctor, while it would endanger me, and it was not impossible that I should be able to give him some sign of warning when he came, which would prevent his exposure on my account. I therefore said to the Prophet, with an apparent submission to his " counsel," that I would go with the doctor, and added that I would take him some other route, and we should finally both make our escape. To this he said, laughing, " I will risk that, Nett. We have too many 'Danites' on the watch, and always engaged in similar expeditions, for that. All the passes of the country are guarded. By the way, I find the doctor has been in town lately, and provided himself with a splendid carriage for the occasion."

The knowledge of this fact took me by surprise, and exciting my pity for him anew, I said, " Brother Brigham, I do not like to do this."

" What is the reason ?" said he, persuasively. " I should like it, as well as to conquer the enemy in any other way. What is he trying to do ? Why he is trying to lead one of the daughters of Zion to hell ;" and he struck the table near him as if he would have demolished it.

" I think I have heard," said I, " my father read in the Bible long ago, when I was very small, that vengeance was the Lord's, and that He would repay, or something to that effect."

"Certainly," said Brigham ; " but do you suppose He will come down and do this thing himself? and that He will become a visible being, playing smash here among the Gentiles? or will he choose the more natural and consistent way of sending His servants to do it for him? According to your opinion, He would not require us to preach His gospel. We are in his hands as our servants are in ours. If I should take a bridge to build, I should not build it with my own hands, but by the hands of my servants, and still I should be the builder of the bridge. So it is with the work of the Lord. We cannot be exalted without Him, nor can he be exalted without us. He was once a man striving, as we are now, for exaltation, and we shall sometime be gods, of different degrees of exaltation, in proportion as we are successful in this world in carrying out the objects of our Church. But you must understand all about this hereafter. I have not time to preach to you longer at present. You certainly understand enough for our present purpose. You will start with the doctor for California, will you not, if he wishes it?"

"I cannot see how I can avoid it," said I. "Do you intend to murder him?"

"Nett," said he, earnestly, "*you* shall not be hurt, depend upon that, except that if you do not go, and carry out our plans concerning him, your blood atones for the neglect."

Summoning what courage I could under the circumstances, I replied, "I am not very easily frightened, but that is sharp talk. Do you mean exactly what you say? And if I go, will that save his life? Come now, promise me this, or I will not go. You will not kill my father's friend? Grant me this. I might as well kill him myself, at my own house, as to detain him from his company, to give you an opportunity of doing it. Rob him if you will, but, I pray you, spare his life. Do. Will you?"

The Prophet made no further reply, but left the house at once, without giving me the least encouragement upon this point.

Not many days after this, a stranger called upon my mother, and represented himself as living at Utah, and as being in want of a school teacher, and said I had been recommended to him as such. Although my mother knew the plans of the Prophet, she dare not expose them to Dr. Roberts, for he was the stranger who had called in answer to my letter. We soon made a bargain, and it was arranged between us tha he should call for me at Captain Brown's, at Ogden city as indicated by the Prophet. I carried out the intention of the latter fully, as I dare not disobey, well knowing my movements were under the constant surveillance of his creatures, by whom I was surrounded, and that the consequences of any attempt on my part, to thwart his plans, would be visited upon my own head in the most summary manner. Indeed the steps of the doctor, were dogged from the time he entered the city, until he left it : and every word uttered by him, while there, was reported immediately to the Grand Presidency. Even his interview with me, and the manner he was received by my mother was likewise reported. My readers can well imagine the agony of my position. As soon as Dr. Roberts left me, I went in accordance with instructions to report to the Prophet; I confess this was the saddest sacrifice I had ever made at the shrine of my faith in Mormonism and its Prophet. It was not only necessary that I should make a faithful report of what had been already effected, but that I should do so with a certain degree of cheerfulness, as an evidence of good faith on my part. For although I knew the Prophet would most likely overlook a mere show of reluctance to do his bidding, as long as it had its origin in nothing more dangerous than a woman's repugnance to violence, or crime, or respect to my father's friend; yet I knew equally well, that the first show of "heresy" or want of faith in him, would be fatal to me.

The real difficulty of my position existed, after all in the influence which he exercised over me in common with all the Church. I could not divest myself of the idea of his divine commission. I could not bring myself to disobey him. He claimed to be my Saviour; and I had been educated to believe that his claims, however extravagant, were not to be disputed; and it was long after this, before I came seriously to question his pretension as a Prophet of God: and even to-day, I sometimes falter in the intention of giving these facts to the public, when some new doubt clouds my future, and my belief in the true God. Often am I startled from sleep at night, with the inquiry, "is he not the Prophet, and will not his curse reach me beyond the grave? Am I not at war with my fate! And if so, will not my future be terrible?" Although I doubted and rebelled against the new forms our faith was assuming, and against that which, among many of us, both men and women, was regarded as of doubtful orthodoxy, yet no question of the legitimate and fundamental principles of Mormonism had ever been seriously entertained by me.

It was not merely a question of my own existence in this life, but of that also of the dread future: I believed both to be under the control of the Prophet.

When I arrived at the Prophet's house I found him there. He said as I entered, "Well, Nett, how is your honor?"

This was a familiar form of address, he was in the habit of

using with those he wished to flatter. To which I replied, "I have none."

"What have you done with it" said he, laughing.

My heart was too full for trifling; but I felt the necessity of disguising the real state of my feelings under an assumed play of words—an airy badinage that should disarm his suspicions of my unwillingness to go on with the work he had assigned me; and I replied, "I must have left it in the waters of the Mississippi where I was baptized, for if I ever had any, it was when I was a child; I certainly have none now."

"And yet," said he, "you are on hand to roll on the work of the Lord. You are aware that a Temple must be built, in order that blessings may be bestowed upon the Saints more abundantly; and you will yet be as clay in the hands of the potter."

I then gave him an account of what I had done: and of all that had been said, and arranged between Dr. Roberts and myself: with which he was very much delighted.

Hiram Clauson was in the room, absorbed in the study of a tragedy, a part in which he was to play at the amateur theatre, kept up by him and others, as one of the amusements encouraged by the Prophet.

He was a young man of good parts, who had one wife already, and was now seeking the hand of Alice, a daughter of the Prophet, for another. The latter turned very much elated and said, "Brother Hiram, you may take my horse and buggy, and go with Nett to Ogden city and leave her at Captain Brown's."

" Your will is my pleasure," said Hiram Clauson, " I suppose you will let Alice go with me, will you not, brother Brigham ?"

" Certainly, my son," said the Prophet, caressingly, " and if you are faithful, you shall have her for a wife some day."

The good humor of the Prophet was judiciously seized upon by the ambitious lover, to secure the prize he had so much coveted. It was very naturally esteemed a high honor among the marriageable men, to win a daughter of the Prophet for a wife : and brother Clauson went off in fine spirits, to get the horse and carriage ready, while I went home to prepare for the journey.

CHAPTER XX.

PREPARING TO ENTRAP AN OLD MAN.

It was with sad misgivings that I prepared to go upon the infamous mission, from which I now saw no escape. It was already well on towards noon, and no time was left for reflection. I was scarcely dressed for the occasion, when Hiram Clauson drove to the door, with Alice in the carriage. He, already the husband of one wife, and now happy in finding himself affianced to another: while she, young and innocent, but little comprehended the cruel future to which spiritual wifeism was about to consign her.

Stepping into the street, prepared to go, I said, " good morning, sister Clauson."

" What do you wish me to understand," said Alice.

" Nothing more than that your father gave his consent this morning, in my presence, to your marriage with Hiram."

"There Alice," said brother Clauson," what did I tell you? you did not believe me."

" How can one believe these Mormons," said I; " but as for you, Alice, being a daughter of the Prophet, and not altogether dependent upon your husband, you may do well enough, for you wil be still under the protection of your father. But

I should advise you to remain single several years yet, as you are very young."

Brother Hiram, who had listened with great patience, and apparent pleasure until now, said testily, "Come, come, it is getting late, and we must be off."

To which Alice replied. "I see Hiram would like to drop this conversation. For my part I have a deep interest in it; especially now that my father has given me away to a man who has one wife already, and is courting another besides me, and both of them much handsomer than I am."

Hiram appeared greatly nettled at the turn the conversation was taking; for what Alice had stated was true. He was courting a third wife, and of the three Alice was the least beautiful. His young head was already fired with the ambition of having many wives, which, next to the favor of the prophet, was the surest passport to public favor and preferment in the Church; and he said with ill-disguised impatience, "Come now, girls, the horse is becoming restive, and will not listen to such folly; I am unable to hold him."

Finding him in earnest, we got into the carriage, and he drove into the country, in the direction of Ogden city. Our course was northerly, and lay for a short way along the bank of the gentle Jordan. It was one of those clear, bright mornings so common in this climate. The balmy breath of spring, which exists nowhere in such perfection as among the snow-capped mountains of Utah, fanned the cheek into a ruddy glow of health, and expanded the lungs to their fullest capacity. The air of Utah appears to have been made for the especial use of the lungs. The simple act of breathing in such an atmosphere, is a pleasure. Under any other circumstances I should have enjoyed the ride very highly.

Once in the open country, when the cloud occasioned by our joint attack upon Hiram had passed away, our little party were in the best of spirits, except that my own soul was secretly upon the rack to provide some escape for the doctor, or to avoid having anything to do with his destruction myself.

It was easy to see that the young people were happy to be near each other. Hiram, evidently intending to call out a reply from Alice, said at length, "What a lovely spring we have!"

"Yes," said Alice, "I hope we shall have a pleasant time. I was thinking, Nett, what an exalted opinion you ought to have of yourself, to be trusted upon such a mission as this. You can hardly imagine how highly my father has spoken of you. He thinks you quite a heroine."

"Indeed. Did he send any further instructions by you?"

"No," said Hiram. "I presume he thinks you are equal to the management of the affair yourself. He says you understand what is wanted, and if you wish, you can accomplish it. But he is getting impatient with you on account of your unwillingness to obey his counsel. How dare you think of not granting any request he may make of you?"

"Oh! as for that, I dare *think* for myself, however it may be with what I have dared to do, or may dare. No one can read my thoughts."

"Except my father?" said Alice.

"Oh, your father? why do you ask such a question? But how am I to get back, Hiram?

"I am going to leave Alice to come back with you."

"That is right," said Alice. "And we are going to run off with the old doctor. Nett is willing I should be first, and she will be second?"

"I see," said Hiram, "you think it quite an object to be the first wife. I cannot see what particular difference it could make. But you forget that Gentiles have but one wife."

"No matter," said Alice, "he will undoubtedly waive that objection for this once for the benefit of romance. Let me see, there will be a moon to-night. It will be enchanting to elope by moonlight along this beautiful road, and then away among the mountains, with a fine old gentleman, whose head is silvered by a good old age. Hiram, do let us go off with him. What inducement can we offer you to keep still until we are too far gone to be overtaken?"

"Inducement? Why, Alice, that would cost me my head. And besides, it would be impossible for you to get away."

Thinking this trifling upon a dangerous subject had been carried far enough, as it might lead to serious suspicions as to myself, I said, laughing, "Hiram, do you think we would go?"

"He knows very well," said Alice, "that I would, before I would be given away like an old mule to a man who has already one wife, and is seeking for others."

By common consent we hereupon dismissed the subject with a laugh; but I detected in the face of each, a trace of serious concern which harmonized with a similar anxiety within my own heart. This sprightly and somewhat precocious girl, although educated under her father's personal influence, and never doubting Mormonism, indeed never dreaming that to doubt was within the range of possibilities with her, yet now, when her budding womanhood was about to assert its sway over her woman's nature, she felt impelled, by an instinct wiser than her own experience, and beyond her own control, to reject that part of Mormonism which ignored her woman's individuality—which cut her off from all the true woman holds most dear—the right to possess, and hold within the silken meshes of her love-enslavement, one man—all her own. Without knowing it, she already stood braced, as all Mormon women do, against this unnatural invasion of her rights. I studied her position carefully, as a commentary upon, and justification of my own refusal to be one of many wives; and as I recognized in her fine appreciation of the noble instincts that stirred within her, an evidence of a superior womanhood, I foresaw a dark shadow rising to becloud her future. And the prospect before Hiram was scarcely less disheartening. The spirit of rebellion, which exhibited itself in Alice, against the claims of the other wives, is still stronger after marriage; and I am of the opinion, that the end of spiritual wifeism is as disastrous in its influence upon the men as it is upon our sex. This unquiet chafing within their own family circles, creates a necessity, as well as a wish, to escape from the annoyance of their little wife communities, and hence the love of home and family is constantly decreasing, and the individual family is becoming more and more absorbed and swallowed up in that greater community of the Church, of which the "Prophet" forms the controlling centre and chief interest.

Nothing has so much surprised me since my arrival in the States, as the quiet and delightful peace which characterizes the domestic relations of the Christian families with whom it has been my privilege to associate; and I am led to believe, that this perfect individuality, existing in each separate famiy in this Christian land, cemented by the love and influence of one wife and mother, is the real foundation on which rests the future good of the State, and that the latter will be safe and enduring, just in the proportion that these families remain as they are—isolated, virtuous, and strong.

We arrived in due time at Capt. Brown's. As we drove up to the door my aunt and the captain came out to meet us, the latter saying, in his pleasantest mood, "Well done, Nett. I knew you would come home at last," which I received as an evidence of a wish on his part to efface, as far as possible, the unpleasant recollections connected with his failure in getting himself sealed to me on a former occasion, and I met him in a similar spirit. The object of our visit was well understood by them, and they were charged, under private instructions from the Prophet, with the general management of this cruel "mission." The captain exerted himself to make our stay pleasant, and as a relief against the harrowing emotions which oppressed me, I accepted his efforts in our behalf. We had what, under other circumstances would have been recognized as a pleasant time, a cheerful and agreeable company of invited guests, mingled with the home circle, while wit and humor enlivened the scene, and plays, and various amusements, were the order of the evening. It was late when the party broke up and we retired, and not till then, when I attempted to address myself to sleep, did it occur to me, how, like a band of brigands, we had demeaned ourselves. Since we had, upon the eve of an expedition of robbery, and may be of murder, resorted to light and airy amusements to stifle reflection. Big and bitter tears came to my eyes, as I reflected that our Church was simply a well organized community of thieves and robbers, who were not appalled by the sight of human blood, when the success of our schemes required that blood should flow. It was enough to know all this. It was enough to be unable to escape from the country, now fully under the control of men who counselled and perpetrated such crimes, and from a religion which justified them; but it was too much to be an unwilling instrument for the accomplishment of the unworthy aims of these religious pirates.

I occupied a bed with Alice, in a room which we had to ourselves, I did not go to sleep immediately and I noticed she was also awake. Not wishing she should know I had been crying, I dried up my tears, and asked her if she was satisfied with her lot. She was not surprised at the question, for young as she was, she had become familiar with this growing discontent among the women, and fully understood the force of it. But as she did not answer me at once, and fearing I had been overheard by Captain Brown who occupied a room separated from ours only by a thin partition, with his young wife Phebe, but eighteen years of age, I added in a lower tone, that after all she had as yet no reason to be dissatisfied, since she was but a mere child, and being a daughter of the Prophet, she had less to fear than the generality of her sex among us.

"Oh! as for that," said she, "I was just thinking of the subject to which you refer. I think if we all do as father directs us, we shall soon be able to conquer the whole world: and then, Nett, we shall be queens: and father says you shall have a great palace, and many servants, chosen from among the Gentiles. He says he knows many Gentiles in the States who are good to work."

"Men ?" said I.

"Yes, and women too. Father says the President of the United States will yet be glad to black his boots, when the thousand years of our reign upon earth commences ; and that he will have him at it before long."

There was a trace of the father's ambition in the soul of the young girl. I knew she had been instructed by her father to tell me this : and not daring to express to her a doubt in his power as a Prophet even if I had felt it, and wishing to change the conversation, I said to her, " but do you not love Hiram ?"

" Oh yes," said she, " I think I do, but then you know that his present wife, Ellen, is much better looking than I am ; and Margaret, whom he is also courting, is prettier than either of us. Don't you think he is fine looking when he plays Don Cæsar upon the stage."

"Certainly, I think a great deal of Hiram myself," said I.

Alice replied; " and I fear he thinks too much of you, for he goes to your house every day, and Ellen tells me he goes there twice a day."

"Don't you understand," said I, "why he comes to our house ? He meets Margaret there, as her mother will not allow him to come near her house, or even speak to Margaret

I do not like to have them meet there, as I have no sympathy with this spiritual wife business; but mother does not think it best to prevent it, as your father favors their wishes, and would most likely be offended. But Ellen seems to be very fond of Margaret herself; and she is said to favor the match." *

It was by this time late: and we were just falling asleep when we were startled by the shrill notes of a female voice at a high pitch of excitement, as it abruptly broke the stillness of the night, loudly berating some one for not going

---

* The spiritual wives are exhorted and instructed to use their influence to win by every possible means other "spirituals" to the home of their husbands; and this they often do, and for this reason, as they say, that if their husbands will have more than one wife, they have a choice, and they procure those most agreeable to them, and under such circumstances, the husband seldom brings home a wife to whom his "home circle" objects. The following is one of the "songs of Zion" used in their public worship, the teaching, of which like much of what is taught in their public meetings, inculcates this doctrine:

> Now, sisters, list to what I say:
>   With trials this world is rife,
> You can't expect to miss them all,
>   Help husband get a wife!
> Now, this advice I freely give,
>   If exalted you would be,
> Remember that your husband must
>   Be blessed with more than thee.
>
> Then, oh, let us say,
>   God bless the wife that strives,
> And aids her husband all she can
>   To obtain a dozen wives.

home with her, "as you have agreed:" said she, at the end of her first burst of indignation. We were very soon enlightened as to the principal ground of complaint: for she made no secret of it. It appeared that Captain Brown had married as a "spiritual," an old woman, one of his neighbors, who was rich in oxen, sheep, and cows, and, as rumor said, he had taken her for the sake of the property. In order to avoid the annoyance of an unpleasant temper, which she was known to possess, he *consented* she should still live in her own house, and superintend the cattle, where from time to time he paid his devotions: and as a general thing he had not failed to do as he had "agreed." On this occasion, he had been expected to be at her house, but on account of having company, or from forgetfulness, had neglected it; and she had now come in person to assert what claims, and to enforce what rights were due under the marriage contract.

When I afterwards saw her, I was not surprised at the discordant tones of her cracked voice; for she was not only old, ugly, and haggish then, but had the appearance of originality, in the marked discord of the form and feature which characterized her. I have no power of words at my command by which to convey anything like a fair description of the character, or state of feeling, indicated by her manner of delivering the following philippic, aimed at Captain Brown.

"You are mean," said she, "you grey headed old villain Mr. Brown, you know very well, that you promised you would pay as much attention to me as to any of your wives: and you have put your brand upon all—yes, upon every one of my cattle and sheep. I have told you over and over again, that I would never submit to be treated as some men treat their spirituals. Now come along, and stay at my house to-night."

"Hush, hush," said Captain Brown, "and go home, and mind your own business. You ought to be ashamed of yourself, to come here this time of night, and raise such a row when we have company. I'll come over in the morning. You know, Mary, the business I have on my hands, just now—that is the reason I did not come to-night."

"Oh, yes; your business—your company, always some excuse * * * Come now with me, or I will——"

"Hold on," said the vanquished man of war, "I s'pose I must go," muttering in evident bad humor, and loud enough to be heard by us:

"You cross-eyed old fool. You will get your walking papers soon, I wouldn't have you for all the cattle and sheep in America."

As he went off with his attractive "spiritual," his wife Phebe, who rather more than hinted that she was glad to get rid of him, had a fine laugh at their mutual expense: and when he was well out of ear shot, the house was in an uproar with the immoderate giggling of the seven or eight women, who were in bed under his roof. They laughed, and cracked their jokes upon the ludicrous events of the night, until fairly exhausted; and would then calm down, and compose themselves to sleep; when perhaps some new criticism upon the valiant captain, and the cows his wife had brought him, would renew the boisterous mirth until the house would explode in a roar of uncontrolled laughter again. None enjoyed it better than Phebe, except perhaps Alice; who although accus tomed to the ever recurring absurdities of Mormonism, thought she had never seen anything more ridiculous in her life. The captain had but few sympathizers among us, for it was well understood he had married the old woman on account of her property, and the assistance it would afford him in supporting his other wives. The house was finally quiet, and, one by one, they fell asleep; but for my own part, I found myself unable for a long time, to lose in the forgetfulness of grateful slumber, the recollection of the sad "mission" now upon my hands.

CHAPTER XXI.

ROBBERY AND PROBABLE MURDER OF DR. ROBERTS.

It was late the following day when we awoke. The calm beauty of early spring by which we were greeted brought not its accustomed joy. Hiram returned to the city, and contrary to my expectations, he took Alice with him. I was therefore left alone with my own thoughts, to work out the dark "mission," assigned me by the Prophet. I waited with no small degree of anxiety for the coming of Dr. Roberts; for whatever was to be the result of the expedition, and whether I succeeded in giving him sufficient warning to save him or not, I wished the unpleasant work off my hands. Time passed slowly and heavily for the first day; but the second was marked by the passage of the company to which he belonged, which consisted of four wagons: oh, how I longed to warn them that the Doctor, who was lingering behind, in order to effect my escape, was in great peril; but there was no opportunity for that. I was watched every moment. A trusty Mormon eye was always upon me. My every movement was under the notice of some one in the interest of the Prophet.

Three days after the main company had passed, if my recollection is not at fault as to the exact time, Dr. Roberts came on, alone, and called at Captain Brown's, and inquired for me.

He brought a letter purporting to be from my mother; which was according to our previous arrangements. I took the letter, and after reading it, told my aunt in his presence, that my mother had sent for me, and that I was going home with this gentleman, who I had introduced to her as Dr. Roberts. He thereupon said he would call for me towards night. While my aunt knew all the Doctor had done, or proposed to do, she received him with well-dissembled indifference, and very innocently asked him if he was a Mormon, and other questions tending to disarm him of suspicion. No one among us was so badly informed of what was going on as the Doctor, and his own movements even were directed by Brigham Young, through Mormons, who under his instructions, pretended to be the Doctor's friends.

About dark of the same day, Dr. Roberts returned with a very fine carriage, from the direction of the city. It was covered, and drawn by two fine horses. The whole establishment was well arranged for the journey for which it was designed, and particularly adapted to the occupation of females. It occurred to me at the time, that I had never seen anything so pleasant and comfortable. I was now racked by the bitterest anxieties. I had supposed Alice was to go with me, as I could not believe they would trust me alone with the victim, for the Prophet knew I would give him warning. But Alice had been sent back to the city, for some reason I did not at the time understand. I now believed I was to go alone; and I trembled with excitement at the prospect of being able to to put him on his guard, if it was not already too late to do so. It was a cloudy night, and was quite dark when I stepped into the carriage, which drove off at once, at full speed, while hardly a word was spoken; and I did not at first observe that I was not alone. I soon made the discovery, however, that I had company, and that Ellen, the wife of Hiram Clauson, was with me. Ellen was about seventeen— small, delicate, modest, and very pretty. It was difficult for me to judge from appearances, whether Ellen or myself was most astonished. At first I was perfectly confounded, but a moment's reflection restored my self-command, and then it occurred to me why Alice had been sent back to the city, and that beyond question she had accompanied us in the first instance, by the Prophet's directions, only to watch me. When my first surprise was over, I said, "Ellen, where are you going?" She pressed my hand tightly, as a hint of caution, and said, in a tone of voice louder than she was in the habit of speaking:

"Oh, you know my father, John Smith? Well he is determined I shall marry Brigham Young, and I accidentally learned yesterday that this old gentleman was to start for California to-day, and I went to him this morning before daylight, to tell him my situation, and that I wished, if possible, to escape a fate I so much dread. He has consented to take me on with him. For which, may he be blessed of Heaven. My family think I am at the lower part of the city, washing at my sister's, and they do not expect me at home for several days, and by the time I am missed, we shall be beyond their reach, and if we are not, then they will be unable to tell whether we have gone east or west. So I think we shall have no difficulty in making our escape."

For an understanding of our position, I have only to state, that Ellen was the daughter of Orson Spenser, a well known Mormon in the city, and not of John Smith, as she had represented. I saw at once the Doctor was lost; at least it was not within my power to save him. Probably the Danites were already before and around us.

The old man, who had listened with attention to Ellen's story, said, when she had finished., "I am aware there is a great risk in this business, but we shall soon be met by two men, who will pilot us to the camp of my party, where we shall find those who will protect us, although at the peril of life. But for the present, not a word; we will talk when in some safer place."

Our course lay directly north from Ogden.

The team sped on through the darkness; the way led us for the most part through the timber. The road was generally good, but there were in some places ditches and small streams to cross, and we bounded on, and over them in a manner, and with a success that was quite miraculous. The horses were well chosen, I should judge, for while they were easily managed by the Doctor, they yet flew over the ground, as if inspired with the high duty they had in charge, even the "mission" of our escape. The Doctor was perfectly self-possessed, and seemed to be nerved to the highest pitch of firm resolve He must have carefully studied the route, with the view of driving over it at night. His whole soul was thrown into the management of the horses. Between him and the noble animals, one would think, there existed a common sympathy; for they obeyed kindly his softest whisper of caution, and sprang forward at his faintest chirrup. On we flew. For a time my soul was in agony. I felt it was too cruel to remain an impassive spectator to the sacrifice of the brave old man, who had so generously staked his all, in order to rescue two women, personally strangers to him; and it wrung my soul none the less, when I reflected, that he had undertaken this on account of the gratitude he bore my father.

The cool night-air that laved my burning cheek and temples, now on fire with despair, whispered consolation at last. For it told me, after the first flush of excitement was over, that so much nobleness of effort could not be lost. A better Providence certainly must, and would interfere to save the good old man. Then the crushing weight of despair gave way to the healthy excitement of hope; and my brain grew calm, and I cooly entered into the estimate of chances. But there was little ground for hope. Indeed, the more I reasoned upon what I knew, the more the visible prospect for his escape lessened. The very fact that Ellen had been sent by Brigham Young, under the pretense of seeking protection, but really in order to watch me, proved the Danites had the matter in hand. Oh, the events of that night, and the swift ride through the darkness, were scorched upon my very soul, to last forever.

I have no idea how far we had been speeding on, when the Doctor, whose ears and eyes were ever upon the stretch, said suddenly, with an air of satisfaction, "All is well now, the men are coming to protect us against the miserable villains that inhabit this territory."

Ellen asked quickly, "Doctor, can you distinguish the color of their horses?"

"Why, yes," said he, after a moment's pause, "one horse is white, and that rather stumps me, for neither of our men had white horses."

She gave me a nudge, and used an expression, which, though it did not reach the Doctor's ears, sealed in my mind the doom of the brave old man. "But," continued the Doctor, after a moment of thoughtful silence, "don't be frightened. If I were a woman, I should much rather fall into the arms of death, than into the arms of these villains. But here they come, and are strangers too; at least to me." The strangers, as the Doctor called them, were two men on horseback, who now approached us, and one of them said, as our carriage came to a stand still:

"I suppose you belong to the company ahead, sir? This is rather a dangerous place in which to be found alone at this time of night."

"I do belong to that company. Can you tell me how far ahead they are?" replied the Doctor.

"Oh, much farther, my friend, than you will be able to get."

"I am quite sure," returned the old man, with assumed indifference, "they are not far off."

"No, I suppose not," replied one of them; "but that is no sign you will ever see them, you old kidnapper."

"Who have I kidnapped?" asked the Doctor, who grew every moment more resolute, as he saw the danger increasing.

"My wife," said Hiram Clauson; "and my niece," roared Captain Brown—both in the same breath, for they were the Danite horsemen who now obstructed our further progress.

I watched the old man closely at this juncture; and if I had respected the honorable benevolence of my dead father's friend before, I now had cause to admire his manly courage. His grey hair, and flashing eyes, were clearly visible in the darkness. His left hand grasped the reins, and the spasmodic motion conveyed to them by the quick panting of the horses, showed how firmly he had them in hand, ready for a dash onward, while his right hand rested upon an inside pocket on the left breast. I saw there was not a moment to be lost, and I said, intending to be heard only by him, "Do not shoot, for undoubtedly there are others near."

"Has he attempted to shoot," anxiously inquired Captain Brown, at the same time sidling off in such a manner as to put us between his tall military figure and the Doctor.

"No" said I, "but I was afraid he might attempt it, but I think I may have been mistaken."

The valiant Captain Brown, now somewhat reassured by finding our persons between him and the Doctor, said briskly enough, "Here, Nett, you and Ellen take our horses, and we will attend to the dimes; and when we get through we will overtake you."

While we were being handed into the saddles the men had left, the Doctor sat as before unmoved, and remained so, as we judged, until we were out of hearing. Whether he afterwards offered any resistance or not, I never knew; but I am satisfied that Capt. Brown would have been sent to his long account, and his eight wives made widows that night, had my caution been delayed but a moment longer.

We moved slowly down the road in the direction of home, until fully out of hearing; and then halted. When we dare speak above a whisper, I said, "Ellen, what will they do? Will they kill him? Oh! if the people of the States knew of the proceedings in this Territory, they would send an army, and destroy us, as we deserve."

"Oh, yes," said Ellen, "if they knew; but they do not, and never will. We are secure among these rocky mountains. Besides, this territory is so remote, that no trifling matter will be noticed by the Government. A great many crimes must be committed, and proof positive must be furnished, which will be difficult, with everything in the hands of the Church, before we shall be called to an account. Much blood has, and must be shed before the Government can get a clue to the facts of the case, as all these murders are charged to the Indians, and there is no evidence to the contrary. More over, the 'Danites' take care that all proof against them is destroyed. Take for instance this case. If they kill Dr. Roberts, even his own company cannot show it was not the work of the Indians—if indeed the company have not been murdered also, as they very likely have, or will be, as they were but a small party, and knew the business of Dr. Roberts at the city. The Danites will regard even this a dangerous knowledge to pass out of the territory in the possession of 'Gentiles.'"

We now listened attentively for some sound, which should indicate the fate of our friend; but nothing could be heard from that direction. The wind began to blow with violence, and moaned dismally through the forest. Of course our imagination conjured up the most horrible images. We dismounted, and cowered close together upon the ground, holding the horses by the bridles.

Although it seldom rains in this climate, yet it did on this occasion. While we were there waiting, I took occasion to ask Ellen how and why she came there. She replied, drawing herself closely to my side, "I came, first, because brother Brigham thought it would be too bad for you to go alone on such an expedition. After you and Alice had left the city with my husband for Capt. Brown's, brother Brigham and Burton came to our house, and told me where you had gone, and explained the object of your mission. They then directed me to go to Hawkin's Tavern, where Dr. Roberts was stopping, and say to him what I have before told you in his presence. The Doctor was greatly moved at my story. He was somewhat embarrassed at first to know what to do; but as he believed what I said, he pitied me, and consented that I should go with him, and I came as you have seen."

Soon after she had finished her account of the matter, we heard the men coming; and when they approached us, Capt. Brown asked if we had been afraid; and to rally and cheer us, he said to me, "Your are a brave captain, Nett; and when you want a larger company, you shall have it."

To which Hiram replied, "She is a better leader now than Porter Rockwell, for he is always *sending* men to do these things, but never goes himself." I listened to this trifling in silence. I had no heart to speak. There was nothing that I could do now, as the Doctor was probably already dead, or at least beyond my assistance; and for the moment I would gladly have died with him. I regretted, in the excess of my grief, that I had interfered to prevent his fighting it out, as he had no doubt designed to do at first. Ellen, now that all was over, regretted the part she had felt herself forced to take in the affair. With a show of sadness I had never before seen her exhibit, and of which I supposed her incapable, she said to Hiram, "What have you done with the good Doctor?"

Her husband was about to reply, and in fact commenced to state what had been his fate, when Capt. Brown checked him, saying, "Silence, Hiram, until we see Brigham. They do not care about knowing yet."

"If he is dead, I do not wish to know it," said I.

No further reply was made, and with a shudder, we each mounted behind one of the men, whose hands as I supposed, and still believe, were stained with innocent blood, and rode through the darkness towards home; and at three o'clock the next morning, we arrived at Ogden city, and were set down at Capt. Brown's door. We glided, like guilty spectres, away to bed in silence; and the next morning, a spring day, calm and beautiful, broke as peacefully upon us as if the night which preceded it had not been devoted to the commission of a crime, which for *deliberate cruelty and premeditation was without a parallel.*

Capt. Brown and Hiram Clauson were absent for several days, as I supposed on some further business connected with our late mission; and we were consequently left during this time at Ogden, as we could not return to the city until they found time to take us. After three days, Hiram came back in company with Capt. Brown; and then we were taken home, where I was glad to go once more, and find myself free from a forced participation in the crimes which I now knew to be the principal business of the Heads of the Church to concoct, and the "Danites" to execute.

It was with bitter tears that I told my mother what I had seen, and what I supposed had been done with the Doctor—with the grey-haired old man, whose only crime had been that he had not forgotten the widow and the children of his dead friend.

We still believed in Mormonism, as we had originally accepted it, and we still believed in the Prophet, as the visible Head of the Church, because we knew no other; but we could not believe the crimes of the Church were necessarily a part of Mormonism. "We have fallen," my mother said, "upon evil times; and if the Prophet Joseph were alive, these wicked men would not bear rule."

But what could two women do? We dare not even speak to my brother Howard upon this subject, and I have no reason to believe he knew of it; and if he did, the control of the Prophet over him was so absolute, that he would have regarded his "counsel" as above crime. I noticed that my mother, who up to this time had held her age remarkably well, began to break; and she never recovered fully from the shock occasioned by the disappearance of Dr. Roberts.*

---

* The author deems it due to the subject of this narrative to state, that he has given the facts of the foregoing case of Dr. Roberts as they

were given to him, without a wish, or an effort to extenuate or lessen the responsibility that justly attaches to all who, even by implication, countenance the commission of such a crime. But the candid reader cannot fail to notice, that while at first sight she is apparently culpable, when adjudged upon a strict construction of acknowledged rules of moral ethics, yet there are many and weighty considerations which may and should be urged in her behalf.

First, she makes an exposition *herself* of this crime. In simple frankness, she reveals a crime, in which she was forced to participate by the Prophet, whose influence she saw no means of evading. This fact alone should secure her, at least, our candid sympathy.

Next, had she refused to render the assistance demanded of her in carrying out the "mission," to which she had been assigned by the Prophet, she would have lost her *own* life, *without saving that of the Doctor*. The Prophet and his "Danites" could, and would have found other means of effecting their cruel purpose.

Again, we have to consider that at this time Mrs. Smith was in a transition state of mind—just emerging towards the light—still within the dark and foggy labyrinths of her Mormon faith, though struggling with a half-formed wish to escape from it. Had she entertained at this time a *clear, well-grounded doubt* of the Prophet's power to curse her in the world to come, as well as in this, there would be a propriety, which does not exist now, in expecting her, a mere woman, to stand up in opposition to the whole power of the Church. On this point she says, chap. 19: "Although I doubted and rebelled against the new forms our faith was assuming, etc., yet no question of the legitimate and fundamental principles of Mormonism had been seriously entertained by me." This shows in a clear light the cruel fact, that a well-fanned fanaticism, and the fear of ghostly penalties, and such like bonds, constitute the magic wand of the Prophet's power among the conscientious adherents to this delusion.

The question is not, whether this was a crime, judged by our standard, for on this point there can be no doubt, but whether it was one when judged by the standard which she acknowledged; and whether to do this, or to disobey the Prophet, was the greater crime—she being still tried by the same standard? And lastly, admitting the strongest possible case that can be stated against her—admitting that she had shown herself on other occasions a woman of firmness, capable of sacrificing her life, even, for what she felt to be right, as when she took the poison in self-defence against the butcher Jones, and admitting that she was bound to do so in this case, yet it should be remembered, that the same human nature that is equal to great efforts and strong self-reliance at certain times, is also subject to its moments of weakness; and at the worst, this was but one of these. Upon the whole, whatever may be the opinion as to *what* Mrs. Smith *should have done*, the story of Dr. Roberts leaves no doubt as to what she *did* do; and it furnishes internal evidence of the highest order of the truth of her narrative.

CHAPTER XXII.

SEALED FOR TIME.

The short time that elapsed between the events narrated in the last chapter and my marriage, passed drearily and slowly enough, notwithstanding my mind was more or less occupied with the preparations necessary for it. That one remembrance of the old man, who, with his firm, honest look, and his white hair streaming in the wind, I last saw in the hands of the "Danites," was ever before me, to disturb my life with a vague fear, that the Prophet might again " counsel " me to assist in the perpetration of some similar crime, I was therefore greatly relieved, when Smith arrived from his farm, with the required recommendation of his bishop.

I have before stated, that no marriage can be celebrated without a written recommendation * from the bishop under

---

* This recommendation must be accompanied by the proper tithing receipts. The following is a true copy from the original one received by Mr. Smith:

"This certifies that I received the following articles of Reuben P. Smith, on Tithing:
September 18th, 1851, by 1 day's work, labor Tithing $1 50

whose jurisdiction the male party lives; and when this is obtained, no legal objection exists to his marriage. With this Mr. Smith was provided, directed to the bishop of our ward, and thus he stood fully endorsed, as a Mormon whose orthodoxy was not to be questioned.

Andrew Cunningham had succeeded Jones as the bishop of the ward in which we lived. He therefore came with Mr. Smith to my mother's house, and " sealed us for time." It will be remembered I had already been sealed to Jones for eternity, which carries with it no wifely obligation, hence I was at liberty to marry a husband for time. The bishop generally does the " sealing " of this kind; but none but the Heads of the Church can seal for eternity, and this is usually done by the Prophet.

We were married in the morning, quietly, in the presence of a few neighbors, not wishing to create any excitement, as we knew the whole Church were watching us with something of distrust. It was generally believed by those who knew my history, that I would not be likely to marry any man who was a Mormon in good faith; at least not one who be-

October	12th, 1851, by	1 day's work, labor Tithing, ...	$1 50
"	13th, "	" 1 day's do do do	1 50
December 18th, "	" ½ ton of Hay, ...	2 50
January 27th, "	" 8 bu. & 11 lbs. wheat on wheat Tithing, . .	12 27¼
"	" "	" 5 bu. & 30 lbs. wheat on Property Tithing, .	8 25
March	31st, "	" 1 day's work abor Tithing, ...	1 50
April 1st & 2d, "	" 1¼ day's work do. do	2 25
"	22d, "	" 60 feet lumber, at 6 cts a foot, . . .	8 60

" Pleasant Grove Ward, Utah Co., U. T.

" GEORGE S. CLARK, Bishop.

" April 20th, 1852.   " Per WM. G. STERRETT, Clerk."

lieved in the spiritual wifeism. The fact, therefore, that I wished to marry Reuben P. Smith, who, it was well known, came to Utah as a Gentile, had the effect to raise a doubt as to the genuineness of his conversion, and to keep us both before the public mind.

After the ceremony was over, we went to my brother Howard's to dinner. When we arrived there, I introduced Mr. Smith to Martha and Howard, as my husband, which was the first they knew of our marriage. It so happened that Luna, a little daughter of the Prophet, was in the room, and when she comprehended what had happened, she ran home at once, and told her mother that "Nett had just been married to that fellow Smith." Children always echo the true sentiment that governs at home, and speak openly what older heads strive to conceal. This remark of the little girl showed the state of feeling in the Prophet's family towards us. In less than half an hour the room was full of goers and comers, to wish us joy upon the occasion. The Prophet sent us word, when he understood that we had been married in that quiet way, that he should insist upon our having a grand wedding yet; and that he would make us one at the Council-house, as this would be the most suitable room for the occasion, being large and commodious. This is the Hall, since used as a court house.

Coming from the Prophet, this had a peculiar significance, as it proved that while he had us under "advisement," he was still willing to treat us openly, as if we were true to the faith. Pacific measures of this kind, gracefully executed, was a leading characteristic of this man, who as Prophet and Chief

Pontiff, has governed the Church, made up of the most discordant elements, for years, with a success unparalleled in the administration of human affairs.

Mr. Smith, while he saw the necessity of humoring the public sentiment upon that subject, which means the sentiment of the Prophet, felt even this to be an intrusion upon his rights. He therefore, with an apparent cordiality, offered to pay the expenses of the wedding, but told me privately he had no idea of giving the thing countenance by his presence, as he should take care not to get back from his farm in time. He however left money to procure for me a proper dress for the occasion, in case he should change his mind upon the subject, and return.

The Prophet had the Hall fitted up in a style of unusual splendor, and when the time arrived, sent his own carriage, known in the city as the Prophet's omnibus, drawn by four fine horses, gaily ornamented, to bring in the guests. When the company had assembled, and everything was ready for the opening of the dance, the omnibus came for us, accompanied by the full band of music. But Smith had not arrived. This was at two o'clock; and they returned in like state at four, and were still more disappointed in not finding him. I then sent word that some unforeseen obstacle had probably prevented his return to the city, and that I trusted the assembled company would enjoy the festivities of the occasion, none the less on account of our disappointment.

Before Smith left I advised him to return, and attend the party, as it would have a tendency to disarm the prejudice I knew to exist against him in the Church; but he had not then fully decided what to do. I therefore had hoped up to the last moment, that he would return, which I then believed to be the most advisable course, and I still think it would have been to our advantage. About dark, Edmond Ellsworth came from the Hall, with a carriage, to inquire further after us, and I begged him not to come again, as I had now given up all hope of Smith's coming. I was by this time much alarmed, fearing the Prophet would divine his real motive in keeping away.

About nine o'clock, Smith arrived, and came in with as much unconcern as if he had no personal interest in attending his own wedding. He said, "they appear to be having a fine time in the Hall at our expense; but they are welcome."

"But are you not going?" said Lizzie.

"Not this time, sis."

"Oh! you must," said Lizzie. "They will never forgive you, after going to so much trouble and expense for your wedding. You will offend everybody."

"I will pay the expense," said Smith, "and as for the balance, the poor old Doctor's bones should satisfy them."

My mother, who was fearful of the consequences, urged Smith to go; but he utterly refused; and while I admired his manly courage, and the generous tribute he thus paid to the memory of Dr. Roberts, I trembled, when I reflected how it might possibly affect us.

The Doctor's fate had made a deep impression upon his mind, and he said it would be barbarous to join in such festivities, with the "brigands" who had robbed and probably murdered the friend of my father. I think I am justified in saying, that Mr. Smith, in this, as in everything else, was actuated by the most lofty sentiments of honor, and true manhood.

He then wished me to dress as if I was going to the party. I did so, and mother spread the cloth for a supper of cold meat and potatoes, and we were not without a pleasant, if not a joyous evening. Although we had no music and dancing, we were acting in good faith with ourselves, and I was content to abide my husband's judgment.

The next day the Prophet sent his daughter Luna, to ask me to come and see him. He had heard that we were going to California, and it was about this he wished to 'counsel" me. I asked my husband what I should do, and after some consideration he directed me to go.

When I arrived at his house, he received me with his usual cordiality, and said:

"Nett, do you intend to go to California?"

"I am not sure yet. Perhaps."

"Well," said Brigham, "you never can go; so you had better not start. Do you understand me clearly? If you set out you will never reach California. That is entirely too much for you to expect. If Smith wishes to go, tell him to go on, but he can't take you."

I was so perfectly astonished at this "counsel," that without making any reply, or evincing any feeling upon the subject, I went home in anguish of spirit, and related to my husband what the Prophet had said. I shall not attempt to describe the effect of this upon Smith. It was a terrible blow to us both. The fact was now fully realized by us for the first time, that the Prophet dare not allow me to leave the territory. He was aware I knew too much to be trusted beyond the influence of the Church.

Smith had a drove of cattle, of which he wished to dispose, and it was at length thought best for him to go on to California alone, and return after effecting a sale of them. H therefore left me for that object about fifteen days after our marriage, and was absent three months. After his return, we made another attempt to go to California, which, as will be seen, **signally failed.**

CHAPTER XXIII.

INTRIGUES OF BRIGHAM YOUNG.

When my husband returned, he was fully determined to leave the territory, and take me with him. But before he had time to take measures for the accomplishment of our wishes in this respect, the bishop of the ward called, and asked him if he intended to settle in the country, and added that in case he did not, he had better go as soon as possible; but that he could not take me along. Smith replied that he had not positively concluded what to do—that it was not impossible that, by spring, he should conclude to settle permanently, but that he did not like to be forced to go or stay.

I was greatly alarmed at this open demonstration against us; for I knew how vain it would be to contend against such fearful odds. After due reflection, we concluded to wait patiently during the winter, and trust to the future and a kind Providence for means of escape. We therefore rented place, and went to housekeeping until spring. The winter passed pleasantly, and without interference from the Church, during which time, my husband made the acquaintance of a merchant doing business in the city by the name of William Mac. He was a Gentile, and had his family with him; but was intending to go to California in the spring. My husband, when he became well acquainted with Mr. Mac, told him how we were situated. Mac said he knew of several similar cases in the city, of men who were forced to remain, rather than give up their wives. "But," he said, "this is the way to manage it. When you are ready to go, bid your wife good-bye, as if you intended to give her up; and when you get to Bear River, wait for me, and I will bring her on with my wife. Let the women manage it between themselves." Smith agreed to this, and paid Mac seventy-five dollars for his promise to bring me. He came home very much elated with the arrangement; and as by this time spring was near at hand, he made preparations to leave. He had a very fine horse, which he did not wish to take with him, and he exchanged it for a valuable gold watch, which he left with me as a keepsake. On the 17th of April, 1853, he bid me farewell, with the understanding privately existing between us, that I was to join him on Bear River within a week; and I have not seen him since. I went with him half a mile, or so, when he set out, and took my final leave at the stream, known as the City Creek. He lingered near me for some time, as if oppressed with a presentiment of evil, and then with a resolute sadness, broke away, and left me perhaps for ever. I recollect well the last view I caught of his manly form in the distance through my tears.

I sat down under the shadow of a wide-spreading tree, upon the bank of the stream, and watched him, until at last he vanished among the hills, and then, crushed with a sense of loneliness, and a vague fear, which, under the circumstances, seemed uncalled for, I returned to the city to begin that ex perience of watching and suspense, which to this day has no end; and He who "tempers the wind to the shorn lamb," alone knows if we are ever to meet again.

A few days after this, Mrs. Mac sent her little boy with a note, saying they expected to go on the next Monday, and directing me to meet them at that time at the bath-house This was a mile and a half from Brigham's residence, on the California road. She also directed me to bring no clothing, except what I wore, in order not to excite suspicion, and that she had made provision for my wants in that respect.

I could not confide to my mother, or to any of the family my intentions, as they would not be likely to favor the enterprise. I therefore assisted Lizzie in washing the dishes after breakfast, as usual, on the morning on which we were to go. While we were thus employed together, she said to me, in her innocent and simple way, "How glad I am, Nett, you did not go to California with Smith, and leave us all alone. I am sure it would have nearly killed us."

When the dishes were out of the way, I quietly put on my sun-bonnet, and took the watch Smith had given me, telling Lizzie and my mother I was going over to Howard's; and bidding them as I went "good-bye," I set out, as I supposed. for California.

After all, it was not an easy matter to leave my young and nnocent sister, and almost helpless old mother, in such a place, and I half relented when once in the street, and out of sight of them. But I thought first of Smith, and then of my Mormon Prison, and went on, determined if possible to make my escape, as I could do them no good by remaining

I had gone but a short distance, when a man whom I had never seen before, evertook me, and with a smile which disclosed at once how much he knew of my business, said, "Good morning, Mrs. Smith. The Prophet wishes to see you at his office at ten o'clock." I stood petrified with horror and astonishment, wondering how the Prophet could have been informed of my intentions. When I looked up at length, the stranger was still looking me full in the face, much delighted at my embarrassment. His quizzical intelligence as to my personal affairs, threw me off my guard, and I said, with an anguish I have no means of describing, "Great God! I am defeated again!" The stranger satisfied with his work, turned and left me, without further reply. Oh! had there been pity in Heaven, or on earth, at that moment for any human being, certainly I was a proper object for its exercise.

Crushed by this failure, and half doubting Mormonism, and yet awed by an overshadowing fear of the Divine power of the Prophet, I knew not where to turn. Brigham had told me often if Smith was not a true Mormon, my love for him was illicit, and for the moment, an oppressive sense of shame came over me, as the bare possibility that Brigham Young was, after all, the true Prophet of God, forced itself upon my mind and checked the doubt which my soul had cherished, perhaps, impiously, as to his Divine mission. "Great God, if there is any to whom I may pray besides the Prophet, direct me now."

When sufficiently reassured, I went directly to the Prophet's office, and as I entered, I said to him, perhaps not in the most agreeable manner, "What are your wishes?"

He looked at me for some moments, with a calm sternness which he had never before manifested in my presence, and said almost harshly, for he was as a general thing conciliatory and winning:

"I wish you to stay with the Saints, and be satisfied. I have a great work for you to do, and a great reward for you after it is done. You are mine. The spirit of the Lord tells me so. You need not be a wife, but you must obey my counsel. I wish your Smith had been scalped by some of our *white Indians* (meaning the "Danites"), before you ever placed your determined and ambitious mind upon him. He is a Gentile at heart; and if you ever live with him, you will commit adultery in the sight of God; and your children, if you have any, will be illegitimate, *and you shall be damned.*"

He said many other things, which I cannot now recall, as the great excitement under which I struggled, had the effect to fix only the most prominent points upon my mind. I made no reply, but when he had finished, I went home, feeling my case was hopeless. I told my mother what I had attempted, and how I had failed. I was nearly wild with excitement and despair, and she listened with patience to my ravings and reproaches.

My tears and physical exertion alone saved me from madness. Towards night, she soothed me into a sound sleep, and I awoke next morning refreshed and calm, and prepared to gird up my soul for a new struggle.

A few weeks after this, the Prophet appointed me a teacher of the ward school; and about the same time, Secretary of the Female Indian Relief Society; the duties of which occupied most of my time, and I had but little opportunity to lay plans for my escape, or leisure to brood over my wrongs We received a letter one day from my brother Uriah, then in California, with the glad intelligence that he was coming home immediately. This gave us all joy, and I was particularly well pleased, as I knew he would assist me in getting away. He was a fine young boy, generous, brave, and manly, and as I had reason to believe, was but little attached to Mormonism. He was the idol of the family. While we were thus daily expecting him, Howard came in one day, looking very sad; and after a while mother said,

"Howard, how can you look so serious when we are all so happy, making preparations for Uriah's return?"

"Mother," said Howard, "do you so certainly expect to see Uriah?"

"Certainly: he has written he will be here very soon."

Howard looked at my mother with great concern, for she had said this in a manner that showed how much her heart was set upon it.

He said, after a little.

"Mother, you would feel very bad if you should hear Uriah was dead."

"What do you mean, Howard? Is Uriah dead?"

We needed no further answer. He took from his pocket a letter, which brought the sad intelligence, which mother read and re-read with speechless horror. He died when just upon the point of starting for home. It was a terrible blow to us all. My mother refused all consolation, and at one time we supposed she would sink under it.

Unnatural as it may appear, our Mormon neighbors rejoiced at this our new calamity; for they said, as we then had no dependence, or protectors, my husband being absent, and our only brother who was unmarried being dead, we should be obliged, Lizzie and myself, to marry some Mormon. Our house, at this time, was truly a house of mourning, and for a few months following this event, we were as sad as can well be imagined.

By the Prophet's dictum, under whose protection I was now directed to consider myself, my marriage was generally considered void, and was thus spoken of in the Church; and I was liable as ever to receive propositions for marriage. This was but a natural result of Mormonism, for Mormon women are not allowed to remain idle in this respect.

Since leaving Utah, I have heard much said about the death of Leonidus Shaver. I knew Judge Shaver well, and recollect the circumstances of his death. He occupied a room in my brother Howard's house; and died there. There were a great many things connected with the trouble between him and the Prophet, which I never understood, and I have good reason to believe, much more than has yet been disclosed. I remember, that one day the Prophet came to the house, and inquired for the Judge. The latter was in the habit of locking the door, and darkening the windows of his room, when not at home, and they were so on this occasion; which led us to believe he was gone.

The Prophet was very much excited about something that had just happened, in connection with the Judge. This was a year or so before his death. I never saw the former more disturbed and alarmed than at that time, and he talked very freely about it. Just as he was in the height of the excitement, we heard the Judge jump out of bed, and this alarmed the Prophet still the more, as he supposed Shaver had heard what had been said, which was probably true. The difficulty between them increased after this, and one morning the Judge was found dead in his bed, in the room just mentioned. But at this time, my brother did not own, or live in the house, for he had sold it to a Mr. Dotson, who was then living there.

The Heads of the Church made a great show of having the case investigated, by which they made it appear, that the Judge had died of some disease in the head, which *perhaps* was true. But I heard the Prophet say before this, that Judge Shaver knew a great many things that he did not wish to come to the knowledge of the Government at Washington, and that he dare not allow him to leave the territory. *He was unquestionably poisoned.*

I think it was in the summer of 1853, that another Judge was sent to Utah, by the name of Brocchus. Soon after he came he was called upon to make a speech, at a public meeting, at a time when the Prophet and the Heads of the Church were on the stand. I suppose Judge Brocchus knew but little of our customs, for he commenced to address the women, large numbers of whom were present, upon the subject of spiritual wifeism. He pointed out to them its wickedness, and the unhappy results that must follow to themselves and their children, if persisted in. He also stated, that it was against the laws of both God and man. I presume this was the first, and only time, that a Mormon assembly was ever addressed in open opposition to their faith and practice. Certainly the only case of the kind that ever occurred at Salt Lake.

The Assembly were greatly excited, and more than two-thirds of the women were in tears, before he had spoken many minutes; among whom, Brigham observed some of his own wives. All were astonished. It was a moment of great peril for the Prophet, and for the Church. One word then, spoken by authority and having the physical support of a military force at hand, would have brought on an explosion.

The Prophet saw this; and, as usual, he was equal to the occasion. The Judge was admonished to desist, and when he sat down, the Prophet rose, and by one of those strong, nervous appeals, which has never been wanting in success before a Mormon audience, he annihilated the Judge and the effect of his speech. In five minutes many of those whose tears had flown most freely, responded to his broad sarcasm in screams of laughter.

When the spirits of the congregation were fully restored, he turned to the Judge, and administered to him a torrent of abuse. Among other things, he said: "I will kick you or any other Gentile Judge, from this stand, if you or they again attempt to interfere with the affairs of our Zion."

The Judge was beaten, and saw the necessity of leaving the territory. The Prophet afterwards threatened, in private, to take his life, but I heard he was permitted to leave.

Judge Brocchus was succeeded by Judge Reed, of Bath, Steuben county, New York; who, profiting by the experience of his predecessor, exercised great discretion in his intercourse with the Mormon leaders, and became very popular with them. The Mormons, on their part, treated Judge Reed with studied attention, hoping to efface the unfavorable impression likely to be made upon the authorities at Washington, by the Brocchus affair, in which they appear to have succeeded in a measure, for it is understood that Judge Reed expressed the opinion, when he afterwards returned to this country, that the Mormons had been misrepresented, and that the charges against them were exaggerated. This, if true, was in pursuance of a line of policy adopted by him, as being the best calculated to meet the difficulties of his position; for beyond question he had studied the state of things at Utah very closely, and though he expressed his opinions with caution, he was certainly not a convert to our faith, nor to the Prophet's administration of the Government.

As he was from the neighborhood of our native place, and was well acquainted with most of our family, we were very intimate with him during his stay at the valley.— It was due to the friendly relations existing between him and the Prophet, more than to any other cause, that we were afterwards permitted to leave Utah, as hereafter narrated. It was through him that we received letters direct from my uncle, Col. John R. Stephens, of Hornellsville, New York; and through this channel came the information which finally led to our escape.

Judge Reed remained in the valley about a year, and then

went home on business, intending to return to Utah, but he died suddenly while there. He was an excellent and kind man, of whom I still entertain the most grateful recollections.

CHAPTER XXIV.

THE STORY OF WALLACE ALONZO CLARK BOWMAN.

ABOUT this period, a young man was coming from Mexico in command of a company of traders; and by chance, he was met by Brigham Young at Utah, who was on his way from Great Salt Lake City to Little Salt Lake.

The Prophet was accompanied as usual by his "Body Guard," and attracted some notice on the route by the display in which he indulged—a kind of demonstration he was fond of making when well protected by his military attendants.

It is said all great men have their little weaknesses, and that of the Prophet is well known to be cowardice. He is great in words, however, and withal is a shrewd manager of men, and when not threatened with personal violence, he is truly great. On this occasion, the state and display affected by the Governor and Prophet excited the curiosity of the young captain of this band of Mexican traders, whose name was Wallace Alonzo Clark Bowman. This young man was a native of the State of New York, and being of a daring and roving turn of mind, had left his home at the early age of eighteen, and was now in the full tide of a successful career, when he thus unfortunately met Brigham Young. He was over six feet in height, stoutly built, and well formed, standing straight as an arrow, with fair complexion and light hair, a broad high forehead, with a keen blue eye and a Roman nose. He was as fine a specimen of manliness as is often met with in real life. He was, moreover, one of that class of men, with whom the emotions of fear, or the necessity of caution, are entirely unknown. He also entertained the most undisguised contempt for double-dealing and of religious affectation of any kind. In short, having no reverence, and unable to comprehend the meaning of discretion, he was the last man to meet the Prophet's approval, but quite the man to awaken his cowardly suspicion, as he was a specimen of the only class of men of whom the Prophet was not a judge.

The two companies met at Utah, and halted to make of each other mutual inquiries as to the state of the roads and the like, while the animals were being fed. Bowman observed that Brigham was a personage of some consideration among the strangers, and upon inquiry was informed that he was the Governor of the Territory, and the Mormon Leader. "If that is so," said he, "I must make the acquaintance of that distinguished adventurer." He then introduced himself to the "Prophet," by saying, he had heard of him and of his religion often, though he knew but little of the latter, and he would like to be instructed in it somewhat. He then asked him to take a seat for that purpose. He told him further that he had heard much said against the Mormons, and their practices, but he presumed they had been misrepresented, as all such sects were liable to be by their opponents; and he should be pleased to know the facts from the Prophet himself.

Bowman said this in that easy off-hand manner, which, had it been addressed to an equally brave and simple-minded man, would have been met in a similar spirit of courteous independence—willing to concede as much as it exacted. But the Prophet was not a man of the generous mould to understand one of that nature. Though a good judge of the kind of men of which his Church was composed, the Mexican trader puzzled him; and he assumed at once the young man must have some villainous design upon him. He thereupon retired to his carriage, with an indecent haste, that betrayed his want of either courage or courtesy, and directed his secretary to inform the authorities of the City, that he wished Bowman arrested upon his arrival there, as he knew by the Spirit of God, the trader was a spy sent from the States to take his life.

The fact was, that nothing could have been farther from the truth; and the pretence of revelation, behind which the Prophet attempted to shield his cowardice, smacked more of unscrupulous *villainy* than of Divinity.

Bowman, unawed by this treatment, stepped to the door of the Prophet's carriage, and said to him, in that spirit of defiant independence which a free rover of the plains feels himself at liberty to assume when treated rudely, "Sir, I have seen Governors before, but I never saw one so little a gentleman, or so much a bigot;" and then turning to his men, with a dignity the Prophet might well have envied, ordered his company to move on.

The whole outfit and other accompaniments of Bowman's party proved he was possessed of wealth, and this was perhaps another inducement with the Prophet for wishing to bring the young rover into collision with his Danite assassins. When Bowman arrived at the city, he was arrested by Robert Burton upon suspicion of various crimes. This was a pretense resorted to for his detention. He was put in charge of John Norton, one of our nearest neighbors, who kept him imprisoned near by, in a place used by the police for that purpose. There was a great curiosity manifested among us to see the man who had made so long a journey to kill the Prophet; and among others, I went to his prison. I was astonished at the courteous good breeding with which we were received. He politely handed us seats, and after some pleasant conversation upon indifferent topics, in which our position and sex were acknowledged, with an easy and graceful address, his eye rested accidentally upon his jailer, John Norton. At once his wild eye flashed fire, and his whole bearing changed to that lofty mien of daring which characterized him when free. For a moment his chafed spirit roused itself into the fierceness of a caged tiger, and yet the while preserving all the dignity of his exalted manhood. He said, "Sir, I presume I have not fully appreciated the extreme humility of my position in the presence of your exalted Prophet, else I should not have taken the liberty of addressing him upon equal terms."

It was amusing to note the effect of this upon John Norton, who, though generally a man of commanding presence, now stood abashed before his prisoner. Bowman's eye rested for some time upon him, during which interval, not a word was uttered. At length, with an expression of disgust, and then of pity, he turned from him to us, and apologized for his rudeness in the presence of ladies, by saying, "Imprisonment under any circumstances is beyond endurance to me, who, since finishing my education in my native State of New York, have seldom slept beneath a roof; but particularly so, when I am deprived of liberty in defiance of my natural rights, and without the pretence of justice." When we left, he bade us good morning, with as much gallantry and unconcern as if he had been doing the honors of the drawing-room. I came away with a full understanding of his position. I knew he was innocent; but I knew equally well that would not avail him. I asked my mother, who had accompanied me, what she thought. Without saying a word for some time, she shook her head, and the big tears filled her eyes. "He is about the age Uriah was, when he died among strangers," said she at length. "How should I feel if this brave boy were mine? But he *is* somebody's boy."

"They will kill him," said I.

"Certainly," said my mother; and then we sobbed in silence, and Lizzie joined in our tears without fully understanding why we wept, for she had not heard the foregoing conversation.

Bowman was held a prisoner for several weeks, as the Prophet had not returned. When he came, a trial was had, and great efforts were made to procure some evidence against him; but all rested upon the revelation of the Prophet, except that the latter stated that Bowman was armed when he approached his carriage. Being armed in that country was not a crime, for no man went unarmed there. But it so happened, that Bowman, although generally provided with, and well skilled in the use of defensive weapons, had, on this particular occasion, left them on his horse, as he expected to remount in a few moments. This was proved by all his men. He was therefore set at liberty, after an annoying confinement of nearly two months. But this did not avert his fate.

The Danites are called in only as a last resort; but are never at fault, when the Prophet's will is known; and in this case, the Prophet had gone too far to think of relenting.

When free, he was directed by some one to our house, to find a boarding place. His horses were kept near us, and he wished to board close by them, while he remained in the city to complete some further arrangements for continuing his journey. My mother was surprised at the request, as we did not keep boarders; but told him to call again towards evening; and in the meantime, she asked the bishop what to do, well knowing Bowman had been sent there by him, or at least by the Prophet's direction. The bishop appeared to be acting under instructions, and told her, as if prepared with an answer before hand, to allow him to take his meals with her, but not to sleep at her house at night.

As for myself, I had become so familiar with the Prophet's way of doing business, that I was greatly alarmed at this turn of affairs; for I saw clearly we were, in some manner then unknown to me, to be forced into the work of Bowman's destruction.

As his prison was in our neighborhood, we had, with most

of the other families of the vicinity, visited him frequently, and had become well acquainted by this time. I had never been approached upon this subject myself, but I knew many of our female acquaintances had been directed to visit him, in order to report to the Prophet what he had to say.

I now felt my time for action had come, and that I was again to be forced into a participation in crime.

In order that my readers may fully understand my connection with what follows, they have only to recollect, that to disobey the Prophet's counsel would have been death to me; and further, I found it would be impossible to effect my escape, until I could disarm the Prophet of all suspicion he might entertain of my *intention* to escape. My object was to avoid, as much as possible, being useful to him; but, at the same time, to obey his "counsel" when there was no way to avoid it, with a show of cheerfulness and good faith; and thus I hoped again to acquire the reputation of being a good Mormon—whereas I was now regarded, as well among the Gentiles as in the Church, as only a prisoner at large. So much was I looked upon in this light, that even Bowman had heard my story, and had publicly denounced the Prophet for thus holding me a prisoner from my husband. This rash advocacy of my cause, prompted as it was only by his generous and manly nature, probably suggested to the Prophet the idea of using me as a decoy to effect more readily his ruin.

Soon after Bowman left, John Norton came to the house in some haste saying, "Nett, I have news for you, of great importance, from Brigham."

"Importance to whom?" said I.

"To the whole Church, and in this way. The Prophet is satisfied that if Bowman is allowed to leave the territory, he can and will give us great trouble, by raising an excitement against us on account of his imprisonment while here. Now, we wish to hear his mind from his own lips, and we can then judge what should be done. When he returns, Brigham wishes you to bring him to our house, and make such advances to him as you may think best, to draw him out upon that subject, and tell him that you would like to go off with him; that, if he will take you, you will be his wife."

"I think," said I, "he would not be likely to take me."

"No fear of that," said Norton, "for we have come to you to do this, from the fact that you are the only person that could approach him. He said only this morning, in the most public manner, in Blain's store, that if he could get you away from this place, he would like to see it sink; and that if he could invent any method of getting you to your husband, he would do so, even at the risk of his life."

At this point of the conversation, William Kimbal, a young son of Heber C. Kimbal, the latter one of the Heads of the Church, came up and said: "John, Bowman will be here soon, for I just saw him go into Blain's store." Then turning to me, he said, "Now, Nett, the Prophet expects you to put in your biggest licks; and if you do not, we shall all know it, for we shall be secreted within hearing of you."

"Do your best," said John Norton, as they both left me, "and tell him I am hunting cattle, if he inquires for me."

John Norton then secreted his brother Wiley in our house,

to hear what passed between Bowman and myself while there. When they were gone, Wiley said, "Come, Nett, go and slick up, for Bowman will be here very soon."

My readers will understand that even the Mormon boys are trained, at an early age, in this branch of the Church service, and soon become adepts in "milking the Gentiles," as robbing outsiders is termed in their slang vocabulary. One of these boys was under the age of fifteen, and was already well versed in crime. It was with a heavy heart that I dressed with unusual care for the occasion, not daring to disregard the counsel I had received. At first, I thought I could place a note in Bowman's hands, by which I should warn him; but this would be attended with greater danger to myself, without a fair prospect of benefiting him; and besides, his known rashness made it hazardous to do anything for his relief, more especially so as I should have no opportunity to explain fully the true state of the case, or how he was threatened—and at most could only give him a glance or a sign of warning.

The distance from our house to Norton's, although but a step, would perhaps be sufficient to convey this signal, and yet I knew many eyes would be upon us.

When I was dressed, Wiley, who had awaited my return with impatience, complimented my appearance, and pronounced me ready "to do the work of the Lord," with the affectation and solemn cant characteristic among the Saints when they do not wish to call things by their right names. I seated myself in the rocking-chair, to await his coming, racked by anxiety. At about four o'clock he came, and I received him in the presence of my mother, Wiley having slid into a dark room within hearing. I must have concealed my agony badly, for he said with a show of alarm, "how pale you are, Mrs. Smith. Mrs. Coray," bowing to my mother, "what is the matter? Has anything new occurred?"

"A little excitement," replied my mother, with an assumed calmness, "always makes a baby of her."

"Her absent husband," said he, "is the subject, I suppose, of a continued anxiety with her."

I was too much excited to act well the part to which I had been assigned; but I made every possible effort to regain my self-command. It was with some exertion, therefore, that I was enabled to say, "I understand you are about to leave us. I wish the Prophet would decide upon my case, and set me at liberty, and I would accompany you." I said this and other things, with a design of encouraging his advances, and he responded with his usual gallantry; and yet, perhaps, contrary to the expectation of the Mormon leaders who had assigned me this duty, in order to corrupt him, he did so with the utmost innocence, and freedom from an improper motive.

The Prophet had, as usual, reasoned upon the assumed fact that all men were open to the seductive charms of corrupt influences; and much of his own success in governing the *men* of the Church is to be credited to a skillful application of this principle: and it is for this reasom that the condition of a Mormon woman is beyond belief horrible, exposed as she always must be, to the danger of falling a victim to the brutal claims of some one of the Prophet's creatures, as the price of some service or obedience rendered to him..

I had expected much from the high-toned honor of Bowman; but he rose still higher in my estimation when he refused to understand the meaning of my words. In order to cut the matter short as possible, and to secure the opportunity of uttering to him a single word of caution, while passing to the house of John Norton, I affected some embarrassment at first, to convey to Wiley an idea that I felt myself refused; and then, as if reassured, I said to Bowman, with an easy unconcern, which I was by this time able to assume, "come, let us go over to John Norton's. As you are about to leave, perhaps you would like to bid his wives, Martha and Rebecca, good-bye."

"Certainly," said he politely. "I reckon those ladies among my friends. They visited me often in prison, and I must pay them my compliments before I take my leave, and I shall have no better time than now."

As we passed from the front door into the street, I was glad to notice that Wiley did not attempt to follow us. We were the next instant *alone*, on the public walk, and although we were together but a moment, and while watchful eyes were perhaps upon us, I said to him in a hurried manner, and in a low voice, "Mr. Bowman, I beg you not to speak, but listen to me for the one moment we are to be alone. I have time to state but one thing, which, if you rightly understand, will be sufficient for your purpose. It is this. I am acting under the direction, and by the instructions of the Prophet. Are you listening? Do you understand me? Whatever I say, think not of me; but that Brigham Young is speaking through me."

He looked puzzled, then astonished, and was about to speak. But we had arrived at the gate of John Norton, and the door was not many feet off. "Hush," said I, and the next moment he mechanically rapped at the door, and we both waited in silence for admittance. I shall never forget the change that came over his smooth, unruffled face, during the few moments he had listened to me. He was in appearance twenty years older in that time. His eyes were bent in anxious thought upon the ground, and his whole great frame struggled to master the words, by which I had opened to him a new source of danger. He would have faced, undaunted, fifty men in the open combat, on a fair field; but now he stood half cowering before a mystery of which his experience furnished no solution. But though at fault in this respect, he was not wanting in intellect; and when our summons was answered from within, he started as if from a painful reverie, and then the sunshine and a clear sky was over him again. Howbeit, I still detected, by certain lines upon his handsome face, traces of anxious thought unusual to it. We were shown into the sitting-room, where we were expected.

CHAPTER XXV.

FATE OF BOWMAN.

PERHAPS the saddest feature of Mormonism as regards its own victims, should be looked for in the influence it necessarily has upon women. It is impossible to convey a clear idea of the absolute slavery of our sex under Mormon influence. It is not enough that all the recognized rights of an isolated domestic life, are invaded by a *community* of wives; but all these women jointly, and severally, are to be the unquestioning instruments in the hands of their spiritual husbands, in carrying out the merciless designs of the Church, forced to this degrading work by the ever present fear of being denounced, and of imprisonment, and even death, in this world, and of being cut off from the Prophet's Paradise in the next. Innocent women, young and tender girls, and honest mothers, with all the instincts of their true womanhood upon them, are expected at the Prophet's, or the husband's bidding, to look crime in the face, without a shudder, and to prostitute all the sweet, and winning graces with which a Wise Hand has endowed them, as a means of exerting a softening and refining influence upon man's rougher nature, to carry out these designs of the Church against their Gentile victims. But female humanity is unequal to the sacrifice while virtue, the real source of all womanly charms, wields her gentle sceptre over the heart.

This was well illustrated by the manner we were received by Martha and Rebecca. The latter, who was the first wife, and was recognized as entitled to take the lead in doing the honors of the house, received us; handing us seats in the sitting-room, where we found Martha.

I had by this time fully regained my self-possession, and Bowman, whose buoyant nature would not bear depression, appeared to good advantage; but the ladies, though evidently making an effort to act well their part, were depressed, and solemn as if assisting at a funeral: and indeed, they well knew they were preparing the way for one.

Bowman, with a tact for which I had not before given him credit, divined, by aid of the key I had afforded him, as to myself, the true state of the case as to *them*, and said in a light and airy manner, yet with a caution that showed every word was well considered, "How is this, ladies? you look as solemn as a Quaker Synod. Martha, has that ungracious husband been treating you unfairly,* by giving Rebecca the finest dress again?"

---

* The above reference to the scenes of bickering to which those households are always subject, where spiritual wifeism is practised, brings to mind a circumstance that occurred at Salt Lake City, about the time of which we are writing.

The family of which I speak, lived in the Temple Block, with Mrs. Whitney, well known there. I do not recollect the name; but the man was from England as was also at least one of his wives. It

This allusion to a dispute, which by the indiscretion of somebody had found its way to the public ear, but a short time before, rallied Martha into the mere shadow of a laugh, as she said,

seems the first wife, who was married before she came to the valley, and who was much attached to her husband, objected to share her household honors and responsibility, with the new spiritual—forced upon her. The latter was not recognized, or tolerated in any respect by the first wife; although she was the favorite of the husband. Things went on in this way, until one morning, the "spiritual" took the liberty of putting on a dress belonging to the first wife, without asking her permission. This exasperated the latter to such a degree, that the other parties, finding the house scarcely large enough to hold them all, attempted to discipline the refractory wife into submission. In order to justify what they were about to do, the unfeeling husband and the new wife, represented the lawful and previous occupant to the Heads of the Church, as being *possessed with the devil*. This put her beyond the pale of sympathy or protection. They then bound her to a narrow bench, *where she lay upon her back, night and day,* until the cords *had cut through the flesh to the bone; and she had unjointed one shoulder in the struggle to break loose.* She was in this condition, when I saw her. Great numbers of the Church visited her, and many believed she was really possessed of the devil. She was pointed out as a warning to refractory wives by the Church authorities. I noticed she acknowledged a look of friendly sympathy, although no one was allowed to speak to her. I went in with several others; and while there, we saw the poor woman's child, something over two years old, come to its mother's side, and attempt to break the cords by which its mother was bound. The little thing was a girl, destined to grow up, and live over again perhaps, its mother's sad life, or to feel what its mother never could, submission. It was the most intensely cruel and touching spectacle I ever witnessed. The

"Oh no. That difficulty is all settled. He sees the folly of treating Rebecca better than he does me, and is becoming quite a good fellow."

"By the way," said Bowman, "where is this husband, John Norton, to-day?"

This was the second time this question had been asked by him, and evaded by the ladies; but now it was so direct that Rebecca replied, "he said he was going over Jordan, to look after the cattle."

My readers will recollect that John Norton and Wm. Kimbal were at that moment within full view and hearing of us; separated from the sitting-room by a partition, so constructed as to be conveniently used for that purpose.

Nothing could reassure Rebecca and Martha, for they grew every moment more and more solemn and constrained, and it was a positive relief to them, when, by a pre-arrangement, Mrs. Burgess, one of the neighboring women, came to the door, and with a dissembled show of haste and alarm said to them,

"Come over at once; one of my children has been burned terribly."

"How," said both at once, and without waiting, for an explanation, the three women ran off together, leaving us alone,

hild rolled its wild eyes—fired with a precocious sense of wrong, the source of which it struggled to comprehend—first to its hapless mother and then to us, as if puzzled as much to know why the mother was confined there, as why we did not release her. Its pitiful moans and appeals for the help we could not give, were enough to break our hearts.

in the sitting-room. The design of this was, that I should be enabled to lead Bowman into some developments of his plans and feelings towards the Church, in hearing of the listeners of the next room. Then commenced a series of attacks upon my victim. I felt I could now afford to act my part well: more especially as I had given him what warning I could. I represented to him in my best manner, how much I wished to escape; and that I should be pleased to do so by his assistance; and that I was willing to submit to any conditions he might impose, and hinted further at other possibilities, in a manner not to be mistaken. As a part of my instructions were to ascertain if possible what amount of money he had, I told him, that in case he could not take me, that with a small sum of money, I should possibly be able to get away, in another manner, which I did not mention. To all this he listened in thoughtful silence; and I was pleased to notice that I had not awakened his interest, until I referred to the money. I then asked him in order to draw out a reply of some kind, what he thought of the Mormons.

"Why as for that," said he slowly, "I have no good reason to think very well of them. I think I know these Saints are making arrangements to take my life. I shall never be permitted to leave this place. I know the man who is to be charged with the duty of effecting my murder. My life is not worth a fig. But should I succeed in getting away, which is now impossible, I should be very glad to restore you to your husband: and then I would come to this accursed den of assassins, with such a company of true men, and such an array of arms, as would sweep this impious Prophet, and his

Danites,' from longer cursing this beautiful valley." While he said this he rose from his seat, and his eye flashed a proud defiance, and his whole frame swelled with a lofty enthusiasm.

"But," said he, resuming his seat after a moment's silence, and falling back into his quiet and thoughtful mood again, "you mentioned just now that money might be useful to you. If so, you can have all you wish; as it will be useless to me. All the money in the world cannot save me, Mrs. Smith: and you may as well have it as any one." I then took the watch Mr. Smith gave me when he left for California, and handed it to him. This was a keepsake, and I did not wish to part with it; but he looked at it, saying as he did so, "this is worth about one hundred dollars. I will give you two hundred for it." I knew he would have given me the money as soon without the watch, as with it: and that he had chosen to give the transaction a business form, from motives of delicacy to me. I appreciated his motives, but I parted with the watch with regret. But there was no remedy for it, and he took from his pocket a purse of gold, which I should say contained several thousand dollars, and counted me the amount, saying at the same time, I could have more if I wished. The fact was I dare not refuse the money or explain to him, why I preferred to keep the watch in the presence of the listeners.

He then said, "Well, Mrs. Smith, I find I am nearer ready to leave this city, than I had expected; and I may as well meet my fate at once. I have concluded to leave to-morrow morning. If I can once reach the open plains, I can defy them. The difficulty will be to escape beyond the cañons and mountain passes leading from this city. I think I shall never pass them; but we shall see. But it is time I had seen my men, that they may be ready for an early move in the morning."

We then returned to my mother's who had tea ready, and when the meal was finished, Bowman went up town to put his affairs in readiness for the journey; and we saw him no more that night. With his company he had three Indian slaves, purchased as he said in Mexico.

That slavery exists not only among these Mexican and Indian traders, but also among the Mormons, and by authority of the Prophet, is perhaps not generally known; but it has been reduced to a regular system, in the territory, under their administration. Young Indian girls and boys, who are captives among the various tribes, are purchased, and trained as servants, and are now as much a recognized item of property there as the negro slaves of Louisiana or Kentucky.

The next morning, our house was filled with our immediate neighbors, the acquaintances of Bowman, as it was generally known he was to leave the city at an early hour, and would bid his friends adieu, after he had taken his breakfast at our house. Notwithstanding great efforts had been made by the Heads of the Church, to create a prejudice against him, he yet had many true friends among us, though none dare to advocate his cause openly.

When the time arrived for his departure, he came to the house accompanied by his party. I noticed among the rest, three very formidable looking Spaniards, who had in charge the pack animals. His packs were large and numerous, and were said to contain valuable goods, and other property and money.

His own dress and appearance on this occasion was very imposing. He wore a sort of over-shirt of brown broad cloth, of very fine fabric, with blue pantaloons, and leggings, fastened above the knee by bands of red velvet, richly ornamented with bead work, which he prized, as having been worked and presented, rumor said, by the fair hands of a distinguished Mexican lady. His buckskin riding gloves, were laced from the wrist to the elbow with silken cords, and the Mexican hat, which completed his graceful, and somewhat ambitious costume, was removed when he came in, with an air of good breeding, and consideration for his friends, and he chose to treat us all as such, that would have done honor to a gentleman of any country or position in life. His whole costume, however, was arranged in good taste, and according to the customs of the country. As he moved among us, he was acknowledged by all to be a model of grace and manly beauty; and more than one heart deplored his fate, from which every Mormon felt there was no reprieve. He wore a sad and even gloomy face at first, and was much astonished to find so large a company. Seeing many whom he recognized as his friends, he brightened up somewhat, as he said with a touch of sarcasm,

"Where is Brigham? He should be here to preach my funeral sermon."

The rebuke was so well deserved, that we *looked* as guilty as we *felt*. He saw the effect of his speech; and generously added:

"My friends, I know who are the guilty ones among you and I have now to bid you a final adieu. I thank you for the honor of your presence here this morning. I wish it was in my power to serve you."

When he had finished his breakfast, he turned to me and aid :

"Mrs. Smith, I trust I may ask you to accept this sash at my hands."

He then put a beautiful sash over one of my shoulders, and around my waist, and tied it there. Then placing his hands one on each side of my face, he kissed me, saying :

"Good-bye, Mrs. Smith ;" and then he kissed all the ladies present, in like manner, and bid them good-bye. John Norton and the bishop of the ward were present, with many other men, and a large number of women. It was noticed that when he shook hands with the men, he did so with less cordiality than when he kissed his adieus to the ladies.

His party moved on at his order, and he left us, bearing with him the sorrowing sympathy of every woman present. I think nothing but the presence of the men restrained our tears.

This was Sunday morning; and after meeting, the Prophet came to John Norton's house, accompanied by General Wells I saw them, and feeling an anxiety about the fate of Bowman that would not be appeased nor brook delay, I went there. I was still in mystery as to the particular manner in which he was to be disposed of. I knew my interview with him had not been attended with quite the result the Prophet had anticipated, and that he had changed his policy with rega to him since but in what way I knew not. It was this I wished to know. I concealed my interest in the matter as best I could, and was well and very kindly received by the Prophet, who complimented me upon the skillful management of my "mission," as he was pleased to call it. He placed his hands upon my head, and as the Prophet of God, conferred a blessing upon me, closing with these words: "You, Mary Ettie, shall yet be mighty in word and deed."

The Prophet then turned the conversation upon the subject nearest my heart. Besides John Norton and family, there were several other persons present of note in the Church, both men and women.

He said, addressing the company generally, "we must make some arrangements as to Bowman at once. We must adopt some plan by which to end his existence. It will never do to allow him to leave the territory: for if he is once at liberty again, he will set the Spaniards and Indians against us, if not half the world besides, and that will never do."

General Wells then proposed that two men should be selected from the private police, for the purpose of carrying out the Prophet's "counsel." John Norton volunteered as one, and the General engaged to find another. With these few words, the matter was settled. Some other unimportant conversation passed, and the trial and condemnation of one of the noblest and bravest of men was accomplished. A young and innocent man, one incapable of the commission of a crime, was thus to be cut off, to gratify the craven bigotry of the Prophet. I had often seen Brigham Young in difficult positions before; but I had never known his unwor thy fears get so much the better of his judgment. The "High Commission" separated, and I went home, sick and disheartened, to mourn for the doomed. A morbid curiosity prompted me to know all the details of the cruel measures taken for his destruction, and circumstances favored my wishes.

My husband, before our marriage, had been employed by Major Holman, Indian Agent for the territory, to distribute the goods, consisting of beads, blankets, brooches, paints and the like, to some of the tribes; and by accident, a package of the paints used by the Indians had been left at our house. This fact, unimportant in itself, was known to John Norton. Just at night, Norton came to our house with James Ferguson, and asked for some of this paint, and made no reserve in telling us what they wished to do with it. The remainder of this story I learned from Norton and Ferguson themselves. This Ferguson had been selected to accompany Norton. They left the city on horseback, and that night, passed, after dark, the house where Bowman had put up. Knowing the route he must take from there, they went on to Salt Creek cañon, where they disguised themselves as Indians, by painting their faces and putting on blankets and horse-hair wigs. It appears that Bowman had sent his main company on, while he remained behind, keeping but four horses and two Spaniards with him. He had purchased a wagon and harnessed two of his horses to it; one Spaniard was driving, and the other was riding one, and leading another horse behind the wagon, and Bowman was riding inside of it. It was in this manner that Bowman entered the cañon, the next morning, nearly alone, probably with the hope of misleading the "Danites," whom he knew would be on his track.

But Norton and Ferguson were in ambush near the road, and as the wagon came on, they both rose from behind some rocks and bushes, and gave an Indian war-whoop, and fired a shot, which took effect in the hat of one of the Spaniards, whom they wished not to kill, but only to frighten. At this, both of these cowards fled with the loose horses, and made their way back to the city, leaving Bowman alone, who now rose in the wagon, and drawing himself up to his full height for a quick survey of the danger, from which he evidently felt there was no escape, looked undaunted upon his assailants. A moment of silence intervened, and the report of two rifle shots rang among the rocks of the cañon, and he fell to the bottom of his wagon dead. Either wound was mortal; one hit him full in the breast, and the other in the forehead. I afterwards heard both Norton and Ferguson relate the circumstances of his death, and both agreed in the statement as above given. The Spaniards, upon their arrival at the city, went before a magistrate, at the suggestion of the Mormons, who affected great alarm, and made oath that Bowman had been shot in Salt Creek cañon by the Indians, one of them showing the ball hole through his hat, in confirmation of it; and this statement was credited as well among many of the Mormons as among the Gentiles, and is so received to this day by the masses.

A posse of the police were sent out to look for his body, and for the property, but returned, after a thorough search, without discovering either; and thus the matter was hushed up with the public. No part of his property, which must have been valued at many thousands of dollars, was ever discovered, as far as was generally known; but the following will indicate its probable disposition.

The first or second night after Bowman's death, John Norton and Ferguson brought his body to the city, in the wagon in which he had been killed, and drawn by his own horses. They took it to Norton's house. When the men had gone out, Rebecca came over and told me what had happened, and I went home with her. We took a light, and went to the back room and saw the body. We had no difficulty in recognizing it. I clipped from his head a small lock of hair with my scissors. I afterwards gave this hair to Dr. Hurt, then or afterwards Indian Agent of the Territory; and this, with a note from Brigham Young, received upon a former occasion, and referring to another matter, were sent to Washington by Judge Kinney, as the Doctor informed me. I had afterwards, and at different times, repeated conversation with the actors in the tragedy of Bowman's imprisonment and death, from whom I have gathered what I did not know of my own knowledge. Norton and Ferguson both acknowledged, in my presence, that they killed Bowman in cold blood; and, what will perhaps appear singular to my Gentile readers is, they did not consider it a crime. Hiram Clauson, who, it will be recollected, assisted at the robbery, and probable murder of Dr. Roberts, told me that the body of Bowman was given to Drs. Andrews and Williams, well-known physicians of the city, for dissection.

I have thus sought to do justice to the memory of Wallace Alonzo Clark Bowman; and as his murderers are still living, I can but hope they may yet meet the reward due their crimes.

CHAPTER XXVI.

MORMON JESUITISM.

WHEN all was over with poor Bowman, I felt the full pressure of my disagreeable position. Mormonism, now doubly hateful, was rendered the more terrible to my imagination by the fact that there was no reasonable hope of escape left me. I wrote to my husband not to return to Salt Lake, as if he did, he would very likely never go away alive.

A little circumstance happened soon after this, which served to render my position still more uncertain and disagreeable.

A stranger came to our house, with a letter purporting to be from my husband's mother, directed to him and myself, giving the information that a valuable property had fallen to the family in Scotland, and wishing him to accompany her to secure it. The letter had been taken from the post office at Salt Lake by the stranger, who represented himself as a brother of my husband. The whole affair looked so singular and suspicious, that I thought my safest course would be to lay the matter before the Prophet. I conceived this to be a plan of the Mormons to test my sincerity.

The stranger afterwards called at our house, and professed to be authorized by my husband to take me to California, in order to accompany him to Scotland, for the purpose named in the letter. The Prophet pronounced it an attempt of my husband to get me from the Saints, and advised me not to go. This did not alter the opinion I had entertained from the first: that the Prophet knew all about it; and that it would be at least safe to follow his "counsel" in this matter, however it might be when I was free to accept or reject it, if indeed such a time should ever come. I give this to illustrate the character of the Mormon leaders, and their line of policy. I soon after received a letter from my husband, saying he had given up the idea of getting me from Salt Lake. That he had made every possible effort in that direction, and had sent two men to bring me away, but that they had never been heard from since; and that he was quite discouraged about succeeding, while Mormonism flourished there. As he made no mention of having sent his brother, I felt myself confirmed in the opinion I had entertained, as to who were at the bottom of that transaction. I was still teaching the ward school, and Brigham Young came to see me very often, and took unusual pains to encourage and keep me in good spirits, as he believed I could yet be reconciled to the Church. I deemed it best to encourage his efforts in this direction; and I was equally industrious in my efforts to convince him I was becoming every day better satisfied; and that even then I was, to a certain degree, contented and happy. Any other course would have been beyond question suicidal; and, as my readers will hereafter learn, it was by the patient pursuance of this policy, that I afterwards effected my escape; not, however, until I had been the victim of repeated disappointments and hardships

CHAPTER XXVII.

THE STORY OF WILLIAM MAC.

On my way to school one morning I met William Mac. It was this man that had been engaged by my husband to take me to Bear River, where he was to meet us, which scheme, it will be recollected, was frustrated by the Prophet Mac had just returned from California with more goods, and his family, to remain during the winter. This was the first I had known of his return, and I eagerly inquired what information he had of my husband; but he knew nothing of him.

It was a few days after this, that I was in his store, to inquire for some small matter, which I had been unable to find at other places. It so happened that no one was in the store at the time, but his two clerks, who were both Gentiles. As I went out, thinking no Mormons were in hearing, he said to his clerks, "I think it a burning shame that Mrs. Smith cannot go to her husband. If she remains until I go in the spring, I will take her in spite of the whole Mormon crew. If she will risk herself with my wife, I will take her." I did not hear these words myself, but there was a Mormon within hearing who did. Bishop Browning, of Ogden City, stood at that moment just outside the door, and heard all he had said. He knew me, and had heard of my marriage to Smith and of course appreciated how important it was the Prophet should also know of Mac's intentions. He therefore went immediately to Brigham's office, and reported what he had heard; and I was sent for at once. When I arrived at the Prophet's office, he was alone, and sat absorbed in deep study. His face was overcast and even sad. It was not unusual to see him thus, when free from excitement. He is probably the most unhappy man alive. I have seen him join the dance with the utmost abandon; and have heard him say afterwards that dancing served to drown for the moment, the crushing weight of care and responsibility under which he groaned. His government is too absolute to be easily administered, and it is believed by his most intimate associates, that the frequent exercise of his assumed prerogative of holding "the issues of life," which he practically does through the agency of his "Danites," weighs heavily upon his spirit, and not unfrequently disturbs his conscience.

He has been often heard to say that his life was not worth the possession; and that if he consulted only his own feelings, he should quit the world at once.*

---

* It cannot be supposed that the Mormon Prophet is the dupe of his own pretensions, and hence this starting back at the remembrance of his crimes, and at the recollection of the many, many victims, whose bones are strewn from Nauvoo to Salt Lake, and through every valley and cañon, and over every plain of Utah, vindicates the divinity within us. It admonishes the wrong-doer, that although "hand join to hand," and notwithstanding "God is slow to anger," "the wicked shall not go unpunished."

He rose as I went in, and giving me his own chair, he assumed at once his usual smile and self-possession, and said, "Well, Nett, I have another tedious job for you."

"What is it?" I asked.

"This," said he. "I wish to send you upon a mission to the Gentiles to get money for us."

"How do you expect me to get money from the Gentiles? Certainly you will not expect me to rob, or steal, nor commit that other sin, which you have always taught us was so wicked.

"I do not wish," said he, "you should break any covenant you have made, and while you do not do that, you will be safe enough. But at present, this is what I wish: that you should go to Mr. William Mac, the merchant, and make such advances to him, as that he shall be induced to believe you are willing to become his mistress, *i. e.*, to live with him without marriage. The Gentiles have but one wife, but they often have others, whom they support privately, to whom they are really more attached than to their lawful wives. Now, you have, perhaps, never understood that this is *one* reason why Mormons are allowed to have a plurality of wives, *i. e.*, to avoid the sin of keeping mistresses. I wish you to do this without delay. You can succeed, I am certain, from what I have heard this morning. I have just learned he takes a great interest in you." He then related to me what he had heard from Bishop Browning, and all Mac had said. I earnestly begged the Prophet would excuse me for this once, and reminded him that I had never refused to obey his "counsel;" but asked that he would send some one else

That I had hoped to serve the Church in some other capacity, and did not feel able to acquit myself with credit in such a mission.

Drawing his small frame up to its fullest height, he assumed towards me that air of severity, softened by a slight margin of patronage which, in his hands, was so strong a weapon, when dealing with those who were entirely within his power. Upon occasion he could rise to something very near the sublime, if by chance no strong arm was near to frighten his divinity and high pretension back within the limits of good manners. He now looked every inch the Prophet and inspired Seer, as he said:

"I wish you to proceed according to the best of your knowledge. That is all I require. I know whether you can do it or not, before I send for you. You trifle too much with my word. I am directed by the spirit of *my* God * when I act."

I saw I had unwittingly aroused, to its fullest intensity, that strong will, which had never yet found its equal within the pale of the Church, and which forms a strong element of his

---

* "I am directed by the spirit of *my* God." In these words the Prophet does not acknowledge the "One only true God" of the Bible; but he refers in the expression "*my God*," to the particular God in whose kingdom he expects to be in the next world, and to whom he is responsible in this.

He teaches that there are many gods, each having a kingdom in the other world, in which each is absolute; but that over all these, the God of the Bible is the acknowledged Head; and that he, Brigham Young, is to be a god there also; and that the God of the Bible was once a man, now risen to the high estate of the central and Ruling Godhead.

government, among those who acknowledge his authority as a Prophet.

I hastily apologized, and made my escape from the inspired presence, with the best grace possible, promising a cheerful obedience.

After seriously canvassing my position, I concluded it was my duty to protect myself, and to obey the Prophet was my only way to do this. As far as Mac was concerned, if he was an honest man, he would not be misled by me. If he believed as he professed, that it was wrong for Mormons to have a plurality of wives, he certainly would not do what both Gentiles and Mormons professed to think a crime, and therefore he would be safe. For if he did not yield to temptation, the Prophet could find no pretext for extorting money from him.

My readers will of course understand that I was expected to go only far enough to get him committed by some overt act or promise, which the Mormons could use as the foundation of charges against him, for which he would prefer to pay heavily, rather than be exposed. This was about the time the Prophet was building a very extensive dwelling for his wives, where he wished to gather those who were especially his favorites, under one roof: a sort of religious harem, to be fitted up with a costly magnificence, worthy of the residence of the Prophet, and the possessor of so many wives. To do this, he was availing himself of every possible resource for raising money.

I have been asked repeatedly, since my return to the States, how many wives the Prophet had; and I have heard it stated here, that he had thirty. Now I suppose if the Prophet himself were asked the question, he could not answer it, without first having an examination of the records, as well of marriages as of deaths, for they often die without his knowledge, as they are scattered over the territory, and often live in places remote from the city. I recollect hearing a story told of him, which illustrates this point.

At one time, when on a tour of inspection at Little Salt Lake, he put up for the night with a family of Mormons, consisting of a woman and her daughter. In the morning, the mother asked the Prophet if he knew that young lady, referring to her daughter. He said he did not. The mother then informed him, that the young woman was his daughter; and stated the time, at Nauvoo, when she had been "sealed" to him. Upon examining the records, it was found to be true.

I heard, at another time, one of the High Priests, whose business it was to anoint the sick, say, that he had that morning anointed twenty of the Prophet's *babies*—all of whom had the measles. If Brigham Young has not a hundred wives, which he probably has not, it is because he never saw so many single women whom he wished to marry. Of course I need not state, that it very seldom happens that his wishes in this respect are disregarded; and I think they never are, among the true believers; for why should they be, since his application is backed by that unanswerable argument: "thus saith the Lord," and that is the end of it.

Going to my school-room, I sent the children to their homes, and set myself to work at once, to carry out the hated "counsel" of the tyrant, whom I dared not disobey.

I fixed my plan of operations, by adopting such measures as should leave no doubt of my intentions, hoping this very boldness might put him on his guard, or at least, astonish him into decency. At first, I drew up a note addressed to him, in which I expressed my proposition, in terms not to be mistaken, and then dressing myself with care, went to his store. Mr. Mac was not in at the moment. The clerks volunteered to show me anything I might wish, but I told them I preferred to see the proprietor; as I was looking for an article used only in the High Priest's office, and that I would wait his return. This excited some curiosity with them, and gave rise to some speculation as to what it was; in the midst of which, Mr. Mac came in. This was as I preferred it should be, for I wished to give the man some chance for his life, and not to use an unfair bait, but to tempt him in the presence of his clerks, and with their eyes upon him, and when he was free from excitement. If he fell into my snare under such circumstances, it would be but the result of his own folly.

Mr. Mac received me very kindly, and with the overacted politeness in vogue among shopkeepers of his class, wished me good morning; at the same time, asked what he could do for me. "Several things," said I. "First, I wish to look at this," going to a piece of carpet near by, and, at the same time, handing him the note in the presence of the clerks. After reading the note, without the least show of embarrassment, he turned to me, and said, as if nothing had happened out of the usual line of business :—

"**Yes, yes**; I think we haven't it now, but we can accom

modate you soon;" as if referring to some imaginary article of trade, which he happened not to have.

"Let me see," he said, referring to the note. "Does the lady expect me to keep this?"

"I believe she does," said I, and then took my leave, sorry to find him so approachable, saying as I went out, "you will please to let me know when you can fill the order," as if still referring to the imaginary article, supposed to have been mentioned in the note. I was the more pained with the result of this interview, from the fact, that one of the strong arguments the few of us who rejected the spiritual wife doctrine were in the habit of urging was, that the Gentiles who believed in Christianity, rejected it, as not being a practice authorized by the Bible. Against this view, the Prophet urged that it was only a *pretence* with them.

"True," he would say, "the Gentiles have *openly* but one wife; but they have in secret as many as they can support."

And here was a Gentile who, by his practice, had confirmed the Prophet's reasoning.

I went with a heavy heart, immediately to report the progress I had made.

Brigham was well pleased, and encouraged me to go on; "but," said he, "after this you had better not come to my office. I will send some one to assist and instruct you, as occasion may require.

"I have been publicly preaching of late, to our women, against associating, in any way, with the Gentiles; and if, Mac should notice you came here, he would be likely to think you visited him with my consent, and hence, would suspect you of bad faith."

Up to this time, it had never occurred to me, that if I should go to my brother Howard, now my only brother living, possibly he could protect me against the necessity of submitting to the Prophet's "counsel," in the execution of these "missions." He was a High Priest, and was much about the person of the Prophet, having been one of his secretaries from the first, and he was said to have influence with him. On my way home, I went to Howard's house, and told him what had happened, and asked him to assist me. I believe him to be an honest man, and that he would in no case, or for no earthly consideration, commit a crime; but the claims of the Church and the word of the Prophet, are to him a law above all question or cavil. He listened to me with patience, and said when I had finished:

"Mary Ettie, I am sorry you are capable of filling missions of that kind: but it is an evidence of the Prophet's divine commission, that he has discovered this talent in you; and the whole Church recognize you as fitted for the work; and many think it is a special grace sealed upon your head. It will be utterly impossible to escape your mission, or to question the Prophet's counsel—you must go on."

I went home sick and disheartened, for I saw there was no escape from this degrading service. I had been at home but a few minutes, when John Norton came to the door, and said, as if he understood the embarrassment of my position, "Nett, I tell you to do as you have been counselled; there is no other way for you."

I knew he had been sent by the Prophet, who had probably been informed of what I had just said to Howard. I made him no direct reply, but went to bed early, to seek forgetfulness for the time in sleep.

The next morning, I awoke refreshed and calm. I wished to make one more appeal to Brigham Young, and I went to his house, and had the good fortune to find him there with Orson Hyde. As I went in he met me at the door, with his best smile, saying, as he patted my cheek playfully,

"Well, Nett, you think you have a hard time of it, do you?"

"I do not understand," said I, "why you have selected me for this kind of work, always ending as it does, if not in murder, at least in something as wicked."

"Because," said he, "I know you have the faculty of gaining the friendship of those with whom you come in contact, and you must do something for the Church. If you will not marry any of us, you must help 'milk the Gentiles.' I do wish you could ever realize how we have been driven from one State to another by these Gentiles, until we have finally reached this stronghold among the mountains; and they would now push us on, and into the Pacific, if they could. But the powers of Hell cannot disturb us here. They are now inventing every possible plan to get away our most intelligent women, while I am telling them plainly every Sunday from the pulpit, they are not wanted among us."

"I understand you, brother Brigham, as to that," said I; "but why are not others, as well as myself, sent to milk the Gentiles, as you term it? I am fearful my husband will not approve of my conduct, if I should go on with this matter."

"Perhaps," said the Prophet, "if your were called upon to do as some females in the Church have done, you would renounce Mormonism outright. You do not know what everybody may be doing, any more than everybody knows what you are doing. When people first come into the Church, they must be fed upon the thinnest milk; but you should now be able to eat strong meat."

I felt a strong inclination to laugh, which he noticed, and checked me, by saying:

"You always trifle with serious matters."

"Do you think it a trifling matter," said I, "to lead a man off, and take his money, and perhaps his life?"

He looked at me seriously for a moment, as if smitten by the inquiry, and said at length, almost despairingly:

"I have a terrible headache."

But without sparing him, I said, "Smith will never tolerate such work."

"Never mention him," said he. "It is a sin to think of him."

"But if he comes back, and confesses his sins," I replied, "you are bound to forgive him—are you not?"

"He never will," said the Prophet, earnestly. "If he does, he shall never have you; but my head aches, and I must leave you to accomplish your appointed work."

"I will not disturb you further," said I; "and if I had the power of healing, I would relieve you. But Saints never have the power of healing and prophesy at the same time—do they, Brother Brigham?"

"No, no," said he, with a show of impatience unusual to him and as I stood in the door to take my leave, his face wore an expression of distrust. I thought he doubted whether, in my simple question, I had not intended to read him a lesson upon the text "Physician heal thyself;" but I did not delay to apprise him of his mistake.

I went immediately to Mac's store to commence operations, for I wished to have done with it. I told him I wished to trade some; but that I had no money. He said that would make no difference. That I could have anything I wished. I told him I could not accept of anything in that way—purposely giving his words a broader meaning than he had intended. But nothing appeared to astonish the fellow, and after a moment's reflection, he said, with a wonderfully knowing expression of face, "Mrs. Smith, I would like to see you alone, if you will give me an opportunity."

With an eagerness I had not before manifested, I replied, "Very well. Nothing could be more agreeable to me, for I must acknowledge I have been much troubled on your account of late." In what way the reader can judge.

"When may I expect to find you at home?" he asked.

"Come down this afternoon," said I, earnestly. I then went home, revolving in my mind whether there was not ome possible means by which I could save this foolish man Dare I trust him so much as to drop a hint of the part I was playing, and why? I feared not, and yet I was half resolved to attempt it. But I soon found that would be impossible: for I had been at home but a few minutes, when Capt. Hardy, who was chief of the city police, and John

Norton came to inquire what had been my success. I told them how things had been arranged. They said the mission had been put into our hands by Brigham, "who has directed us," said Hardy, "to recognize you as captain, and to render you such assistance as you may wish."

"I think I do not need any assistance. I can do all that is necessary to be done alone," said I.

"Oh, no, madam, we must help you. We are coming to hear what he has to say."

They then directed me to arrange a bedroom, that opened into the parlor, for them, and they would return before Mac came, to *assist me*, as they termed it. The real object being to keep me under espionage. There was now no escape, as I was under the eye of the police, and I felt I could do no more to protect the victim. To attempt it would be to trifle with my own existence.

CHAPTER XXVIII.

MILKING A GENTILE.

The chief of the police returned in a few minutes, accompanied by John Norton, and both secreted themselves within the bedroom; and very soon after this Mac came, finding me, as he supposed, alone. I was engaged in doubling some yarn, and he took the swifts and set them away, saying, as he did so, "Mrs. Smith, you can afford to live without work, if you are willing to grant what I expect of you. You were never intended to live with these Mormons. If you will go with me, I will enable you to live in a society you are so well qualified to grace. Do you wish to go to California?"

"I certainly do," said I.

"Let us understand each other," said Mac. "Would you be willing to go with me wherever I go?"

"Nothing could suit me better. I will go anywhere with *you;*" and I could have added, "with any one else, if I could but get away from Utah."

"You cannot well imagine," said Mac, "my astonishment when you handed me that note the other day. I have often thought before that I should be willing to give any amount of money if you could accidentally fal' into my hands in this way; but I did not expect one like you could be induced to look favorably upon such a man as I am, and I am even now at a loss to account for it."

Apprehensive that his inability to "account for it" would lead him to make some awkward inquiries, I called his attention from that point by mentioning his wife.

"On *her* account I cannot marry *you*," said he; "but I have as good a right to live with you, I suppose, as Brigham Young has to live with any of his wives."

"I think you have," said I " quite as good."

The idea that a Gentile should seek to justify a violation of his own faith by quoting *our* "Prophet," seemed to me very strange.

Emboldened by an apparent success, and by a seeming willingness on my part to meet his advances half way, he attempted a nearer approach to my person; but thrown for the moment off my guard, I met the movement with a shudder of disgust and aversion so undisguised that he paused disconcerted by it, and said, " Why, Mrs. Smith, what is the matter? you act strangely. You are really shivering, too!"

Seeing the necessity of reassuring him, I laughed, and said:

"Oh, that is nothing but one of my whims. Be seated, and let us talk over matters;" and handing him a chair, I continued: "How would it be if I should ask for some money? Are you liberal?"

"Not very," said he; " but I do not forget my friends."

Affecting great satisfaction with him on this account, I gave expression to a willingness to be his, as soon as it was convenient; but that he must be aware how liable we were to be discovered, and that such conduct in a Mormon woman was deemed in our Church a very high crime, punishable with death.

He was aware of that, and expressed himself willing to abide his time. He was particularly happy in his commendation of my prudence, and hoped I would manage the thing discreetly.

I then told him he had better leave me for the present, and that the next evening we would take a walk to some quiet and unfrequented part of the town, where we could have a moment by ourselves undisturbed.

With this he was satisfied, and he took a very affectionate leave of me, contenting himself, however, with the simple demonstration of kissing my hand.

When once rid of him I found relief in tears. How was it possible for human nature to endure such tortures? Captain Hardy and John Norton came from their hiding-place, and essayed to cheer and comfort me. Their compliments were so extravagant and ludicrous, that it was soon difficult to determine whether I was suffering most from my excess of contempt or tears. The captain said I was a model coquette, and the Prophet should know how well I had performed my mission, and many other things too disgusting to admit of tears; and I dried them up.

"That is a good arrangement," said John Norton; "and you must meet him to-morrow evening as you have engaged. But where had she better take him, Captain Hardy?"

"I have been thinking of that," said the Captain. "I think the south side of the adobé yard, by the slough, is the place for them. We will be near to protect you, Nett. That is a lonely place, but you may have no fears. Go on, and we will always keep you in sight."

My gallant assistants then withdrew, and I was once more left to myself. I thought the matter over, and came to the conclusion that this man Mac was undeserving of sympathy; and as they probably aimed to take only his property, I would go through with my part cheerfully.

Just before dark the next evening, I left home, prepared for the enterprise. The clear calm twilight, always enchanting in Utah, was fast closing in; and the moon soon after rose with unusual splendor above the rugged mountains, back of the city, revealing the silver crowns of their snow-capped summits, far to the north and west. I had seldom seen a more lovely night, and never before found the pure air more delicious. It seemed desecration to taint such an atmosphere with works fitting only for demons. I walked leisurely down the street on which Mac lived, and passed his house. He was sitting with his wife by the door. I had proceeded but a short distance, when he overtook me, and said, as he came up:

"Mrs. Smith, you are faithful in the performance of your engagements."

"I fear I have been but too faithful," said I. But not to him, as my readers by this time understand.

"What a lovely evening," said he. "Such a night is favorable for us. Shall we go down by the trees, and find a seat among their shadows, where we can hold a whispered interview unnoticed?"

"No," said I; "we shall be less exposed by the adobe yard. Let us go there, if you are willing."

"Anywhere you say," said he. "And I must say this is the happiest moment of my life." He took my arm, and observing that I trembled, he said: "Mrs. Smith, how is this? you are crying, as I live, if this moonlight does not deceive me. There is some mystery about this."

Forcing myself into self-possession with a success I hardly hoped to achieve, I said, smiling through my tears : "Mr. Mac, is it possible you understand so little a woman's heart? Did you suppose I could forget my husband so readily, even without a tear or a regret? It was along this very street we walked, the night before he left me."

This effort at coquetry had the effect I wished; for while it silenced his suspicions for the moment, it gave me a shelter behind which to retreat in case of emergency.

"Yes," said he, "I think I can understand you;" as if relieved from an unpleasant fear—that his hold upon me was uncertain. "I can appreciate your feelings, and it does you credit; although I had flattered myself that I should be able to supply his place, at least in some degree; and in the end to supplant him, not only in possession, but in that more tender relation of the heart, and I hope I am not deceived. Am I? If so, tell me, and I will try to bear in silence the most cruel disappointment of my life."

The pathos of his words, and the earnest concern they evinced, excited my pity for a moment; for I reflected that perhaps the accursed practices of our Church had had the effect to weaken the bonds of good faith as well among the

Gentiles as among us. It was perhaps but another form of the bitter fruits of our errors, destined, may be, to corrupt the world.

I had seen as yet nothing of the police, and was growing more and more nervous every moment about being left alone, when I saw two men not far from us, one of whom I recognized as Captain Hardy. I therefore felt at ease, and replied now without restraint.

"Mr. Mac, I am very much flattered by your professions of attachment, and I accept them as being made in sincerity; and judging from my own heart, I think you would not wish me to take any step that could have a tendency to injure me."

He was not quite prepared for this, and made no reply at first, but at length said: "Let us go down by the adobe yard, the place for which we started, and talk it over."

I now had the cards somewhat in my own hands, for the police were near enough to protect me, in case I needed them; while they dare not come so near as to be within hearing of us. I therefore refused to go further, and we discussed the question for a long time. While he urged, I refused. The police very naturally supposed, in the meantime, the reverse was true, and that Mac was the faltering one. We at length started towards home, slowly, all the while disputing the point. I took care on my part to leave the impression, with those who could only see us, that I went unwillingly. As we passed a schoolhouse Mac saw the policemen, as I supposed for the first time; but it seemed otherwise, for he said:

"Who are those men? I have seen them several times since we have been walking."

"One of them is a policeman, I think," said I.

"What can they be doing here?" said he. "They are never on guard in this quarter of the town until after midnight. Mrs. Smith, I half suspect they are watching us."

Wishing to alarm, if possible, without explaining to him my true position, I replied: "Oh dear, such a life will kill me. I am going home."

"Hold one moment, Mrs. Smith," said he, as if startled by a new idea. "Have you been playing a part to-night? Tell me now; is it not true that you have been acting under the instructions of these Mormon devils, to lead me into some trap? I have heard of such things among these Saints before; but I could hardly believe it of you women—and yet why not; for I know enough of Mormonism to comprehend that the women dare not disobey 'counsel.' Come, tell me how it is, that I may prepare for the worst. I shall not blame you. I know there is something wrong, for you have had an opportunity of doing as I expected you, and yet you fairly shrink from my touch. How is it? Are these policemen sent to assist you?"

I looked upon the poor man now with positive pity—for he was greatly alarmed; and yet I dare not answer his questions fully for I doubted his discretion. Still determined not to lull his suspicions, I said, with a significance of tone which should have been clearer to him than an open avowal: "Mr. Mac, all is right. But if it were not, what then? You know I dare not tell you, even if it were wrong.

But I must go. Good-night!" I left him thus abruptly, hoping his good sense, if he had any, would come to his rescue. I went home quickly enough, attended at a safe distance by my police guard.

The next day Captain Hardy and his assistant came to the house, much elated, and rallied me greatly upon what they called my *failure* to get Mac down to the adobé yard.

"How did it happen, Nett?" said the Chief of Police, in high glee. "Why would he not go on? I fear you are losing your skill as a coquette. Perhaps the frogs of the slough croaked too loud for his nerves. How vexed and disappointed we were when we saw you turn back. But it has turned out for the best, and shows the hand of the Lord was in it; for this morning Mac has sold out his whole property, and is to receive the amount in cash on Monday. What could have given him such a fright? But no matter. The Prophet wishes you to get him out again, immediately after he receives the money, before he goes home, and take him near Mr. Judd's, by Simpson's shed, we will have a seat arranged for you. He will not object going there. Tell him as an evidence of your sincerity, that you will grant any request he may make, if he will meet you at your own gate at seven o'clock on Monday evening. That is about the time he is to receive the money. He will not be likely to go home until after seeing you; and he will have the dimes with him—but not long, for we will try to relieve him of them."

I was sorely disappointed at the new form the affair had assumed. It seemed, these Mormons with their spies that never sleep, were always ready to turn everything to their own advantage. I had hoped the business was ended. This new demand upon my endurance sickened and discouraged me. I made the Captain no reply; but looked at him in silence. Thinking he had gone too far, he hastily apologized, begging to know how he had offended me.

"In no way except by your presence, sir. Am I no longer to have even time for sleep? Say to the Prophet that I obey; but I trust you will leave me for the present, as I have need of rest."

"You shall not be disturbed; you shall have everything your own way, Nett. Good day."

Sick and disheartened, I went to bed, and fell into a sound, though not untroubled sleep; for my victim, half rescued and yet half within the meshes of the entanglements which surrounded him, disturbed my dreams. I have had occasion more than once to thank Heaven for the sweet influences of sleep. I awoke towards night, and at once applied myself to the accomplishment of my ungracious task.

Going to Mac's store, I found him alone; I said, "Mr. Mac, after thinking over our interview of last night, I have concluded, that if you will call on Monday—say at seven o'clock—I will take you where it will be convenient for us to be by ourselves." I assured him further, of my entire good faith, and made myself agreeable. I was prepared for being repulsed, as I supposed he would hardly fall into the snare a second time; but instead of showing he had learned wisdom from the past, he received my proposition gladly. After a moment's reflection, he said he could not come at that time, as business of importance would detain him.

"Any other time you can name," said he, "I will be with you."

"Any other time will not do," said I. "This is the .ast proposition I have to make."

"Very well, Mrs. Smith, I will meet you then at seven o'clock. You shall have it as you wish."

This was Saturday: and on Monday, at the appointed time, Mr. Mac called at our gate and found me, with bonnet in hand, ready to go. "I suppose you intend to take me to the adobé yard this time," said he, as we moved down the street.

"No, we will go down past Mr. Judd's, and find a seat by the vine-covered shed near his house."

"Very well, I shall follow, and be content;" said he, watching me, however, very closely, as if something in my appearance troubled him. He finally said, with some impatience—

"I think you are an enigma. What can be the matter now? At one moment you seem very fond of me, and the next, one would think, I was the object of your special hate. The more I do to please you, the farther I am from it. You are unlike most women. Am I so very disagreeable after all, that you cannot endure me?"

"Oh, the truth is, Mr. Mac, my whole life thus far has been but a quick succession of vexatious ill luck, and I am fast becoming a confirmed misanthrope. I owe you an apology. But here we are. Let us occupy this seat. Have I not been happy in my choice of a rendezvous? you must give me some credit for this."

"I will give you credit for anything you ask, if you will put off that long face;" he said in a more cheerful tone.

The seat we now occupied had been prepared for the occasion by the police. The shed at our backs was owned in common by Mr. Judd and Mr. Simpson, and was near the house of the former. It was inclosed, and more or less covered with vines on the side next to us : and one part of it was occupied as a hen-house. Captain Hardy, with his police force, had thoughtlessly taken possession of the inside, without notifying Mr. Judd of the fact : which act of indiscretion he soon had reason to regret. As for us, we fell into a very interesting conversation at once. Mr. Mac, pleased and embarrassed by the novelty of his position, and elated with the prospect of success, exceeded himself in a laudable effort to please.

We had been thus engaged for some time, when an unlooked for event disturbed our interview. The police were so near, being separated from us only by thin boards, between which were spaces, more or less wide, that I was entirely unconcerned as to my own personal safety ; and I did Mr. Mac the honor of making myself an excellent listener, joining in the conversation only when I found it necessary in order to draw him out upon some point, on which I knew by previous instructions, the Chief of Police wished his opinion, or when growing too confidential and subdued, or personal in his remarks, it became me to open to him a new field of thought by a suggestion or a query, and thus to hold him in check. Upon the whole, he was an exceedingly happy man, and I should have pitied him, in view of the disappointment by which I foresaw he must soon be overtaken, had he not deserved my contempt. But it came in a manner more ludicrous than I had expected, and I found myself as much astonished by it as I had expected him to be.

It appeared the Chief of Police and his assistant had both allowed their dogs to follow, and it had not occurred to them, how much inconvenience this oversight might occasion, until all the parties of the drama had taken their places, and it was then too late to correct the mistake. But, in order to make the best of the matter, each secured and held his own cur, listening at the same time to the conversation in progress between Mac and myself. While thus engaged, one of the dogs, by some sudden impulse, effected an escape from the hand of its master, and in the effort to regain possession of it, a support on which several broods of chickens were quietly at roost, was thrown down, bringing with it a score of frightened birds.

In a moment all was confusion. The squalling of the chickens, and the wild clarion notes of alarm sounded by the cocks, joined with the unearthly yelps and barking of the dogs, raised a din and clamor which for the moment carried everything before it. The abrupt and unexpected nearness of the uproar rendered its first advent terrific. And over all, soon rose the sputtering yells of Mr. Judd to his wife, to bring the rifle which he said was loaded, and he would shoot the thieves. I started at once at full speed in the direction of the city, fast followed by Mr. Mac, who was too much frightened to think or act for himself. In passing the house, I saw the aged pair in their night clothes, bounding from place to place, more hopelessly alarmed than any one else, except Mr. Mac and the hens, for these were the only parties not in the secret. When at a safe distance up the street, I paused to look back to see the policemen, plunging from the hen-roost amidst the unabated cackling of hens and the yelping of dogs, and making good use of their heels down a by-street, the gallant chief losing his hat in the scramble. The whole posse was hotly pursued by Mr. Judd, shouting loudly " Hold, you roost robbers; it is the Mormon law to shoot thieves; and I will fire. Quick, woman, with the rifle ;" but every moment putting a greater distance between himself and his weapon. The female head of the house the while, some two rods behind in hot pursuit of him, with rifle in hand, screaming at the top of her cracked voice: " Here, man, take the gun. Do take it."

Before Mr. Mac had time to recover from his astonishment sufficiently to ask an explanation, I effected a safe retreat from the scene of action and reached home alone, greatly amused at the comical termination of the affair. But this was not the end of the matter with Mr. Mac; for the next day the police, after letting Mr. Judd into the secret, had Mac privately arrested, and confronted him with the witnesses to our conversation; and the unlawful proposals he had made to me, threatening an exposure, not only to his wife, but to the world, and he paid roundly to avoid it. When this was done, Mr. Judd threatened to have him arrested for robbing his hen-roost; and then the " Gentile" was " milked" again, and so on, until every pretext was exhausted. He afterwards said to a Gentile friend that he had paid about one thousand dollars for this indiscretion. Captain Hardy and Robert Burton, when all was over, came to our house and told me, how they had succeeded in "milking" him, and they were highly gratified with their success.

A few days after this, the Prophet sent for me to come to the house of Hiram Clauson, where he came, as he said, to compliment me upon my success in "milking the Gentile Mac." When I went in, he received me very cordially, saying: "Nett, brother Hiram was saying as you came in, tha you deserve to have your name written in the chronicles and archives of your brethren, and your acts and miracles also, and so it shall be done. You have been a faithful servant."

It was to extort this expression from the Prophet, and to lull his suspicions and to gain his confidence, in order that he would trust me beyond the limits of the city, that I might thus sooner or later find the means of making my escape, that I had submitted to obey his " counsel," and had assisted him in the perpetration of crime. I therefore said to him:

"Brother Brigham, I am very glad if my conduct has met your approval; and I shall improve this opportunity to ask a favor of you. I wish to spend the winter in Tooille Valley, with my brother Howard."

"Certainly," said the Prophet, graciously; "you shall go, and I hope you may enjoy yourself immensely."

My brother had lately moved his family to that settlement, where he had a farm; and I soon joined him, by permission obtained as above mentioned, to spend the winter, hoping that something would turn up in the meantime by which I could effect my escape. But before I proceed to give my adventures while there, I will pause in my own personal narrative, in order to give in the next chapter a few facts in the history of other persons, with which I was not immediately connected, yet which fell under my notice, having a tendency to illustrate the influence and general working of Mormonism under the government of Brigham Young

CHAPTER XXIX.

PUNISHMENT OF HERESY.

The following episode in Mormon life I give, not because it has any peculiar interest over many others which I have neglected to narrate, but because it illustrates the idea indicated by the heading of this chapter, and for the further reason, that the facts are well authenticated.

About the time referred to in the last chapter, Jesse T. Hartly came to Great Salt Lake City. He was a man of education and intelligence, and a lawyer by profession. I never knew where he was from, but he was a Gentile when he came, and soon after married a Mormon girl by the name of Bullock, which involved a *profession*, at least, of Mormonism. It was afterwards supposed by some that his aim was to learn the mysteries of the Church, in order to make an exposé of them afterwards. At all events, the eye of the Prophet was upon him from the first, and he was not long in discovering, through his spies, good grounds for suspicion. Hartly was a fine speaker and a man calculated to make friends, and he was named by some one, unacquainted with the fact that the Prophet regarded him with suspicion, as a fit person to be appointed missionary preacher among the

Gentiles. As is customary in such cases, he was proposed in open convention, when all the Heads of the Church were on the stand; and the Prophet rose at once with that air of judicial authority, from which those who know him best understand there is to be no appeal, and said: "This man, Hartly, is guilty of heresy. He has been writing to his friends in Oregon against the Church, and has attempted to expose us to the world, and he should be sent to hell cross lots." This was the end of the matter as to Hartly.

His friends after this avoided him, and it was understood that his fate was sealed. He knew that to remain was death; he therefore left his wife and child, and attempted to effect an escape.

Not many days after he had gone, Wiley Norton told us, with a feeling of exultation, that they had made sure of another enemy of the Church. That the bones of Jesse Hartly were in the cañons, and that he was afraid they would be overlooked at the Resurrection, unless he had better success in "pleading" in the next world than in this, referring to his practice as a lawyer.

Nearly a year and a half after this, when on my way to the States, I saw the widow of Jesse Hartly at Green River. She had been a very pretty woman, and was at that time but twenty-two years old. I think she was the most heart-broken human being I have ever seen. She was living with her brother, who kept the ferry there, and he was also a Mormon. We were waiting to be taken over, when I saw a woman, with a pale, sad face, dressed in the deepest black, sitting upon the bank, alone. The unrelieved picture of woe which she presented, excited our curiosity and sympathy. Accompanied by my sister, I went to her, and after some delay and the assurance, that although we were Mormons, we were yet *women*, she told us her brief story, without a tear; yet with an expression of hopeless sorrow which I shall never forget. Oh! Mormonism is too hard—too cruel upon women. Can it—will it be permitted for ever?

It was not until I had suggested to her, that perhaps I had also a woe to unburden, as the result of my Mormon life, which might have some comparison to her own, that she commenced by saying:

"You may have suffered; and if you have been a Mormon wife, you must have known sorrow. But the cruelty of my own fate, I am sure, is without a parallel—even in this land of cruelty."

"I married Jesse Hartly, knowing he was a 'Gentile' in fact, but he passed for a Mormon, but that made no difference with me, although I was a Mormon, because he was a noble man, and sought only the right. By being my husband, he was brought into closer contact with the members of the Church, and was thus soon enabled to learn many things about us, and about the Heads of the Church, that he did not approve, and of which I was ignorant, although I had been brought up among the Saints; and which, if known among the Gentiles, would have greatly damaged us. I do not understand all he discovered, or all he did; but they found he had written against the Church, and he was cut off, and the Prophet required as an atonement for his sins, that he should lay down his life. That he should be sacrificed in the endowment rooms; where human sacrifices are sometimes made in this way. This I never knew until my husband told me, but it is true. They kill those there who have committed sins too great to be atoned for in any other way. The Prophet says, if they submit to this he can save them; otherwise they are lost. Oh! that is horrible. But my husband refused to be sacrificed, and so set out alone for the United States: thinking there might be at least a hope of success. I told him when he left me, and left his child, that he would be killed, and so he was. William Hickman and another Danite, shot him in the cañons; and I have often since been obliged to cook for this man, when he passed this way, knowing all the while, he had killed my husband. My child soon followed after its father, and I hope to die also; for why should I live? They have brought me here, where I wish to remain, rather than to return to Salt Lake, where the murderers of my husband curse the earth, and roll in affluence unpunished."

She had finished her sad story, and we were choking down our sobs of pity in silence, when she noticed her brother, of whom she appeared to stand in awe, coming toward us, and she rose saying, "I trust you will excuse me," and then went her way, still wearing the same stony expression of agony, and as unrelieved by tears as when we first saw her. But this is but one case among a thousand others, that have never seen the light, and never will, until the dark history of the "Danites," or the "Destroying Angels," as the Prophet was sometimes pleased to call them, is unveiled.

It was about one year previous to the death of Hartly

that the following incident occurred. Wiley Norton was going by our house one day on horseback, and calling at the gate, said he was on his way to assist in burying a dead body, that had been found a short distance out of the city, by two of the herd boys. These were smallish boys, employed in looking after the cattle, and to assist the herdsmen. They had reported the fact of finding the body when they came in the night before, and by this time the Gentiles had heard of it, and a great number of stories were in circulation. Among others, that a Gentile had been murdered by the Mormons, which was probably true; but there was no evidence of it. Wiley said he would call when he returned, and tell us what he saw, and all he could learn about it. In the evening, Wiley, as he had promised, called and gave us the following facts. He said:

"We went out with the boys to find the body, who took us to the log, behind, and partly under which, it was hidden. When we came near it, and the boys pointed where it was, brother Jeddy (Jedadiah M. Grant) told them, there was no dead man in that place. And this was true, for we had already removed it. He then attempted to make them acknowledge they were mistaken; but the boys persisted in the statement first made They said they saw it yesterday and knew what it was, although it was now gone. Brother Jeddy's object was to have the boys return to the city, and report that they had never seen the body, but that they had told the story as a joke; which coupled with the fact, that it was not to be found, would allay the excitement among the 'Gentiles.' This the boys refused to do: 'for how could we?' asked the honest little fellows, 'for we did see it.'

"Brother Grant told them, if they would not, he would take them to the slough and have them drowned. Still they refused, and we took them to the water, and brother Jeddy put one of them in, and held him there until he was quite exhausted, and when he could breathe again, he said as resolute as ever, that the man was dead; for he saw, and could smell him. He knew it. This was repeated several times, with a similar result. We then dug a grave, and told the other boy we would bury him alive if he did not go to the city, and contradict the statement the two had first made. What a time we had with them. The boys were good blood, I tell you. Although the one that we were about to bury consented, the other was silent, and so brother Grant let them off for the present; and one of them has set it right with the Gentiles, who now believe the story of the dead body was a hoax, got up by the boys. I believe the boy that brother Jeddy put in the water, avoids having anything to say about it."

When the reader reflects that it was but the merest *chance* that brought this fact under my notice, and that a hundred such incidents might, and probably did occur, unknown to any one, except to the perpetrators of them, he will be able to form something of an estimate of the amount of crime committed by the Heads of the Church, and by their authority Certainly there must be a day of reckoning for such as these. The Mormons recognize the *right*, and inculcate the *duty* of the father to slay his daughter or her lover, as a last resort to prevent her marriage with a "Gentile."

Many facts are within my knowledge, illustrative of this point. Several occurred of some note, the winter Colonel Steptoe was at the valley with his regiment. One of his soldiers became attached to Amanda Tanner, a Mormon girl, with whom I was well acquainted. Her father forbade their meeting, and confined her to the house, until he supposed the attachment had been forgotten; and she was left alone one day, for a few hours, and the girl sent for her soldier, who came of course. Unfortunately, the father returned sooner than expected, and finding the Gentile there, took his sword and charged upon the lover, before he knew the enraged father was in the house. But fortune favored the soldier; for Mr. Tanner, in his haste, and in the act of striking, brought the point of his sword against a beam, breaking it in several pieces, and the Gentile escaped.

The father, still holding the handle of the shivered blade, said to the trembling girl: "Listen. When you are caught in Gentile company again, you shall die;" and she knew he would do what he said, and she gave up the Gentile. The soldier was prosecuted, and heavily fined.

The same winter one of Col. Steptoe's officers formed an acquaintance with a daughter of John Taylor—Mary Ann. She was a very interesting girl; and the intimacy ripened into a mutual attachment. Her father is one of the Twelve Apostles, and a man of great influence in the Church; and was, at the time, living in New York, where he edited a paper known as the "Mormon."

On account of her beauty, as well as the position of her father, Mary Ann was much sought after, both by old greyheaded Saints among the Heads of the Church, and by younger aspirants for saintly and matrimonial honors. But the budding instincts of her young womanhood naturally revolted against the dark future promised her by Mormon wifeism; and she preferred the Gentile. She succeeded in getting before Judge Kinney with her lover, and they were married. This was a termination more fortunate than she could have expected, had the father been at home. For when he heard of it, he wrote to the Prophet, blaming him very severely for not preventing the marriage by the sacrifice of her life. He wrote that he should always feel dissatisfied because the blood of his daughter had not been shed to atone for the sin of marrying out of the Church. She was afterwards cut off from the Saints, and publicly traduced by Orson Hyde, who had been one of her admirers before.

This precious man, Hyde, whose number of wives was great already, had urged the mother very strongly to force Mary Ann to marry him, even against her own consent, which extreme measure might have been resorted to, had Col. Steptoe's military force not been at hand. When the regiment left the valley, she accompanied her husband.

That the strictness as to the intermarriage with Gentiles was a question of policy, and not one of principle, was shown by the course pursued by the Prophet, in relation to the Indian chief, Walker. This chief was at the head of a powerful tribe in the western part of the territory. Some cause of quarrel had interrupted the good understanding before exist ing between Walker and the "Mormon Chief," as the former called Brigham Young; and the Prophet, wishing to reëstablish friendly relations, and also to found a permanent influence favorable to the Saints within the tribe, attempted to induce some of the Mormon women to marry Walker, as a means of effecting that object. I heard the Prophet say one day, to a young girl, that the Mormon woman that would volteer to make that sacrifice for the Church, should have a crown of Immortal Glory in the celestial kingdom. The matter created great excitement among us at the time, and it was expected that some of the girls were to be "counselled" to accept this "mission," as none were found so reckless of peace and womanly "glory" in *this* world as to volunteer to hazard it for the *prospective* glory of the next. But either on account of some misgivings on the part of the Prophet as to the policy of forcing the acceptance of the dusky warrior as a husband upon an unwilling maiden, or for some other reason, the matter was delayed until the chief suddenly died from some cause unknown. It was remarked, however, at the time, that the Prophet was seldom at fault in knowing how to accomplish his aims, and the death of the chief, whether by natural or foul means, was followed by a new line of policy, *i. e.* by the marriage of the Indian women by the Mormon men sent to preach among them, and this has now become the settled policy of the Church, pursued not only in that, but among all the Indian tribes within the reach of Mormon influence. So successfully has this policy been pursued that not many years shall pass before all the Indian tribes west of the Rocky Mountains, and probably all the others, between whose hunting grounds and Utah, civilized migration has set up no barrier, will acknowledge the Prophet's sway. And when that day comes, the United States Government shall find in the Prophet and his people a more formidable adversary than is now dreamed of. Will the warning be heeded in time?

After Walker's death, he was succeeded in the government of the tribe by his brother, Squash Head. I knew but little of the character of this chief. He was looked upon as being not very sagacious, but at the same time, remarkably obstinate. He soon fell under the censure of the Prophet, who had taken offence at the obstacles Squash Head interposed to the influence of the Mormon missionaries sent to his tribe.

The Prophet intrigued to decoy the chief to the city, and then upon some charge, either real or trumped up for the occasion, had him arrested, and thrown into prison, where he remained for a long time.

The chief was attended in his prison by a "Danite," by whom he was regularly furnished with food. This attendant represents that one morning he took his breakfast to him, and left with it, thoughtlessly, a case knife; and that when he returned an hour after to remove the dishes, and the remains of the breakfast, he found the chief dead. He had cut his throat with a *very dull case knife!* This was a version of the story first circulated; but it was very soon after this generally understood that the poor old Indian was murdered by the Prophet's order, as his influence among his tribe was considered an obstacle to the spread of the faith among them; and for that reason, was held to be justifiable by the great body of the Church. This circumstance was freely spoken of among us at the time, and I never heard these facts questioned.

I deem this a fitting place to mention another circumstance, which occurred while I was at the valley. I refer to the massacre of Capt. Gunnison and his party, as was supposed at the time by the Indians. I have heard the circumstances of this atrocious murder discussed frequently at Great Salt Lake, by the Heads of the Church, and by the Prophet, and others. In all these cases, it was exultingly claimed by them, and unquestioned in well informed circles among us, that Capt. Gunnison and his party were murdered by the "Danites," disguised as Indians, by, and with the knowledge, and "counsel" of the Prophet. It was, however, believed by some that the massacre was perpetrated by the Indians in fact, but instigated by the Prophet—all parties agreeing in this, that it was done for the good of the Church, which justified the act. My belief is, that the first theory is the true one. I could state many facts going to prove this. The generally received opinion in the Church upon that subject should have some weight; and I never heard any other opinion expressed, until I came to the States, about one year since. I was one day at my brother's house, where a small company were assembled, when this subject came up; and Edmond Ellsworth said, among many other things, "I think Uncle Sam will get sick of sending officers here, when we serve a few more as we served Gunnison."

Ellsworth is a son-in-law of the Prophet, having married for his first, and only wife, Elizabeth, the oldest daughter of Brigham Young.

Thus, his statement should be entitled to the more weight as he was known to be familiar with the Prophet. There was, in fact, no effort made at concealment, and it was freely talked of among ourselves, although it was scrupulously kept from the knowledge of the Gentiles, and from those Mormons whose discretion or orthodoxy was doubtful.

CHAPTER XXX.

TOOELE.

ONE day, soon after the termination of my adventures with Mr. Mac, when I was busily engaged in making arrangements for my journey to Tooille, one of the wives of Jedadiah M. Grant came to our house and urged me very hard to go home with her. Although unwilling to spend the time, as I was very anxious to escape from this city of abominations, I consented, and when there, I found the Prophet, Orson Hyde, J. M. Grant, and several women, pleasantly employed in the enjoyment of a social party. As I went in, the Prophet said very graciously: "Well, Nett, I am happy to see you. I was thinking that when we met last, you felt the influence of a bad spirit. Evil spirits make one feel discontented. The spirits of the Gentiles that have died in our midst are always about us, waiting for another tabernacle to enter."

"I trust you do not expect to assign to me the mission of looking up 'tabernacles' for them."

"I see, Mary Ettie is getting discouraged," said brother Jeddy Grant. "You must give her a blessing; and here is one of my first and best wives, Rosetta, who is almost ready to leave me, and run off with a Gentile. If you will bless them, I will write for you, and hereafter, when they get the 'horribles,' they can find encouragement in reading these and be consoled."

Brother Grant then took a pen and wrote the words of the Prophet, who blessed us both, first one, and then the other. The following is an exact copy of mine from the original still in my possession. The Prophet rested his hands upon my head as he pronounced it:

"SISTER MARY ETTIE:

"I seal these blessings upon your head, that will be given by me, or by my Heavenly Father through me. Treasure them, as words of wisdom. Get wisdom and understanding. Take no thought beforehand, what you shall do, for the Holy Ghost will teach you; and thou shalt be mighty in word and in deed, shalt confound all that oppose you, and put the tongue of slander to shame; have a posterity that will hold thy name in honorable remembrance through all their generations. Thou shalt be able to stop the mouths of lions, quench the violence of fire, escape the edge of the sword; shall have wisdom to direct you at all times, shall live to see the 'winding up scene of this generation,' shall have a companion suited to your condition, and inherit all the blessings of the Redeemer's Kingdom, forever and ever. Amen."

I then gave place to Rosetta, who received one similar to mine. She was a quiet, uncomplaining victim to a faith and practice, to which she had submitted in an evil hour, without fully comprehending its hardships.

Although no word had passed between us, and she accepted the blessing with a becoming grace, I knew she estimated it as I did, as but a mockery; and yet there lingered within the heart of both a recollection of the time, when the Church to us was pure. When the Prophet Joseph administered and wrought seeming miracles before astonished multitudes. And for the moment the crimes of the present Heads of the Church were forgotten, and the ancient enthusiasm and faith which stirred our hearts in the earlier days and in the wilderness, or when threatened by the menacing shouts of Gentile mobs, returned to cheer us. But this enthusiasm was but momentary. We reasoned with our own hearts thus. Grant that double wifeism is right, notwithstanding its practice involves, as a necessity, the cruel sacrifice of all a woman holds most dear; yet crime—positive crime, is not, cannot be right. What the Church clearly demands, the true believer should doubtless concede; but the commission of robbery, murder, and treason to the government cannot be necessary to a pure Church. Yet these men, now before us, on whose shoulders the government of the Church has fallen, on one of whom has descended the mantle of our Prophet Joseph, of blessed and martyr memory, were guilty of all these, and worse, if worse were possible. Was it wrong, then, to doubt these men? And yet, if the Church were ever genuine, is she not so still, albeit wanting purity?

Floating thus among doubts and dear old remembrances, was it strange that the gracious benediction thus received should have been invested by us with some degree of sanctity, or that for the moment we looked upon these men in their self-exalted capacity of ministrants in Heavenly offices, and sadly remembered afterwards, *they were but broken vessels?* I trust those of my readers who regard Mormonism as a delusion, and who have never been swayed by its enthusiasms, or felt its fascinations—for it possessed originally both these elements in an eminent degree—will not judge us too harshly. Human nature is essentially the same, under similar circumstances; and if many Christian people were to look closely into their own hearts, possibly they would find *their attachment* to orthodox and approved systems, resting upon no better foundations than ours; and many would find they were indebted, *alone*, to a more kindly interposition of Providence, that they had been reared and were yet under the influence of a better faith and a truer system; and that they *adhere to it*, for reasons little better than those which bind an honest Mormon to his. I have deemed it proper to urge this modest claim to the sympathy of the civilized world, not on my own account, but in behalf of the many thousands of innocent persons in Utah, who would forsake Mormonism, as I have done, if they were once left unawed by the power of the Prophet, from which there is no hope of escape, until the General Government shall interfere, with a strong arm, for the protection of civil rights in the territory. But it is more particularly in behalf of the *women* of Utah, for whom I bespeak the active sympathy of all Christian people. There are to-day from fifteen to twenty thousand mothers and daughters within the territory, suffering under a cruel enslavement within those Mormon harems, who would make any sacrifice for freedom; and many a mother there who would deem the emancipation of her children cheaply won, if secured at no greater cost than that of her own poor life. Indeed, the only bond that holds many to an unwilling existence there, is the mother's instinctive love of her offspring. Will the mothers and daughters, who owe all they have and are to the influence of the Bible, disregard the cries of these suffering women coming from the far off Mormon land, the agony of whose groans, if made audible to the world, though but for a moment, would rend the heart of Christendom?

The next morning found me on the way to Tooele. This beautiful valley, though no great distance west of the city as the crow flies, is, by the wagon road, twenty-two miles. We have before stated, that Salt Lake city was built on the east bank of the River Jordan. Ten miles, or more, from the west bank of the stream, and facing the city, rises abruptly to a great height, a rugged and barren ridge, known as West Mountain. With its base separated from the placid waters of the gentle river, by a wide interval of grassy bottom, and its summit whitened by snows that know no summer, this range would have offered an insurmountable barrier to direct travel west, had it not been suddenly terminated some miles to the north by the waters of Great Salt Lake, on the brink of whose briny shore it rises in an abrupt headland, as if, when suddenly arrested there, it had gathered itself up to give fitting expression to the bold protest it meant to frown for ever from its frosty top against the unnatural intrusion of this inland sheet of brine.

After crossing the "bottom," in a westerly direction to the mountain, the road wound its difficult and narrow way northerly to the lake, and thence, clinging to its base, close to the water's rocky margin, it rounded the headland, and then turning to the left, swept back to the south again, and soon debouched into a smiling valley, on the other side of the mountain. This is Tooele. My brother lived about one mile from the lake, at E. T. city. This stake was named after Ezra T. Benson, one of the " Twelve;" where he (Benson) owned a mill, and kept several of his wives. The land at the lower part of the valley is not fertile, on account of the salt with which the ground appears to be saturated; but farther up, where this does not exist, it is said to be very productive, and everyhere it is well adapted to grass. As well on account of the soft and genial air of the mountains, which circulates through the valley, bearing health to the inhabitants, as of the simple beauty of the landscape and to its general productiveness, this is a most delightful region, and, uncursed by Mormonism, would be an earthly Paradise.

In rounding the headland we passed the mouth of an open cave, extending deep into the mountain. Nearly opposite E. T. city, the bosom of the lake is broken by a beautiful island several miles in extent, remarkable for its spring of sweet fresh water, although surrounded by the salt and bitter waters of the lake. This delightful island is devoted to the pasturage of cattle having the "Church brand" upon them. The cattle of all who have consecrated their property to the Church, bear this brand. The island is partly wooded, and is a great resort for every species of wild bird. Brant and other geese, ducks and sand-hill cranes crowd here, mingled with other game, in uncounted swarms; and often the noise of their calls, and flutterings, and wild screams, comes over the waters of the glassy lake like the noisy murmur of an excited multitude; as if to invite the sportsmen of the world to the slaughter.

I passed the fall here very pleasantly with my brother and the society of Martha, his only wife. She had thus far successfully fought spiritual wifeism from her door, and still preserved her isolated household; and until winter set in we lived comparatively free from the usual disquietude of Mormon life

Colonel Steptoe had made Salt Lake City the headquarters of his regiment for the winter; and it had already transpired that he would allow such Mormon women as threw themselves upon his protection, to accompany him from the territory in the Spring.

This state of things was creating great anxiety among the male members and heads of the Church; for there was already a flutter among the inmates of the harems; and the affair of Mary Ann Taylor, before referred to, proved they had reason for serious apprehension. There were, in fact, several other similar cases under advisement. Various rumors of these things reached our quiet valley; but it had never occurred to me that I could avail myself of this opportunity to make my escape, until the idea was suggested by an uncalled for severity on the part of the Prophet. He sent Orson Hyde to the president of our stake, with an order to keep me under the strictest watch, and on no account to allow me to leave my brother's house without his permission—which would not be granted until the Gentile soldiers left in the Spring. It was but a short time after this, that my brother was directed to keep me confined mostly to my room, but to afford me, otherwise, every thing necessary to my comfort. I deemed this a sort of violation of the tacit understanding between us; and I resolved to meet it by an effort to accomplish the very thing the Prophet wished to place beyond a peradventure of happening. A circumstance soon occurred which opened the way.

My brother's principal business at the valley was to look after his farm; but at this time he was engaged in selling goods for Mr. Hockiday, a respectable Gentile merchant, from one of the States. This man spent a part of the time at the valley, and was a friend of Mr. Mac's. The latter had given him an account of the manner he had been decoyed by me, in the milking affair, and expressed the opinion, that I had been prompted to it by a Mormon influence which I dare not resist, and wished him to inquire of me how it was.

Mr. Hockiday came to my brother's house one morning, and after exchanging the usual salutations with Martha, inquired for me. He had already learned that I was confined to my room, and the reason why. Martha told him where I was, but gave him no encouragement about seeing me; and, in fact, showed a disposition to evade the subject. Seeing which, he replied: "Then I think I will step in and see her a moment." And without giving Martha time for reflection, came in, unattended, with an assurance that proved he had an object in view. I was at first greatly astonished, but I soon recognized in his straightforward manner of doing business, an honest purpose, and a wish to serve me.

"How do you get on, Mrs. Smith?" said he, bluntly.

"Very well, I thank you."

I knew Martha had not consented to his coming in, and although she was every way friendly to me, she still dreaded to disobey the Prophet.

"I understand," said Mr. Hockiday, "that quite an event has taken place in our Gentile community. That you, and other important characters, have been taking advantage of my friend Mac, who is as good-hearted a man as was ever victimized in this Mormon land. How is it?"

"It is true," said I; "but it was his own fault. He has no one to blame but himself."

"No doubt. But you know, Mrs. Smith, what an influence women have always exerted over men. Since the world began they have plied the vocation of Eve, with a success beyond that of the first mother, and it is all natural and right within its legitimate channel, and for proper objects; but it is a new thing under the sun, and an abomination, that this weakness of our poor human nature, should be turned into a source of profit to these Mormon pickpockets, through the agency of an organized band of female decoys, trained by the heads of the Church to do this business systematically. Is not this so, Mrs. Smith? Are not these things done by direction of the Prophet? We understand you women do them unwillingly, but with none the less effect on that account. Your victims will, of course, pay heavily, rather than be exposed: hence these cases are seldom heard of. But I can assure you that a knowledge of another class of crimes cannot be suppressed. Murder will out, in time."

At this point, Martha, who had heard our conversation

came to the door, and said: "Mr. Hockiday, I think your pony is loose." I suspected at once Martha had unloosed his horse that she might give me a word of caution; and so it proved, for when he had gone out to look after the animal, she said to me, with some degree of earnestness: "Nett, you must avoid all conversation with that man. Doubtless every word you say to him will go to Washington to be used as evidence against us."

I made no reply, and she gave me a look of sad sympathy, on leaving the room, just as Mr. Hockiday returned to it; who said as he came in, "I cannot understand how my pony could get loose. But no matter, I must be off, I think." Then lowering his voice, he added, "there will be a good chance for those wishing to leave the territory in the spring, with the family of Mr. McClure, a gentleman now boarding with Judge Kinney, at Salt Lake. And then, giving me a look full of intelligence, he added there are several women of your acquaintance, who desire to go. They will be under the protection of the military force of Col. Steptoe; and every thing will be safe and snug as could be wished. But I must be on my way."

I made him no reply; but my heart, now quite in a flutter of hope, must have made itself understood; for in taking his leave, he repeated, over and over, certain nods, and expressive winks of encouragement.

I went to bed that night with my head filled with floating visions of this new project. Too much excited to fix upon any feasible plan of operation, my mind sifted and rejected, over and over again, every possible and impossible scheme, which promised to crown the enterprise with success; until quite prostrated by the chafing and fretting of my caged and overtaxed spirit, I fell asleep, and dreamed I had made the attempt, by climbing, on foot, the high ridge that separated our valley from the Jordan; and that when I had gained the snowy top of the mountain, beyond the foot of which flowed the gentle river; and was about to commence the descent to where I saw the army of Col. Steptoe in waiting for me, the snows beneath my feet gave way: and riding upon an avalanch, I slid down the mountain side, with a rush, and a roar of thunder: and landed, as I dreamed, safely within the Endowment rooms, in the presence of the Prophet, and the Heads of the Church: who were assembled for the purpose of celebrating the horrid rite, of offering human sacrifices, and were only waiting for the victim; which had now arrived, for I was to be offered.

The wood upon a huge stone altar, in the centre of the roofless room, crackled and burned with a fierce and merry roar; and the white robed-priests, with the Prophet at their head, approached to lay me upon the altar, to be slain. And when I saw the polished blade of the knife, gleam and flash in the light of the fire of the altar, I woke with a scream before it descended to do its work: and found myself in my own room, cowering under the remembrance of the terrible vision.

Does the spirit, disturbed by a high state of nervous excitement, sometimes flutter beyond the range of our grosser faculties, and make discoveries and investigations into truth; and ferret out hidden secrets, from which, under ordinary circumstances, we are, by the very necessities of our frail humanity debarred? I have no theory of my own upon this subject; but the remembrance of that night vision is still before me; and when the dark and bloody history of those mystic ceremonies of the endowments are revealed and laid open to the day, then will be realized, as I still believe, the original of that dream, vague rumors of which are even now floating upon the public mind, at Great Salt Lake, among those who have never *dreamed upon the subject.*

CHAPTER XXXI.

THE FLIGHT AND RECAPTURE.

For several day's I had serious misgivings as to the possibility of success, should I attempt an escape. But after giving the subject a fair canvass, and weighing the chances, I found the balance to be in favor of the undertaking; and when my mind was thus once settled, I was calm: and then, bending the whole energies of my soul in that one direction, I soon settled upon a plan of operation. A portion of the house occupied by my brother, had been dedicated to the use of public worship; and this part was in the end furthest removed from the room in which I was confined.

The view from my room, in the direction of the mountain, was uninterrupted by dwellings, and the window opening that way had never been fastened; and thus it will be seen, that to reach the mountain east of the valley, would be an easy matter, if a time was chosen when the mass of the inhabitants were not much abroad.

On the following Sunday morning, I said to Martha: "I do not wish to attend the meeting of the Saints to-day. I am not well, and would seek rest. I shall lock my door, in order not to be disturbed; and I wish you would not call me to dinner."

"Very well, Mary Ettie, you look sick. You shall take your rest, my sister, if there is any rest for you. I will see that no one disturbs you."

"If there is rest for me I hope to find it soon," I replied, and returned to my room.

Fastening the door, I waited patiently the assembling of the Saints, which was to be in the afternoon: until then I must remain quiet. I had before this provided myself with a loaf of bread and some matches from the pantry.

This was in the month of February; and the hills, and the ground in some places in the valley, were covered with snow. I put on my brother's boots, and packed up my husband's portrait with the bread and matches, and laid them aside with an Indian blanket; and thus prepared myself to sally forth, upon the perilous adventure.

There was no one in sight, except some Indians with their squaws, who were usually sauntering about the buildings, for the purpose of begging. Some of these squaws came to the window and asked for food, and I gave them some bread. Then, disguised as one of them, with my Indian blanket over my head, I removed the sash, and passed through the window to the ground; and asked them, by signs which they appeared to comprehend, to accompany me. We all set out for the mountains, with the Indian lope peculiar to these tribes, in single file.

As we hastened on to gain a point of the mountain nearest to us, which should, when once passed, protect us against observation from the settlement, my heart leaped with joy under an inspiring sense of freedom, and the bracing influence of this unwonted exercise in the open air, yet disturbed somewhat by the chilling fear, lest, by some mischance, my escape should be discovered before reaching the mountains. This once passed, I left my dusky friends, and plunged alone nto the nearest cañon, little comprehending, in my eagerness to evade my human foes, how great the peril I was braving among the wild beasts of the mountain. I wished to secrete myself here until after dark, to evade pursuit.

Let the reader imagine a lofty and barren range, with its top in the clouds, and covered with snow, having its side split by a deep, narrow gorge, little wider in places than a fissure, and at others, yawning deep and broad, and winding apparently into the very heart of the mountain, and sometimes quite through it; with the ragged jaws thus laid open, partly covered with a light growth of timber or stunted shrubs, the bottom drained by the fretting current of a stream, tumbling from the melting snows above, so far down among the rocks, as to be at some points beyond the reach of the sun's rays, and he will have a faint picture of a cañon These celebrated cañons are a peculiar feature in the scenery of Utah. They are the sources from whence the settler in the valleys draws his supply of wood for fuel, and whence flows the water necessary for irrigation and similar purposes. But they are not untenanted. Here the terrible grizzly bear, famed as the fiercest denizen of these wilds, makes his home with the wolf, the cougar or mountain lion, and many other beasts of prey, scarcely less dangerous when pressed by hunger.

It was up one of these wild passes I now made my difficult way; but not liking the appearance of the one I had entered, I passed over the sharp point of a hill, which separated it from one farther to the north. Gaining this with ease, I picked my way among the vast rocks, and in some places, over the loose sand until it was quite dark. By this time, I had made a headway of some two miles, as I judged, up the dismal pass. Fatigued by an exercise to which I was unaccustomed, and fearing the wild beasts, I built a fire close by a huge rock, and on that side of it furthest from the mouth of the cañon. The night was closing in, cold and chill; but I found the cheerful blaze, which soon lit up the broken rocks about me, very comfortable; for when the heat and excitement of my sharp walk had subsided, I felt myself pinched and stiffened by the cold, almost to numbness. I had not until then comprehended fully the hazard of my undertaking. Though at first appalled by the wild scenery suddenly revealed by the blazing fagots I had hastily collected; with the thousand shapes, which I dared not scrutinize too closely, for fear they would assume some real and living form of danger, yet I preferred my present prospect of freedom, with all its hazard and discomfort, to the bare possibility of returning to my Mormon prison.

When warmed and sufficiently rested, I began to cast about for some plan for future operations. I had succeeded thus far; but the next problem was to reach the city, which was a long way round the mountain. My best chance of success was mainly dependent upon the amount of headway I could make the first night; for if I could pass the narrow road along the lake, which turned the headland, before daylight, my prospects would be fair for reaching the city sometime the following night.

I therefore decided to set out at once, and make the most of the darkness. At all events, I dare not remain in the cañon all night alone. I was fully refreshed, after having eaten some bread, and warmed my stiffened limbs by the fire. I waited sometime after nightfall, and then trusting to my disguise, and a good fortune, which I felt ought not to desert me at a time when I stood so much in need of its protection, I retraced my steps down the cañon, to find the road leading to the city.

Though familiar with the locality of the road by daylight, I found it a difficult thing to find it in the night; and I was obliged to return, until within sight of the buildings from which I had fled before I was enabled to regain it. But I succeeded at last, and then took up my line of march in good spirits. I travelled on easily, and without mishap, until about midnight, when I heard two men coming towards me, from the direction I was going. I quickly hid myself in some sage bushes by the road, and listened to their conversation.

I soon recognized the voice of my brother Howard, who was accompanied by Mr. Maughn, the President of the stake. He was speaking to the latter with a tone of sadness which went to my heart. It appeared they had been in pursuit of me, and were now returning quite disheartened.

" After all," said Howard, as if in continuation of the conversation between them, "Mormonism has not quite broken the chords of nature, which bind me to my sister. Oh! where is she? It is injustice that has driven her to seek refuge among the wild beasts of the forest. To think of her wandering in this horrible place alone. She must certainly perish with cold before morning, if she is not destroyed by beasts of prey. I am almost frozen myself."

They had halted near me; and Mr. Maughn, of whom heartlessness was characteristic, said:

"Brother Coray, there is no use of hunting further for her. The courage that prompted the act will not desert her. She has the advantage of me, for I am almost alarmed to be in such a place. She cannot be far off, but it will be useless to look for her."

"She has fortitude," said Howard, "and has been schooled to danger her whole life. Mr. Maughn, we little know how much the girl has suffered; but I fear she has gone now."

In the few moments that I listened to this conversation, I ran over the chances of success, and asked myself the question, with the seriousness befitting one who discusses a point on which hangs his life, if I should embrace the present opportunity to return to my home, or hold on my way. I chose the latter. When they were out of hearing again, I travelled on cheerfully and hopeful.

It was not until about daylight that I discovered I had missed my way, and that I was still not far from the settlement. I was greatly disheartened by this discovery, and after resting myself a short time, I found the right road, plain enough by daylight, and with what heart I could muster, I went on again.

I soon began to meet the goers and comers to and from the settlement; but I was so well disguised with my Indian blanket that I was not recognized, although many were known to me. But my long night's travel and want of rest began to tell upon me; and I found myself so much exhausted that I was obliged to seek rest by the roadside. I was now in an open prairie, with no cover near; and it was with some alarm that I saw two horsemen coming up the road towards me. As they were evidently from the "stake," I felt certain they would not pass without looking into my face, and if it should turn out that one was my brother, nothing could prevent my being recognized.

I rose from the ground before they saw me, and moved off leisurely from the road to the right, hoping to put such a distance between them and myself, by the time they arrived opposite me, as to mislead them.

I was confident of my disguise as against the eyes of every one except my brother; but it proved that he was one of the horsemen. They were already a little passed me, and I began to breathe freely again, when Howard said to his companion, George Bryant, "that is Ettie."

"Ettie," said Bryant, impatiently, "that is a squaw."

"At all events," replied Howard, "I must see, for I think that is the walk of my sister."

Leaving brother Bryant, he came near me, and said, with a tone that proved he was not fully certain he was right·

"Nett, you had better ride."

I turned round at once, and said, "Possibly I had, for I am nearly tired to death—too tired to get up behind you."

By some effort, I succeeded in getting on to the horse with his assistance; and when we rode back to where Mr. Bryant was waiting in the road, he said, "Well done for us."

"But not so well done for me," I replied.

"Oh, I think you will be satisfied in a few days, said he; that it is better even for you. We have had every man in the settlement out looking all night, and they are still scouring the mountains for you.

"Did you take Smith's portrait with you?" said my brother.

"Certainly."

"It is owing to the influence of that portrait that she cannot forget the original," said Bryant. "Hand it to me, Nett."

I told him I preferred to keep it; but he insisted upon having it. I looked to my brother for protection, but finding no sign of sympathy for the portrait in him, I was forced to yield, and I handed it to him with a presentiment that it was lost to me. I asked him to return it.

Opening it, he said, "Well, he *is* good looking. I am not urprised at your efforts to get to him. I am sorry to injure your feelings, Nett; but you can never see this again."

Dismounting, he dug a hole in the ground, with a long knife he wore in a scabbard at his side, and buried it—buried all I had left of my husband.

Little was said between us, as we slowly returned to the

settlement. It seemed that every desire of life was crushed out of me.

A man soon overtook and passed us, by whom my brother sent word to the president of the stake that I had been found. We saw, before reaching home, a large flag elevated upon a pole, in honor of the "capture," and carried through the settlement, and heard the firing of guns; and when we arrived, the streets of our little stake were full of men, women, and children, and Indians, to see a conquered woman.

"This will be a lesson to her, as well as to other women," said the president of the stake, heartlessly, as we came to dismount; and he added, "May the spirit of the living God hereafter direct you, Nett."

But I heard little more, and was indifferent to what I did hear; for, half famished and exhausted by excitement and long travel, and exposure to cold and want of sleep, I was carried into the house, and put into the possession of Martha. I recollect seeing her kind and gentle face, beaming upon me with pity, as she received me with a tenderness peculiar to her, and sent back the crowd from the door. Days of suffering, of burning fever followed, of which I have but little recollection, save that Martha was always near, and her soothing presence was the good angel which wooed me back half reconciled to life again. She told me afterwards that I had spent much of the time in pleading with the Prophet, who I imagined to be present, that he would not have my husband buried alive—an idea traceable to the loss of his portrait, taken from me, and buried by Bryant.

I awoke one morning, as if from a long and troubled sleep,

and heard Martha in conversation with Howard; and I soon understood that I was the subject of it. I was free from pain, and calm; but it was some time before I was fully able to call to mind the events connected with my attempted escape.

Martha was representing in a subdued and earnest manner to Howard, how cruel it was to keep me imprisoned thus from my husband. She said, "If Nett is ever well again, she shall be restored to her husband. Mormonism of late blights whatever it touches, and is fast becoming past endurance. Don't you think you men, who claim to be our saviours, run some risk of being called to an account in the next world?" She said many other things which I do not recollect.

Howard listened thoughtfully to the strong good sense of Martha's plea in my behalf; and evidently struggling against the bonds of his implicit Mormon faith, said at length:

"Brother Brigham must be counselled as to Nett at once. I cannot bear this state of things. It makes me wretched. I wish she could be satisfied to make what sacrifices the Church demands of her; but if she cannot, we must try to lighten the load for which her faith seems to be too weak."

As I slowly regained my usual health and tone of mind, it became a question of serious concern with me, what effect my late adventure might have with the Prophet. I knew that, on my brother's account, he would be disposed in a measure to overlook my fault; and yet a due regard to dicipline among the women would force him to hold me up as an example.

While thus debating with myself what line of conduct to pursue, the Prophet directed me to return to the city. I obeyed him, and when we met, I explained frankly, why I had attempted to escape; and I judged it best to indicate to him, that now I had no further wish that way. That I was disposed to content myself with Mormonism as I found it; and hoped he would impose upon me no serious burdens again.

He received me graciously, and seemed to accept my professions of reformation as if made in good faith. I felt, however I could not expect him to believe in me fully at first: and he soon gave me reason to know he did not; for after this, I had frequent opportunities to leave the territory; but I positively declined them all; fearing they came from Mormons in disguise, although professedly of Gentile origin. The event proved this was true: the hand of the Prophet was at the bottom of it. He wished to test in this way, the sincerity of my return to the true fold; but he was not long in coming to the conclusion, that I could really be trusted again. I well knew that my only hope of a final success lay in such a well dissembled contentment, as should in the end, regain his confidence; and I pursued this line of policy until it paved the way for my success, at length, when I had nearly abandoned myself to despair.

THE OATH OF THE ENDOWMENT.

SEE CHAP. IV.

CHAPTER XXXII.

HOPE.

It was in the spring of 1855 that I returned to the city from Tooille. My sister Lizzie had been married the previous year to Richard Cordon, an Englishman by birth and a Mormon. He was a member of a military corps known at the valley as the "Minute men." This is a body distinct from that of the "Danites." The latter are set apart for secret assassinations and such other acts as have no foundation in right but the Prophet's will and order: while the former is a well drilled corps of picked men, taking more the character of a militia, held in reserve for general defence. Both however are equally subject to the Prophet's control; and their hands are perhaps equally stained with innocent blood. The Danite band, however, being a smaller body of tried and devoted adherents of the Prophet, who render an unquestioning obedience to his counsel, have, individually, committed by far the greatest amount of crime.

The darkest annals of the world can scarcely furnish a more terrible record, than would the simple biography of a few of these Danite leaders. When that record is written, the names of Porter Rockwell, Wm. Hickman, Hiram Clawson, Captain James Brown, John and Wiley Norton, James Furguson, Robert Burton, and others, whose names I do not recollect, will be found linked with the most cruel and bloody acts, that have ever disgraced humanity.

Rockwell was the leader of this band at Nauvoo; but Wm. Hickman is now supposed to fill that post; having won this distinction, by his daring and success. It is said, that his soul knows no pity; and he fears no law but the Prophet's will. It was this man who won for his band the title now proudly borne by them; viz., "Destroying Angels."

Some time in the following summer, my mother received a letter from my third sister, Mrs. Phebe Knapp, still living in Pennsylvania, near the old homestead.

The letter stated, that a piece of land, which for some reason my father did not sell when he moved from Pennsylvania; but which he had left in the possession of his relatives there, was without a legal claimant. That this land until recently, had been regarded of but little value; but was now supposed to contain valuable deposits of coal: and advised her to return, for the purpose of securing it for herself and children.

We paid but little attention to this at first, as we had never known much about my father's affairs; and had no knowledge of this particular property. Moreover, we had no reason to hope the Prophet would consent to our leaving the valley But my brother-in-law. Richard Corden, went to him with this information, which excited his curiosity so much, that he sent for Howard, who was still at Tooille

About this time, we obtained some account of the same thing through Judge Reed who was from Bath, Steuben Co., N. Y. He was one of the Judges of the territory, and an acquaintance of my mother's brother, Col. John R. Stephens of Hornellsville, N. Y., from whom he had learned these facts. My uncle had requested the Judge before he left the States, to inform my mother, that it would be necessary for her to return before she could regain possession of the property.

This information, coming from different sources, confirmed the Prophet in the belief that there was something in it.

When Howard came to the city, brother Brigham laid before him what he knew of the matter, and advised him to attend to it at once; "for," said he, "the time is near at hand when the Gentiles and the Mormons will dissolve partnership, and then it will be too late."

He referred in the above words to the time, never lost sight of by the true Mormon, when it is expected the Church will throw off all allegiance to the General Government, and raise the standard of a Mormon theocracy: when an appeal to arms will be had, for the mastery in Utah.

Mother was at this time over sixty years of age, and not in very good health. She refused to attempt the journey, unless Lizzie and myself were both allowed to go with her: "for it is not unlikely," said she, "that I shall die upon the plains, and I do not wish to be alone. If the Prophet insists upon it, I will go, and bring him the money for the property, if we find any; but I must take my children with me."

This appeared but reasonable. When Lizzie and myself were consulted, we both discouraged the enterprise. We professed an unwillingness to go, and attempted to convince the Prophet, that as to the property, it was a question of great uncertainty whether there was any, and a still more doubtful one, whether we should be able to obtain it. But as we had expected, this only fixed more firmly in his mind the determination, that we should make the attempt. He is not easily baffled when upon a money scent. He had set his mind upon it, and we submitted to the will of the " Prophet," and set about making preparations for the journey. I was questioned very closely by different persons, as I well knew by the Prophet's direction, with the secret intention of sounding my state of feeling. But I was never off my guard. I always regretted the necessity, and doubted the policy of the enterprise; I had become satisfied with the Church, and given up my husband; and I had no wish to leave Utah. So long and tiresome a journey, over the plains and back again had no attractions for me. I did not wish to undertake it, and I consented only on my mother's account. Elizabeth consented with the more cheerfulness, as her husband was to accompany us. And thus it fell out, providentially, as I have since believed, that we were to leave by the open consent of the Prophet, this Mormon prison: of course under a promise to return. But we were going to a land where the will of the Prophet was not the law. I was so much elated with my prospects, that I trusted myself to speak upon the subject only with the greatest caution, and always with a sigh, and a long face.

Mother had a city lot, on which her house stood. These lots contain an acre and a quarter of land, one fourth of which she had given to me. She obtained the permission of Brother Brigham to sell her place, to defray the expenses of her journey. I went to him to obtain his consent to sell mine; giving as a reason that we might need the money before we returned. But to this he objected. He said to me, "leave your lot in the care of brother Judd, and I will have him ornament it with trees and shrubs, and when you return you shall find it a little paradise. If you need anything for your journey, let me know when you are ready to start, and I will furnish what you lack, to make you comfortable."

I therefore consented to this arrangement with apparent cheerfulness, and thanked him for the interest he took in my affairs. The following winter passed quickly enough; for we were employed in preparing for the journey, and in joyful anticipation of it.

When the spring arrived we were nearly ready. It was by this time generally known that we were about to leave; and our friends called to bid us adieu, and many of the poor women, whose better instincts told them our sorrow at leaving the society of the Saints was feigned, pressed our hands, and with tears expressed the wish to go with us to the land where the rights of woman were respected: and where the high and the low, were alike governed by written laws, founded in right; and not dependent upon special revelations.

Could my countrywomen of the United States have listened to the moans of these crushed and broken-hearted women, could they be made to understand the hopeless despair that weighed them down, a despair that sent a shudder even through my frame, who had spent my life among, and had suffered with them: could they but for one moment mark the effort to crush back into silence the rising sob, and stealthily dry the tear, that nevertheless *would* flow, I am not sure, but they would rise in a body, and if there was no other remedy for these wrongs against the sex, they would march to their relief. They would at least shame the authorities into the right.

About the time we were to set out, a discussion arose in certain quarters, which threatened to break up the expedition altogether, or, at least to prevent my going with it, and nothing but the firmness of my mother, and my assumed indifference to the result, averted this disaster.

Robert Burton, the two Nortons, Mr. Judd, and others of this class, mostly Danites, went to the Prophet to remonstrate against my being permitted to leave the valley. They represented to him how hazardous it would be to allow one who knew what I did of the secret history of the Church, to go among the Gentiles, and beyond a "restraining" influence. I was at least *liable* to apostatize; and there was no knowing what I might be led to divulge. I took occasion to see the Prophet when I heard of it, and to second their appeal with such apparent good faith, that he said, laughingly: he thought I could be trusted, and he wished to hear no more about it.

Some of the Danites became very much excited, and it appeared to me with reason, for I thought of the case of poor Dr. Roberts, and Bowman, and many other similar ones, which if known to the Government, must make it difficult for some of these men to keep their necks safely between their heads and shoulders. Wiley Norton went so far as to say, that if the Prophet allowed me to accompany my mother, our party would not go far, that we should be followed to the mountains, and if the worst came to worst, they would break up the expedition. To this my mother replied firmly, that she was willing to have the expedition broken up, and now was the better time to do that; but if she went, both her children should accompany her.

Nothing ever came under my notice during the fifteen years of my sojourn among the Mormons, amounting as it has to the best part of my life, which so well illustrates the absolute authority of the Prophet as the discussion growing out of this difference of opinion between him and his "Danites." What makes it a still stronger case is, that common sense and right, estimating right by their standard, were clearly against him; and yet his simple dictum, without reason, was submitted to by strong full-grown men.

He was evidently blinded by his overweening greed for money, otherwise he would have seen that the mere prospect of meeting my husband once more was a good reason why I should wish to go anywhere to get away from Utah, and that finding him would be a sufficient bar against returning to the valley. But it is due to the sagacity of the Prophet that I say; I had ample reason afterwards to believe, that my brother-in-law, Richard Cordon, was privately charged with the duty of preventing a meeting between myself and husband; and also to apply the antidote so familiar to a Danite, in case I should attempt to apostatize or make dangerous developments.

Everything was now ready except to procure our letter of recommendation. The following is a true copy of mine, which is still in my possession:—

(*Copy.*)

"GREAT SALT LAKE CITY, *May* 25, 1856.

TO ALL WHOM IT MAY CONCERN:

"This is to certify, Sister Mary Ettie V. Smith is a worthy member in the Church of Jesus Christ, of Latter Day Saints; we therefore recommend her to all good people where God in his Providence may call her, or where her lot may be cast.

(Signed) "THOMAS A. JUDD,
"*Clerk.*"

My mother and sister had similar ones.

CHAPTER XXXIII.

GOING TO THE LAND OF MY BIRTH.

AT one o'clock in the afternoon of May 26, 1856, our little party left the city to commence the long and tedious journey, over mountains and plains, to the land of our fathers.

It occurred to us, as we looked back upon the city for the last time, that it was a few months over ten years since we had followed the Mormon hosts from Nauvoo, slowly and sullenly moving towards the setting sun, in pursuit of an asylum from Gentile mobs and persecutions; and we were now fleeing back to the east to find a refuge against Mormon cruelty and crime. What changes had come over us and over the Church since that time!

There was the capital of an empire, which the Heads of the Church had founded and reared within the short space of ten years, and which they and their trusting followers believed to be as firm and lasting as the snow-capped mountains by which it was shut out from the Gentile world. A new empire grown so strong and confident as already to bid defiance to the General Government. Was it strange that, before we had shaken the dust of the city from off our feet, we looked upon the rising capital of this daring and ambitious people, and felt the oppression of a vague fear in view of the *future* of a sect whose short *past* had been so remarkable? And that we asked ourselves with some concern what wonders it might not be expected to develop hereafter? We encamped that night at the foot of Little Mountain, a few miles northeast of the city. The next morning we commenced the tiresome ascent. It was a slow and tedious journey of two days to the summit. On the night of our first encampment at the foot of Little Mountain, the weather had been warm as midsummer. Our third encampment was made in the snows upon the mountain-top. I had my feet and one of my fingers frozen in getting supper that night. We had labored incessantly in making the ascent with our ponies and light wagon. Before we reached the snow line, we were obliged to unload the wagon, and go up empty, and even this was effected with difficulty, as our little ponies found the wagon alone a sufficient load. Then to return with the ponies, and packing the luggage upon their backs, and upon poles fastened to their sides, and trailing behind, after the Indian fashion, to drag this up also. We were thus scorched and blistered with the heat of the first day, and half frozen the third.

The next morning, we commenced at an early hour the descent, and cooked a late breakfast at the foot of the mountain, in a warm and genial climate.

Perhaps nothing could better illustrate the character of the country, and the usual incidents of travel in it, than an account of this beginning of our journey, and its quick changes from smiling valleys, green with rich pastures, to the lofty mountain-top, covered with snow.

Our route for several days was among the mountains, and lay, for the most part, through the narrow cañons, which form so wild a feature of the country. One of these, I recollect, was remarkable for its wonderful combination of simple beauty and imposing grandeur. For miles, perhaps, the pass would be little more than wide enough for the free passage of the team ; with a smooth and perpendicular wall of rock rising on each side to an immense height, which would glisten far above us in the rays of the sun, like polished marble. The mind is lost in astonishment in attempting to account for the peculiar formation of these passes, and is kept continually upon the stretch of expectation while travelling through them; surprised, at each turn of the crooked way, by some new wonder, or some more imposing point of view. Perhaps when the senses fairly ache with the effort to comprehend the rocky labyrinth—when they are ready to droop with exhaustion, they are relieved as the way opens suddenly, may be, upon a green and narrow plat, where the clear, pure stream, which before had fretted and lashed its bright waters into fury by throwing itself madly against the rocks from side to side, now gently sings a pleasing tale among bright flowers and grassy borders.

In the afternoon of the fifth day, we overtook a family by the name of Hunley, who were leaving the Mormons to return to a deserted home in Texas. We found them in camp, and as our team was somewhat jaded, we concluded to join them.

As their history was a peculiar one, and serves to illustrate Mormonism, I will give it as I received it from them. Mr. Hunley was a planter, living in Texas near Galveston, and had married an educated and accomplished young widow, by whom he received a large amount of property. She had at this time one daughter. After becoming the mother of three other children, Mrs. Hunley became a convert to Mormonism, under the preaching of a missionary saint, at that time wandering through Texas. She was endowed with an earnest and trusting nature, joined to a strong tendency to enthusiasm; and at once felt it her duty to leave her family, her husband not sympathizing with her, and accompany the missionary elder to Great Salt Lake city. She therefore set out, upon the spur of the moment, with her daughter, then about fourteen years of age, leaving the other three children with the husband, and arrived at the valley, strong in the faith that Brigham Young was the only true prophet. She had adopted Mormonism in good faith, purely from a high religious conviction; but when once at the valley, she was not long in making out the true state of things. She had no sympathy with the gross and sensual. When the Prophet understood how she had left a devoted husband, for the love she bore the true faith, he insisted upon having her "sealed" to one of the saints. When it was too late, she made the terrible discovery that from the will of the Prophet there was no appeal, and she was forced to submit. She, however, found means to get word to her husband in Texas, as to the state of things, and implored him to come for her. Mr. Hunley, who never doubted his wife's integrity, regretting only her error, flew at once to her succor. When he arrived, Mrs. Hunley, who was after all a shrewd woman, contrived some story by which she induced the Prophet to consent to her leaving the valley with her husband, under a strong promise to return.

He pronounced a terrible curse, which he said should follow her, in case she apostatized. She did not tell me what the Prophet expected her to accomplish, but it was something connected with her husband's property, as I suppose.

She had with her a young child, the fruit of her Mormon marriage. Mr. Hunley was fond of his wife, and appeared glad to regain her; but he would take no notice of the child.

They left the valley, but a few days before us. There were several other families at the valley who had joined the Mormons from the neighborhood of Galveston, some of whom were less successful in making a safe retreat. Some of these families had been there several years, and were all very wealthy. One of them named Grier owned near Galveston large possessions in land, most of which he had sold, taking the proceeds with him to the valley.

Old Mr. Grier had five sons if I recollect right, and one daughter, and took all with him; but dying on the plains, he never saw the new Zion himself. His wife and six children, arrived in the valley in due time; and on account of their great wealth were graciously received by the Prophet. He required first a tenth of all they had, which amounted to a large sum, and the next spring required them to "consecrate" the balance. To this they objected, and they were soon involved in difficulty with the Heads of the Church, and began openly to express a wish to return to Texas.

This was the signal for the faithful to pounce upon them.

Their great wealth made them a conspicuous mark. When they went to drive up their cattle and mules, they found the Church mark upon them: and thus they were lost, for that consecrated them to sacred purposes; and no one could question that mark, or how it came there. They were harassed in every possible manner, and finally they attempted to get together what cattle and mules they had left, with the view of leaving the valley; but at night they were scattered again by the "Danites." The more effort the five brothers made to get away with their property, the less they had to take away, and the chances of escape lessened, in the same proportion. They had a great amount of money when they came, which had been loaned to different members of the Church. But wishing to collect it again, the Prophet absolved the debtors from payment. Thus the more they resisted, the more they became involved in difficulty.

The daughter had married a Mr. Johnson before leaving Texas, who had joined his fortunes with that of the Griers, and was now involved in their embarrassments. They had a large store of goods at Salt Lake city, which they sold to a Mormon at a great sacrifice, and were making great efforts to leave the valley in company with Mr. Hunley. The Griers found it impossible to do so; for besides having their mules and cattle scattered and spirited away whenever they attempted to collect them for the journey, they were involved in lawsuits, which threatened not only to absorb what property they had left, but to detain them indefinitely.

Things were in this state when Hunley left the city; and Johnson, seeing the Griers were not likely to get away soon quietly arranged his affairs to accompany the former. Taking only those things most needed, and the items of his large property least likely to excite notice, and his wife, he set out, hoping to overtake Hunley.

We all remained in camp the next day. As for us, we were glad to give the ponies a rest, and at the same time, to keep in the company of Hunley; but we afterwards learned, that his object was to give Johnson time to join him, about whom he was very anxious. As Johnson's party did not come up with us, we went on the next morning.

Nothing of importance occurred to us during that day, and we went into camp at night, without hearing from Johnson. The next day, sometime after noon, we arrived at Webber river; and were greatly disappointed in finding it at full banks, and impassable, except by means of rafts. My brother-in-law and Hunley, assisted by the two men the latter had with him, at once set to work to construct one, by which they hoped to cross.

Towards night we saw two women on horseback approaching the camp, attended by an Indian boy. They looked fatigued and disheartened, and their clothing was torn and soiled. When they came up, they were at once recognized by the Hunleys. One was Mrs. Johnson, and the other a Mrs. Dana. The latter it appears had joined Mrs. Johnson's party, when on the eve of quitting the city. Her husband was a Mormon elder, then on a mission to England, and during his absence, she had made some new discoveries, which disgusted her with the Church, and she attempted to make her escape with her two children; but she was forced by the Mormons to leave them at the valley; and she was now inconsolable at their loss. She was always crying while with us, and did nothing but mourn for them. Hers was but one of the many sad and cruel cases of injustice and wrong, that claimed our sympathy on the way.

All were anxious to hear Mrs. Johnson's story—and she gratified the company at once—it was as follows:

She said, "we had a terrible time in getting out of the city, and when once upon the way, we were dogged by the "Danites," until we lost everything but two wagons, and the horses and property belonging to them; and a few spare mules and ponies. They were bent upon killing Mr. Johnson, and he thought it best to leave us, in order to avoid them, and take another route over the mountains, hoping to meet us again at, or beyond Fort Bridger.

Accordingly, taking one of the mules, he set off alone, and that is the last we have seen of him. But I am anxious to get on, to find him. After he had gone, the "Danites," made another attack; but not finding Mr. Johnson, they contented themselves with using only threats, and then left us. They evidently came with the intention of killing my husband; but luckily his absence saved him. We were greatly frightened, and when they were out of sight, our men advised us to get upon the ponies, and come on and try to overtake you with the other families, known to be somewhere ahead. I told the men I dare not attempt that, as I was unacquainted with the way. Whereupon our Indian boy said he had been upon this road many times before he was sold to the Mormons; and he recollected the way. We therefore started with my Indian slave as guide, who has led us by one of his Indian trails, unknown even to the "Danites," over the mountains and through the bushes, and here we are with our dresses nearly torn from our backs."

We all sympathized with the new comers, and after listenng with interest to their story, and while the men were in the meantime busily engaged in arranging the raft to cross the river, we employed ourselves in rendering them what assistance we could.

As for me, I was happy to interest myself in others' woes, rather than my own. From what Wiley Norton had said to us before leaving, we had expected the "Danites," would have followed us. But having escaped thus far, we felt at ease, thinking that as they had so many others to pursue, they had either overlooked us altogether, or had concluded to obey the Prophet's " counsel," in relation to us.

CHAPTER XXXIV.

CROSSING THE WEBBER—PERILS BY THE WAY.

BEFORE the raft was finished, a party of men with three wagons and several mules, appeared upon the other side of the river, having in charge the U. S. mail going to great Salt Lake city.

When every thing was ready, one of these men, named Mitchel, swam a mule to our side, with some ropes, which were tied to the raft; and then returning, he drew it over, loaded with Mr. Hunley's wagon, safely. He then returned with the rope to our side, and the raft was drawn back, with a part of the U. S. mail, which was also safely landed, and our wagon, with all the property belonging to us except the ponies, was taken back with it, in good order. The balance of the mail was now placed upon the raft, and several men with it, and it set out for another voyage to our shore. But when in the middle of the stream the ropes broke, and the raft, with its valuable freight, went rushing down the stream, borne by the mad current at a bounding speed, and was quickly out of sight. The men had the presence of mind to throw what they could of the mail bags ashore, as the raft passed near the land at a sharp turn of the river just below us; and in this way, a part of them were saved; but most of the bags went down. The men saved themselves with difficulty by swimming.

We had been in high spirits until now, as we had expected to get over that night. All our provisions and bed-clothing were on the other side of the river, while the men, women, and children, of both parties, were on our side. Over twenty persons in all, with nothing to eat, and many, with but little to wear. One of the men from the other side, had put on linen pantaloons for greater convenience in working about the raft; but when the night set in he felt terribly the want of warm clothing. The day had been warm, but the cold winds came down from the mountains in chilling blasts, and we all suffered immensely; but this man especially was nearly frozen before morning.

The men gathered what fuel they could and built a fire, about which we crowded to make ourselves as comfortable as possible; but all wanted food. Finally, my brother-in-law, Cordon, took a mule and swam the river, and returned with some crackers and tea, and two bed-covers, which were shared with the company. This was a but a meagre supply, but it was all we had.

It was a long weary night for most of the company; but the morning came at last, and then Mitchel swam his grey mule over the river again, and brought back some bread and coffee, and other articles in such abundance, that we all made a very comfortable breakfast.

Then the question arose how we were to make the passage

of the river. It was decided, after much discussion, that one of the men should go over with the mule belonging to Mitchel, which by this time had become quite the hero of our party, and cork one of the wagon boxes, to be used as a boat. This was accomplished with such success, that after running it over and back, loaded with harness, and whatever loose property there was left, a call was made for volunteer passengers, but none were willing to risk the frail bark.

Thinking it would be as well to drown in the attempt to cross, as to remain with the prospect of starving, for we had already devoured what had been brought over, I offered to go for one, and Mrs. Hunley for another; but no more of the women dared to venture, and the boat, such as it was, was pulled off by the men having hold of the rope on the opposite side, and the next moment our fortunes were cast upon the angry current.

We had with us one man, who baled incessantly to keep the wagon box from sinking, and yet the water gained upon him. We watched with untold interest, the water slowly rising inside the box and the opposite shore which we were approaching *slowly*.

The problem was a very simple one, and it was this: whether our boat could reach the opposite shore sooner than the water could reach the top of the box, and the chances appeared to be evenly balanced for a time. We gained upon the shore, and the man, encouraged by us, redoubled his efforts; but the water was gaining also; and now the scene became to us one of the most absorbing interest. The box was nearly full, and the man looked up from his work as if he thought we were really past hope. Then the men on shore gave a strong pull at the rope, and for a moment we flew towards the land, and the next, the box went under But it was fortunately too near the shore to sink far, and we held on the sides with the strong current rushing against us, until the men pulled us to the land, with no further damage than getting thoroughly wet. They had built a large fire, around which blankets were hung, where we dried our clothing, and were soon comfortable again; gratefully acknowledging our narrow escape.

The wagon box was so much swelled, by this time, that it leaked less and less, and Alice Hunley and my mother and sister were next drawn over with safety, although the rude boat was nearly full of water before it struck the shore. Then Mrs. Johnson and Dana, with a Mrs. Coward, another fugitive from Mormonism, who had arrived at the crossing since daylight, were taken over.

The ponies and mules were after this turned into the river, and it was a novel spectacle to see them with their heads just out of water, moving faster down the stream than they did across it, swim to our side. But they all came in at last, though at some distance below.

When all were over, preparations were made to resume the march—to encounter perhaps new dangers. Mrs. Johnson, now that the perils of crossing an angry river were passed without harm, became anxious again about her husband. He had left word that she must not expect to meet him until the party arrived at Fort Bridger; but unable to brook the delay of travelling so slow with the teams, she took the pony and the Indian boy as guide, and providing herself with some crackers and matches, a blanket, and rope to tie the horse, she set out in search of him the next morning, though remonstrated with by all the company. It was in vain they represented how dangerous the undertaking would be——that it was little short of madness——she bravely galloped away to find a husband on whose track, perhaps even now, the "Danites" were prowling, anxious to shed his blood.

We heard nothing more from either of them until in the afternoon of the following day, when we met Mr. Johnson coming back to learn, if possible, what had been the fate of his party. He had seen nothing of his wife.

Successful in eluding the "Danites," he had arrived safely at Fort Bridger; but unable to restrain his anxiety, had returned through a by-way to seek his wife, who had gone to seek him by the regular road; and they had thus missed each other. But, sick and fatigued with long travel, watchfulness and exposure among the mountains, he thought it best to remain with the teams, believing Mrs. Johnson had gone on to the fort, where he would be likely to find her. In fact he was already too sick to ride on horseback.

He had not been with us long before a man was seen coming down the road, who was soon recognized as Lewis Robinson the keeper of the fort, which was occupied, I believe, only by himself and family. Robinson was a Mormon, and Mr. Johnson thought it singular that he should follow him from the fort, for he had been allowed to depart from it in peace that morning. He therefore secreted himself in one of the wagons, hoping to escape his notice; not knowing what he might want. It was not impossible but some of the "Danites" had arrived at the fort since he had left it; and if so, he was certainly not very safe. It was with the greatest anxiety that he listened as Robinson came up, for his first inquiry, expecting it would be for him; and then he imagined his wife to be already in the hands of the "Danites." In fact he nearly gave himself up as lost; but he was at once relieved when he found that Robinson not only asked no questions about him, but in reply to the anxious inquiry of Mrs. Hunley, informed her that Mrs. Johnson was at the fort, safe, and waiting for her party to come up. Robinson was about to pass without further delay; but as he came near our wagon Richard Cordon said to him, in a tone that proved how much his heart was in the ugly deed, "I say, Robinson, do you know Johnson is in one of these wagons, and that our boys are after him?"

Robinson looked at Cordon, surprised at first, and after a moment of hesitation his face wore an expression of contempt, then laughing, he said: "Oh, I don't care; I am not on that mission to-day." And, as if as anxious to escape from us, as we were to flee from the "Danites," he went his way.

Covered with chagrin and mortification, Cordon for some time stood looking after the generous man, who had so nobly scorned to do a mean action, and I took care not to lessen his embarrassment by any very gentle notice of his cowardly aim.

From this time, I watched him closely, and had reason afterwards to distrust him still more, as to myself.

The next day we arrived at Fort Bridger, where we found Mrs. Johnson—and we all shared in the joy of her meeting with the husband for whom she had shown such heroic devotion. It was a scene of touching tenderness worthy the success her unselfishness had won. She was too much occupied with her new joy to gratify our numerous questions, but still clinging to her husband as if fearful of losing him again. She modestly stated, as if there was nothing remarkable in it, that after leaving us, she had pursued her way with what speed she could until dark, and then finding the ponies must have rest, and that it was too dark to keep the road with ease, she picketed the animals, and building a fire, remained in the cañon until morning, comforting herself with the reflection that perhaps Mr. Johnson was not far off, and possibly he might be attracted by the light of the fire before morning, and come to her.

She said the wind blew cold as the snows that overhung the cañon from whence it came; but daylight appeared at last, and then she hastened on, and arrived at the fort, only to find Mr. Johnson had returned to look for her.

Fort Bridger was to me an object of great interest, as I had often heard the story, which associated with it the fortunes of a man whose name it still bears, told by some of the men who were actors in the wild adventures connected with his disappearance. This interest was not lessened, perhaps, by the mystery that still hangs over it; for the real fate of the daring man who first built the fort is even yet unknown—like a thousand others who have gone down before the fiat of the relentless Prophet among the lonely passes of the mountains of Utah.

This is not properly a fort, but several adobé buildings arranged for the purpose of defence. They were built, and long occupied by a Mr. Bridger, a man of whose early history I have never heard much. He had a family, and was well provided, it is said, with retainers, and stores of arms, and ammunition, and at length became powerful. He was not a Mormon; but was, at one time, on good terms with the Church. But in an evil hour, he incurred the displeasure of the Prophet from some cause not generally known. The matter created great excitement at the time, and an expedition was long talked of to bring him to terms. I recollect the matter well; but nothing more was said about it than necessary; and this is the reason why much of the transaction is still shrouded in the same secrecy.

When the dispute came to the worst, an expedition was fitted out from the city to take the fort, with orders to bring back Bridger a prisoner. The city was in a high state of excitement for several weeks, and in constant expection of the arrival of the captive. I knew many of the men who were members of this party; and I heard James Ferguson, Hiram Norton, and Wiley Norton, and Andrew Cunningham, and many others, relate all they were at liberty to tell of it, after they returned.

The party, with Andrew Cunningham in command, arrived at the fort, and found Bridger gone. But his wife was there living quietly as usual. She knew nothing of her husband. Cunningham judged rightly, as it afterwards proved, that Bridger was concealed in the mountains not far off, and that he must either return occasionally to the fort for food, or that those at the fort must communicate with him for this purpose.

He therefore withdrew his party, professedly with a view of giving up the enterprise, and returning to the city; but afterwards came back with a number of his men, and stationed them in secure positions, from which strict watch could be kept upon the movements at the fort. The measure was well taken; but Bridger was not easily decoyed, and it took an experienced ranger of the mountains to mislead him, or to conceal the signs of what was passing from his practised eye. It proved therefore to be a long siege. Many weeks passed, and no trace of Bridger was found; but the faith of the Mormon leader was strong, and he was content to abide his time—and he redoubled his watchfulness.

The wife was at last detected in holding communication with the proscribed man, no sign of whose whereabouts had before been discovered. It was a short work to make out his hiding-place after that. What was his fate, or that of his family, none but the few "Danites," who were engaged in that "mission," can tell; and for some reason, the same men who had spoken freely to me of other crimes, were silent upon this point. When asked what became of him, they did not know. A large amount of property was taken from the fort to the city, among which were arms, and powder, and lead.

These circumstances made a deep impression upon my mind at the time; but with the great mass of the Church, other and newer excitements took their place; and now the fate of Bridger is seldom mentioned. But there are those in Utah who will still shudder at the mention of his fate; and though it would be unsafe to question thus anything "ordained" of the Prophet, yet many of these still hope to see the time when the mystery, of which Fort Bridger now stands the dark and frowning monument, shall be unsealed through an investigation by Governmental authority. Shall this day ever come?

Not wishing to attract unnecessary notice, we made but a short halt at the fort, but drove on several miles that night before going into camp. This was the first time since leaving Salt Lake we had felt anything like security. Our party had now swelled to a large and promiscuous company of Gentile merchants and adventurers, and Mormon fugitives; and if the Danites had not already given up the pursuit of Johnson or others of the party, we thought they would hardly think of attacking us; for if our numbers did not deter them, the presence of those having the United States mail would at least have that tendency. From motives of policy, these carriers had always been respected, as far as was then known.

A few days of easy travel, undistinguished by any event of importance, brought us to Green River, which we crossed without difficulty by a convenient ferry.

At this point our Texas friends left us. They took the Cherokee trail for home, and we knew nothing more of their fate, but presumed they arrived safely at Galveston, a success they had well deserved.

I regarded the escape of Mr. Johnson and his wife the most remarkable of any that came under my notice while at the valley. To attempt an escape when the Danites are in pursuit is like disputing the decrees of fate.

CHAPTER XXXV.

CROSSING THE PLAINS.

NEARLY the whole route from Great Salt Lake city thus far had been associated in my mind with sad reminiscences similar to that of Fort Bridger, most of which I have necessarily neglected to mention. Several of these were connected with the Green River Ferry, one of which, the case of Mrs. Hartley, I have already referred to in a former chapter. Another case now occurs to me, an account of which I received from Richard Cordon, and others who were concerned in it.

It would seem that some years before this, an American, known as Big Bill, had erected a ferry at this point. What his real name was, if I ever knew, I have now forgotten. The Mormons had one here also, and from motives of interest growing out of the ferry, or from other causes, they wished Big Bill, who was a Gentile, to transfer his interest in the place to them. Whether they could not agree upon the terms, or whether Big Bill had offended the Heads of the Church in some other way, I never knew. At all events, a party was sent by the Prophet, under the command of Robert Burton, to bring him in a prisoner. The pretence under which he was to be arrested, I think, was in some way founded upon a refusal to accept from the Prophet, who claimed jurisdiction over the matter as the civil Governor of the territory, a license to keep a ferry there. Big Bill not only denied the jurisdiction, but claimed that the fee fixed by the Prophet was unequal and exorbitant; and that it discriminated to his disadvantage in favor of the other ferry.

He was a bold and daring man, of great size; trained to the free life of the plains, and young in years, though probably not aware of the kind of foes he had to deal with, and still less accustomed to submit to oppression. Hence when the Mormons came to arrest him, he positively refused to accompany them, but resisted the arrest.

Burton gave him no time for reflection, but ordered his men to fire at once, and he fell mortally wounded upon his own premises. Big Bill had evidently not anticipated things were to be pushed to this extreme; otherwise the Mormons would have found him a dangerous foe, on account of his great strength and experience in border warfare. Though crippled by his wounds, and unable to rise, he was still alive, and it was considered unsafe to approach too near the struggling giant, and the men fired into his breast while he lay upon the ground till he was dead. I have heard those who shared in this cowardly act, describe it. One of them was Richard Cordon. But why multiply cases of this kind Human nature revolts even at the recital of them; and yet every corner of Utah is stained by the innocent blood of these victims.

When we were again upon the way, we found ourselves

nearly alone, accompanied only by a merchant from Weston, Mo, named Gilbert, with a clerk in his employ, whose name was Henry Blood. They were returning from the valley, where they had been with a stock of goods. They had a man to look after and pack the mules, and these three men with Richard Cordon, now constituted the male force of our party, with which we were to cross the Indian country and that too when the savages were understood to be uncommonly hostile.

As I kept no memoranda of our journey home, I am obliged to trust mostly to recollection for the principal events, and I shall not attempt to be accurate as to time and distances, and indeed I do not propose to give a detailed account of it; but shall seize only upon the most notable events of what remains to be told of this narrative; already grown to a bulk much beyond the original design.

We travelled many days with nothing unusual to break the monotony of the journey, until we arrived at the South Pass. After this the Indian signs were more numerous and threatening. Several of the tribes were at war with each other, as we soon learned, and they thus had but little time to devote to emigrants; but more than one party had been cut off, as all were liable to be when unprotected. We travelled in constant fear of them by day, and at night we built no fires, not wishing to attract their attention.

Our load was very heavy for the small ponies over the sandy roads, and through the day, all except mother walked most of the time; but during the long drives after dark, often continued deep into the night, to reach safe camping grounds convenient to water and pasture, my sister Lizzie was obliged to ride, in order to hush her child and keep it still; for at these hours stray Indian bands were likely to be prowling along the trail to pick up defenceless parties like ours.

Mr. Gilbert one day rode up to us as we were seated upon the ground, to rest the team and ourselves, and said, "Mrs. Smith, I notice you do not ride much. Is your wagon heavily loaded?"

"It is," said I, "and our ponies are light."

"Let me see," said he, "you had better ride one of my ponies; you shall do so in welcome if you think you can."

I was very much fatigued, and had answered him with indifference until he said this. I then rose and said to him with animation, "I shall be but too happy to try; I have been accustomed to ride Indian ponies all my life, and I would just now dare to attempt anything to avoid travelling these sand hills, and over these plains on foot."

The pony of which he spoke, was one he had bought of the Snake Indians, and was one of the most vicious and restive of its kind. Mr. Gilbert was leading it by a small cord beside the one he was riding, and I went to the wagon and took a Spanish saddle which Richard Cordon had there, and put it upon its back. I was so intent upon the one idea of riding, that it did not occur to me that the pony had no bridle on, and no sooner was the girth of the saddle securely fastened, than with an easy spring I took my seat in it, and the next moment we were careering over the plains at the top of pony speed. We were under motion, before the full state of the case flashed across my mind. I was upon the back of a loose and half-tamed pony, upon the verge of a boundless stretch of prairie and sand hills, with no bridle to guide or control the animal.

This part of the country was often frequented by the Snakes, the tribe from which the pony had been purchased, and possibly we were not far from one of their villages now ; and if so and should the pony chance to remember it, which it was very likely to do, it would not be long in taking me there.

This was about the middle of the afternoon, and Blood had gone forward with Gilbert's man, to look out a camping ground for the night, and the pony took their trail. But there was no certainty as to how long this would continue, for the instincts and recollections of these animals are strong, and my prospects were good for a swift ride to the nearest Indian camp.

During the first mile my spirits rose fully equal to the occasion. Holding easly to the pummel of the saddle, with my hair, which the first bound of the pony had unloosed, streaming wildly back, and my dress fluttering in the wind, I felt the inspiration of an untrammeled ranger of the plains, and for the first time since leaving the land of the "Saints," did I appreciate the sweet joy of freedom lately won. But reflection soon succeeded. Looking back, I noticed we were already nearly out of sight of the wagon ; while Gilbert was a long way off in pursuit, but instead of gaining upon me he was fast falling behind.

I took but little time to calculate the chances. Gathering up my skirts to free them from the danger of entanglement, then waiting for a favorable show of sand on which to cast my fortune, I vaulted lightly from the saddle and went rolling and spinning rough and tumble along the ground, until the velocity I held in common with the pony was broken. I arose unhurt, although *somewhat* disordered and soiled in dress.

When sufficiently collected to look about myself, I found the pony standing near me, apparently much astonished at what had happened. Mr. Gilbert soon came up, and by means of a lasso secured it. Waiting till the wagon arrived, Richard gave me a bridle for the animal, and I then remounted, secure in being able to guide it, and I had a delightful ride the remainder of the afternoon in company with Mr. Gilbert. We rode a long way in advance of the wagon, expecting each moment to overtake the men who were seeking a camp-ground, but at length the night closed in upon us, and we saw no signs of them.

The sky now began to thicken overhead, and the muttering of distant thunder, with flashes of lightning from the southwest, indicated rain. I had been so long unaccustomed to riding on horseback, that I began to tire of the unwonted luxury. With a headache that was every moment increasing, I was scarcely able to keep the saddle, while Mr. Gilbert, who wished to get into camp before the rain came on, urged the necessity of riding faster. This I was unable to do, and I asked him to ride on to find the camp, and leave me to sit down by the trail till the wagon came up. But as he was generous and manly, he at first declined. He said we were liable to stumble at any moment upon a band of Indians, and he could not think of leaving me, a woman, thus exposed upon the open prairie at night. But I insisted upon his doing so, as I should be less liable to attract attention thus, than with company; and if anything happened, I would mount my pony and fly, or hide in the grass as I thought best. He therefore went on, but handed me his revolver before he left, saying; "You had better take this, as you may find occasion to use it.

When he rode away, my pony was inclined to follow; and instead of being at liberty to crouch quietly down by the trail until the wagon overtook me, I now found myself engaged in a fierce contest with the vicious animal to prevent it from leaving me. I held him firmly by the bit, while, by rearing upon his hind feet, and plunging from side to side, and shaking its impudent little head, it was nearly successful in it. Then, to make the matter worse, and almost desperate, it commenced to rain. The thunder had slowly increased in nearness, until now it bellowed directly overhead, and rolled in wild volleys, rumbling and clattering away off upon the wide prairies, and as if there met by an opposing wave of sound, it was forced, with a deafening roar, back again, just in time to meet other similar ones from the four quarters, to surge in broken howlings, about the struggling pony and myself, as a centre. But if the thunder was terrific, the quick succession of light that flashed from the sky, and broke in jets of fire along the plains, was appalling. Blinded one moment by the fierce lightning, and the next, stunned by the thick darkness, and deluged by the rain, awed and subdued by the crash and the strife of the terrible forces that tore among the maddened elements, the pony and myself, as if impelled by a mutual sympathy, gave over our puny strife, and looked with astonishment upon the sublime and awful drama.

The sagacious animal, with ears pointed and head erect, and nostrils distended, with eyes that reflected back the fire from the clouds, surveyed the storm from every point of the compass; and when satisfied, and after repeating a wild snort at each fresh volley of the thunder, nestled close by my side, with apparently no wish to leave me; and as the uproar began to subside, turned his face from the storm, and was quiet again.

At length the storm passed away, leaving me thoroughly drenched and chilled. I cannot tell how long I shivered beside the pony, waiting and listening for the wagon. It was something after ten o'clock, that while looking carefully into the darkness on every side, I discovered a single light a great way off in the direction we were travelling. It was faint at first, but soon increased in brightness, and gave me great uneasiness; for as we were not in the habit of indulging ourselves in the luxury of camp-fires at night, I was certain this could not be the work of our party; and hence it must be that of the Indians, who, I imagined, had discovered and massacred Mr. Gilbert and his men, and had now built this fire to decoy us to a similar fate. I was still revolving in my mind the probabilities of the case, when the welcome sound of wheels slowly trundling along the trail gave me new hope; and soon after, Richard drove up, with my mother and sister, and were saluted by the pony with a sudden snort, which brought the party to a stand. I was not long in making myself known, and found them as much alarmed about the light as myself. We all came to the conclusion, after exchanging views upon the subject, that escape was impossible, and that probably our trail had been dogged during the day by the Indians with the design of cutting us off at night.

It was suggested to Richard that it would be as well to know the worst state of the case at once; and proposed he should take the pony, and go as near the fire as possible, and see what we had to expect. To this he consented, and when he rode away into the darkness, we had but small hope of seeing him again. "God help my child, if he does not come back," said Lizzie, as she strained the sleeping infant to her anxious breast.

I got into the wagon and held the reins, and we waited with what patience we could for the result. We were at least two miles from the light, and some time must necessarily elapse before he could accomplish that distance and return. We waited a long while, and heard nothing of him. I held the lines in one hand, and the revolver in the other, determined, if we were molested, to make the most of what means of defence we had at hand.

We grew every moment more anxious, and were about to yield ourselves up to despair, when a slight noise was heard in the grass near us. It was like the soft step of a moccasined foot; and we could well imagine it to be the stealthy tread of an Indian. We were sensible that it came towards us, and yet so intense was the darkness of the night, that we found it impossible to recognize each other, and much less could we make out the cause of our alarm.

We held a whispered consultation; but were quite at a loss

to know what course to take. Lizzie said she knew it was an Indian, and mother added, "We shall all lose our scalps, if it is."

We all felt our case to be desperate. As for myself, I thought this to be but a fitting termination of the extraordinary adventures of the day; but the reflection of a moment, convinced me there was no time to indulge in childish fears. Giving the lines to Lizzie, I prepared myself for whatever might come; and getting the revolver ready, and in hand, waited the result, with such calmness and self-possession as I had in command. Mother said, in a low whisper, "Perhaps it may be Richard."

"No," replied Lizzie, "it is an Indian, and you must be certain and kill him the first fire, or we are lost."

"What good will it do?" said my mother, whose strong good sense never forsook her, even under excitement. "For if there is one Indian, there may be twenty, and you cannot expect to kill them all."

But I had made up my mind what to do. The object of our alarm was now so near, that although I was unable to see it, I judged it would not be difficult to send a ball through the miscreant, as I could mark with certainty the direction; and drawing the revolver to a rest across my left hand, I was about to pull upon it steadily, and, as I believed, calmly, with the intention of firing, when the stillness of the night was broken by the gruff voice of Richard, saying, in a petulant tone, "There, cuss the fools, I met them coming back to meet us, before I reached the fire."

"Richard!" exclaimed Lizzie and my mother at the same breath.

I lowered the muzzle of the revolver, and dizzy with the reaction which followed the sudden relaxation of my overstrained spirit, I said, choking with disgust and emotion:

"Richard, your folly had nearly cost you your life. Why did you come up so still?"

"How did I know but you were all dead, and the wagon was in the possession of the Indians?" said he, heartlessly.

The coward had evidently chosen to frighten us, rather than take the precaution to investigate the state of the case, which he could have done with safety to himself, and without harm to us.

After overcoming in a measure the excitement, we began to comprehend the cause of the fire, which Richard said had been built by Gilbert's men, while the former was absent to picket the horses in some fine grass he had discovered by a stream not far from the camp. "They wished me to tell you," he added, "they are very sorry for having frightened you; and they have made some coffee, and prepared a good supper, which is now waiting for you."

We were not long in arriving at the camp; and after warming our chilled and stiffened limbs, and accepting cheerfully the apologies of the two men who had built the fire, we had an excellent supper, which we all enjoyed with great relish.

It was after midnight before the fire was put out, and we were asleep. The day had been one of unusual adventure and peril, but its close had left us pleased and satisfied, and nothing short of a genuine alarm of Indians could have disturbed our heavy slumbers for the remainder of the night.

I have thus given in detail the events of this one day, not only because they were remarkable in themselves, but as I have before intimated, because I do not propose to detain the reader with a minute account of this journey; and since it so happened that many of the marked features of it were thus crowded into a single day, this may perhaps serve as a general index to our life upon the plains.

The next morning found us unharmed, and the march was resumed with the more courage, as we were now nearing Fort Laramie. Two days before arriving there, Mr. Gilbert left us, as he wished to push on at a greater speed than was within the power of our ponies to accomplish. We were now so near the fort that we had little to fear from the Indians, and we parted from him with emotions of deepest gratitude, for the protection the presence of his party had afforded us.

I take pleasure in saying of Mr. Gilbert, that he appeared to be a kindly and honorable gentleman, inclined to noble and generous impulses.

After making two encampments alone, we arrived safely at Laramie, where we found Lieutenant Foot, and several other officers of the army, who with their wives had boarded with my brother Howard at Fort Kearny several years before this; and we were received with great kindness by them on that account.

These ladies greatly commended us for leaving the Mormons, and took it for granted we were not to return to the valley. As for my mother and myself, we had but little to say upon the subject. We were yet too far from the borders of civilization to feel ourselves safe; and moreover we had learned to distrust Richard too much to confide to him our real intentions, and we were still in his hands.

CHAPTER XXXVI.

WE had been at Laramie I think two days, when an express came in from Fort Kearny, asking for a few soldiers; and giving the information that several emigrant trains had been cut off, between that and Laramie; and that the Indians were out upon the trail in force. This was very discouraging news for us. The army officers advised Richard by no means to attempt to make the journey alone, but to wait, and join if he could some party going to Kearny, sufficiently strong to afford us protection.

Notwithstanding we had expected some delay from this state of things, it soon transpired that a company of Government wagons employed in drawing corn from Kearny to Laramie, was to return to the former place the next afternoon.

A party of U. S. soldiers was to leave also for the same place the next morning, in answer to the summons by express but these last would move too fast for us, and we were recommended to join the wagons, as that party was sufficiently strong to ensure our safety.

The wagon master was a grey-headed old man from Weston, Mo., with whom the officers kindly used their influence in our behalf, which proved to be of great service to us afterwards. His name was Samuel Foster, and he rendered us all the assistance needed.

This party, which we joined next morning, moved but slowly, and we were thus enabled to camp by them at night, until so near fort Kearny as to be past danger from the Indians. After this, we made our way alone, without further accident or delay, and had the great good fortune to arrive at Perry, Pike county, Illinois, about the middle of August, 1856, having made the journey from great Salt Lake city within the space of three months. Here we met, after a separation of years, my oldest sister, Mrs. Deuzenbury, with a joy those who have followed us thus far can well imagine. My mother, now well spent in years, and broken in health, and above all, bowed to the dust with the sad conviction that Mormonism, for which she had sacrificed so much, was not only an error, and a cruel delusion, but a wicked fraud : she—my mother, now stood where fifteen years before she had made this sacrifice in good faith, and where she had buried my father ; and wept such bitter tears as should have silenced the voice of censure : howbeit, when once in the midst of these tears and unavailing regrets for the wrong she had done her children a soft voice which she had heard that day for the first time, for many years, whispered in her quick ear, doubly quick to words of blame, "How could you, my mother, have taken the family to such a"—— But the sentence was stayed, and my mother's tears ceased to flow, as she said with a strange mingling of enthusiasm for the faith as she first received it, and mortification at its prostitution since—" My child, but for Mormonism, I should not be able now to hear your question, or feel the pain of your censure. You do not remember that a Mormon elder, through the divine authority conferred upon him by the Prophet Joseph, restored my lost hearing. And though I now sadly mourn the perversion of our noble faith to unworthy purposes by the present Heads of the Church, am I to be blamed, that I still remember the time when it was pure; or that I accepted at the hands of the great Prophet Joseph, the evidence of his exalted mission, confirmed by a miracle wrought upon my own person ?"

We spent two months at my sister's, in the full enjoyment of a reunion with our kindred, and in the free exercise of our natural rights in a Christian land; a boon to which we had been strangers for the last fifteen years.

It would be difficult to convey anything like a clear notion of our experience during these two months. Everything was new, not only in the manners and customs, and dress of the people, but in all their aims and ideas. I was particularly struck with the remarkable fact, that they were in the enjoyment of the absolute right of acting and thinking indepenently; and governed by established laws; it was not easy to free myself from the oppressive habit of squaring my conduct and wishes to comply with the Prophet's " counsel." But as yet I had heard nothing from my husband. This was now the only corroding care of my life. I supposed him to be in California, but had heard nothing from him for the last two years. The Prophet told me before I left Salt Lake city that I must never think of seeing him again : and now Richard Cordon watched me with untiring care, evidently with a view to prevent my holding correspondence with him. I managed, however, to get other members of my family to write, and used every precaution not to arouse Richard's suspicions as to my aims.

About the last of October we left Illinois for Hornellsville, Steuben county, N. Y., where we arrived in safety. Here we found a large number of my father's connections, as well as those of my mother, by whom we were well received.

Remaining here until February of the following winter, I heard from my husband, with a joy, compared to which all other joys are but nothing. He was alive ; I could wait patiently while he was unharmed. He sent me assurances of his love, and said soon, very soon, he would be with me.

When Richard knew what information I had received from my husband, he was at first furious, and said: "*You shall never see him.*" But he had forgotten he was not in a Mormon land, where no law but the will of the Prophet is recognized ; and very quickly afterwards he saw the necessity of greater caution in speech while I was surrounded by the friends of my family. He at once assumed a different line of conduct. Treating me with the greatest attention, he wished to induce me to go back to Illinois, where he hoped to keep me under his control ; and if I could not be induced to return to Utah, I have no doubt as to what he designed my fate should be.

Feeling myself unsafe while near him, it was arranged that he should go on to Illinois with his wife, where I was to follow with my mother at a specified time. But when he was gone, I took care to put myself beyond his reach; and since then my whereabouts has been a subject of some speculation and uncertainty as far as he was concerned.

When my new-found connections heard my story, they insisted that its publication was due the world; and I have, by their advice, and under a high sense of duty, made written and verbal statements to a friend who has prepared the foregoing narrative.

When Richard Cordon heard of my intention to publish an account of my Mormon experience, he returned at once to Steuben county to find me, and being unable to do so, was very much exasperated.

In conversation with one of my uncles, George Stephens, he said: "If Mary Ettie attempts to expose us (the Mormons), she shall rue it. It will be a dear job for her. Her blood shall flow."

About two months after this, some excitement was created within the circle of my immediate friends by the appearance of a rough looking stranger among them, who, upon various pretences, wished to find me. He was described, by those who saw him, as every inch a villain in appearance; and was so persevering in his search, that measures were about to be taken for his arrest when he disappeared.

I think my readers will not fail to sympathize with me when they are informed, in these closing lines of my story, that as yet, I have not seen my husband. That although I am in daily and hourly expectation of his coming, I wait as one whose hope is well nigh exhausted. The Prophet, Brigham Young, said I should never see him, and the Danite to whose care I have been intrusted in this land of the Gentiles, has said the same. Will they kill him? September was the latest point of time beyond which he would allow any earthly consideration to detain him, as he has written me; and this is the first of October, and he comes not yet.

CHAPTER XXXVII.

CONTINUATION OF THE NARRATIVE.

The "closing lines" of the foregoing Narrative, went to press about the middle of October, 1857, by which the sad story of Mrs. Smith and her mother was brought down to that date. Since then, events of the highest importance to them have transpired. With a view of giving completeness to these personal histories, as well as to furnish full and satisfactory answers to the numerous inquiries from various quarters of the country, it is deemed proper and advisable to add the following new facts.

Early in the fall of 1857, Mrs. Smith went to Old Forge, Luzern County, Pennsylvania, to the residence of her sister, Mrs. Phebe Knapp, near the place of her birth. The life of the mother was slowly ebbing away; and it was fitting she should seek a tomb beside the crystal waters of the noisy Lackawanna, where much of her early life had been passed. Before leaving Hornellsville, Mrs. Coray had been bleeding violently at the lungs: and although she rallied somewhat at first, under the bracing influence of the pure air of the mountains, and the kindly attentions and sympathy of her kindred, yet it was soon evident that her race was nearly run.

She went to Pennsylvania still strong in her Mormon faith: and still believing in the "Prophet Joseph." The state of mind indicated in the "concluding chapter" (page 385) was yet applicable. But toward spring, as the signs of an immediate dissolution thickened about her, that confidence in the "Prophet" slowly gave way; and as the memories of childhood, which the sight of former associations recalled, rushed back upon her, with their thousand gentle and touching recollections, there came with them the image of the Cross, and her childhood's hope of salvation through Christ; and when the summons finally came, she received it with joy, and died a Christian. The seed that had "fallen among thorns," had at length struggled into the light; and at the last moment bore fruit abundantly. By her own request the "Endowment robes" were laid aside, and she received a Christian burial by the side of her ancestors, at the hands of the Christian associates of her youth.

But during all this time, Mrs. Smith, in addition to the anxieties incident to the care of her mother, was watching and waiting the return of the husband, for whose safety she entertained so many fears.

With repeated assurances of his safety and his good faith, month after month rolled away, and still he came not. Then followed cruel rumors which she was unable to reconcile with his known character. Time, and this continued suspense began to tell fearfully upon her health. But she had yet to meet other forms of Mormon intrigue for which she found herself but ill prepared.

About the last of April, while watching by the sick-bed

of her mother, she received a letter purporting to be from her nephew, Warren Duzenbury; who lived at Perry, Pike Co., Ill. Although, upon further examination, the letter was found to bear the unmistakable marks of Mormon influence, if not of Mormon origin, yet at the time, it was received by her as genuine. The letter stated with apparent frankness that the writer had seen a man then living near him, but lately returned from California, who knew her husband, Reuben P. Smith, and that he knew Mr. Smith had married into a family of wealth and position in Oregon, and was then living with his new wife in California. This was too much. Absence from her husband, while hope of his return yet remained to her, she could bear. But the idea that Reuben P. Smith could desert her, was a new horror, so completely overwhelming, that it cut off even the wish to fathom the mystery involved in the web of contradictions among which she found herself entangled.

She who had successfully baffled the intrigues of the "Prophet," and had risen superior to danger, and fatigue, and suffering, during the fifteen long years of her sad Mormon experience; now sunk without resistance before a fact—if fact it was—that rendered her life simply worthless. Her strong will, which had borne itself so heroically through so many difficulties, for the first time faltered; and her physical energy, wanting this support, faltered with it. Obstructed circulation intervened, and the delicate machinery of the heart refused to do its office. Danger of a permanent disease of the heart was imminent, and a fatal termination was only averted by copious bleeding and other timely treatment, skillfully administered by the attending physician

(Dr. Henry A. Dorr, of Pittston, Pa.) When immediate danger was thus averted, it occurred to her that possibly this story of the infidelity of her husband was a Mormon invention. She then took measures, by availing herself of the assistance of her brother-in-law, Burier Griffin, then in California, to solve the problem at once. It was better to know the truth, whatever it might be. Nothing could be more fatal to her than continued uncertainty. But, as will be seen by Mr. Smith's statement, while Mr. Griffin was thus making his investigations in California, and before he had found Mr. Smith, the latter, by a rare good fortune, happened to receive one of the many letters his wife had written him, which had the effect to render the assistance of Mr. Griffin unnecessary.

The reader will understand, that up to this time, most of their letters sent through the mails had been mysteriously diverted from the channel intended and indicated by the direction; but that both had received, at various times, letters, which as has since been ascertained, misrepresented both; with the apparent intention of keeping them apart.

In a state of mind which it is impossible for those fully to appreciate who are not well versed in the mysteries of Mormonism, Mrs. Smith was still waiting, with but small hope, the return of her husband; yet having confidence in his good faith. Whatever else had happened or might happen, she still clung to a belief in that honest manliness which at one and the same time had won her to himself, and had been instrumental in bringing her to doubt the "Prophet" and Mormonism. Time wore on, and with it wore away the life of the mother.

One evening Mrs. Smith sat by the mother's bedside, and watched her slow and troubled breathing with unusual anxiety. The physician had just told her what she might expect within the next three days. The journey of the mother's eventful life was about to end. It was the 14th of August, 1858. A calm twilight had followed a quiet sunset. The hush and silence which hung upon the creeping shadows were relieved only by the impatient murmur of the river near by—the bright and fretful Lackawanna, which "uttered its voice" from its rocky bed that night, with all its wonted earnestness.

Who shall fathom those two human hearts! The crushed and nearly broken spirit of the silent watcher by the bed of death—and the dying mother. The world had dealt harshly enough with both, but with one it had nearly lost its hold.

There is something infinitely touching in the going down to the grave, slowly, and sedately, and alone, of a well balanced mind and a strong will; with its full load of errors—crippled by age, and disappointment, and that stern necessity which knows no relenting—if haply the fall be broken by the Rock of Ages. It resolves the enigma of life, and the mystery of death—submission—faith! "Christ receive us."

But who shall analyze the emotions of Mrs. Smith! Why does *she* yet tarry? Why does the mother go alone? Had they not suffered, and explored, and believed, and doubted, and apostatized, together? And now, had they not come back together to the faith of their ancestors? Had not she *too* finished her work? When strong men of the world, who were governed merely by the questionable maxims of political prudence, had wanted the courage to say frankly to their fellow men what they knew of the abominations of Mormonism, had she not spoken openly the truth, and trusted the issue to God?

What, though the public authorities may be misled for the time by officious Mormons in disguise; and what though injudicious "Proclamations," and "Peace Commissions," may compromise the national dignity by unworthy negotiations with outlaws; and by making terms with crime; shall not the future public sense avenge the outrage?

Truth has nothing to fear from the future. It is only the truckling importunity of the hour—at once audacious and time-serving—that is liable to overpower it. That "Book of Martyrs" is defective which records only the *deaths* of the sufferers for truth's sake. It is the living and unscrupulous present that can roast most cruelly, while it spares with ostentatious show; and pursues absolutely without mercy for the attainment of momentary ends; with entire indifference as to what possible opinion posterity may entertain as to it.

Were these her thoughts? Perhaps. Whatever they may have been, they were interrupted, when it was near dark, by a knock at the door. Then followed the inquiry by a manly voice: "Does Mrs. Smith, lately from Utah, live here?" That voice could not be mistaken. She had last heard it in Mormon land, more than five long, long years ago; and she had not forgotten it. After looking for several moments at the stranger standing in the open door, where he was partly obscured by the darkness, she said: "Oh, Smith! Reuben!!" Mrs. Knapp, who had heard the knock and was about to answer the summons at the door, was nearly paralyzed when she heard this exclamation from her sister; for she felt she was about to realize the fear which had of late oppressed her, viz., that Mary Ettie would in the end go mad, if her husband should not return. She therefore said to her: "Ettie, come with me. You need sleep. You have watched with mother so long, you are worn out. That is not your husband."

But it did not matter Two true, human souls, long separated by Mormon intrigue, were now face to face. Who shall understand the mute investigation which their brief communion vouchsafed them? It had been represented to each that the other had married again; and now both silently questioned of the past. But good faith needs not the intervention of words to make itself understood. The stranger faltered, but not long, for he saw how it was; and as Mrs. Knapp essayed to lead her sister away, he said, in a tone of voice wanting somewhat the firmness it possessed at first: "She is right. I am Smith. She is my wife!"

We leave the reader to imagine the scene, and the explanations which followed. Although the mother was already too far gone to speak with ease, she gave Mr. Smith a smile of recognition, as she felt his hand and heard his voice; and afterwards she was able to say, "I always told Mary Ettie you would come." These were her last words. She lingered, however, for three days longer, and died on the 17th.

Her funeral was attended by a large concourse of her sympathizing friends and old neighbors, as well as by many strangers who had heard her story, from the Wyoming and Lackawanna valleys and the surrounding hills; and, as was very fitting, the religious services were conducted by Elder

Mott, the Baptist minister at Hyde Park, Luzern county, Pa., who had known Mrs. Coray and her husband when they were young, which he stated from the pulpit; he also said, he had kept track of the family most of the time since.

The little that yet remains to be told, in order to a full understanding of the foregoing, will be found in the statement of Reuben P. Smith, annexed.

DANSVILLE, N. Y., Sept. 30, 1858.

Statement of REUBEN P. SMITH, *in continuation of the account given of him by his wife,* MARY ETTIE V. SMITH; *from page 242 of her Narrative, entitled "Fifteen Years among the Mormons," etc., made at Danville, N. Y. August* 28, 1858.

STATEMENT.

I propose to give a brief account of my personal adventures since my separation from my wife, so far as it is connected with her Narrative, and particularly so far as it may serve to illustrate and expose Mormonism; but before doing this, I deem it proper to give some account of my birth and parentage.

I was born near West Union, Adams county, Ohio. My grandfather, Reuben Smith, had three sons: Joseph, Joel and John B. The last-named was my father. My uncle Joel is now living on Brush Creek, near my birth-place; and Joseph at Selina, Ill. My father moved to Stringtown, Iowa, where he died in 1847. My mother was Elizabeth Chapman, and a sister of Joseph Chapman; the latter somewhat celebrated as a politician and stump orator at the West. He

CONTINUATION OF THE NARRATIVE.

was an old-school Democrat, and edited and published a paper entitled the "Koon Skinner," at Indianapolis. He was better known there as "Crowing Chapman." He commanded a company of volunteers in the Mexican war, and died on his way back.

Since my return from California, I have examined carefully the foregoing Narrative of my wife, Mary Ettie V. Smith; and as far as I have been able to discover, it is correct; with the unimportant exception, that she appears to have confounded my *object* in going to California, mentioned on page 240, with that mentioned on page 242. It was at the latter time that I went on my own business. At the time first mentioned, I was in the employ of Major Hollman, Indian Agent of the Territory. I accompanied him to Humboldt River and Carson Valley, where he went to distribute the goods due the different Indian tribes in that vicinity. We were gone about three months; and before our return to Great Salt Lake, we crossed the Sierra Nevada into California, to sell some extra horses the major had on hand. Our party was composed of young men, Mormons and Gentiles picked up for the occasion at Great Salt Lake. The Indian interpreter on this expedition was a Canadian Frenchman, named Papa, between whom and myself there soon grew up a strong friendship. Papa was an old mountaineer, one of that celebrated class of rangers who knew the mountains and the plains, and loved them immensely. He wore under his greasy hunting shirt a brave and true heart, and was influenced only by honest purposes. He had conceived a strong dislike to the Mormons, and was always seeking some way to thwart their aims.

He once said, in his rough and droll way, that he would give twenty years of his life, for the privilege of playing for as many minutes upon Brigham Young's house with a cannon, if he only knew his precious "Twelve Apostles" were with him. When he found how I was situated, he volunteered to get my wife away. He said, if I would go on to California, he would bring her to me within the year, which I have no doubt he would have done, had he lived. His family were with his father-in-law, at Devil's Gate, on the Sweetwater, near the South Pass. He left us at Salt Lake, to go home; but we soon heard of his death, and I could never learn the cause of it. His imprudence in speech had probably brought him under the notice of the Mormon authorities.

It was in the fall of 1852 that Major Hollman's party returned to the city. The major, immediately after this, went on to Fort Bridger, to look after something connected with his official duties; and having been delayed unavoidably, he was overtaken by the snows, and was obliged to pass the winter there.

He had left his horses and mules in my charge, and in order to procure good grass, I took them to Utah, forty miles south of the city. I left a man to look after them, and returned to Salt Lake City; and soon after, two of the mules were stolen.

The mules were missed about the time of the passage of the Mormon train from the city to San Bernardino, in charge, I think, of Charles C. Rich and Amasy Lyman, by whom I have always believed they were taken. I advertised for them in the "Deseret News," but the only thing that ever came of it was, the knowing laugh it occasioned among the Mormons. This was one of the many things that opened my eyes to the real state of things in Utah, and more fully determined me to leave the Territory.

As will be seen by the beginning of chap. 23 of the foregoing Narrative, I had made arrangements to go to California with Mr. Mac. He could not delay; and although Major Hollman had not returned, I went on to Bear River leaving the horses in the care of John Hammer, a Mormon,* expecting Mac would join me there, and bring my wife. But it appears that after I had left the city, some horses, and other mules were stolen, and when Major Hollman returned, late in the spring, he was told by the Mormons that I had taken them.

The major, after some trouble, found them all, except the two mules first mentioned, in the possession of Mormons, who claimed they had bought them of me before I left, which I afterwards heard Major Hollman at first believed, but I am well satisfied he finally understood how it was, for he afterwards came to California, and passed within two miles of where he knew I was stopping; and although he spoke of me, and expressed a wish to see me, he said nothing that indicated a loss of confidence. Had I been informed of his being there at the time, I should have taken all pains to have met him; and I know I could have shown him that the hand of Mormonism was at the bottom of it. Indeed, I have since learned by my wife and others, that the mystery of the

* This Hammer is the brother-in-law of John Norton, the "Danite;" whether he is himself a "Danite" I never knew. As to Norton, see Chap. xxiv. and xxv of this Narrative.

disappearance of Major Hollman's stock, was a standing joke among the Mormons at the city for a long time afterward. He is now in the States, as I understand, and I should be glad to have this statement meet his eye. My relations with him in Utah were of the most pleasant and agreeable character.

It was the middle of April, 1853, that I left great Salt Lake City for the last time. I had some young cattle which I wished to take with me, and I joined my drove with one of about the same size, owned by Charles Hunt, and we travelled in company for mutual protection. We were also accompanied by Captain Mott and his family, who were going to Carson Valley. This Captain Mott is the man mentioned on page 55 of the foregoing Narrative. He had brought the bell there mentioned, with his own team all the way from Nauvoo, and when it was delivered safe and sound at Salt Lake, the Prophet, contrary to Mott's reasonable expectations, refused to pay for this important service. Mott thereupon grew dissatisfied, and sold a claim which he had on the American Fork, about ten miles north of Provo, and prepared to leave, thinking, that if he went to the Mormon settlement at Carson Valley, his design possibly might not be understood. But the Heads of the Church were not deceived, and when we had arrived at Willow Creek, sixty miles from the city, he was taken back, upon the pretence that the title to the claim which he had sold was defective. After he had shown this to be untrue, he was permitted to rejoin his family; but he was again arrested when we had proceeded fifteen miles further, upon the pretence that his tithing had not been paid.

We went on to Bear River, where we all encamped, to await the result as to his case, as well as to watch for the coming of my wife, where Mac had agreed to bring her. We were now eighty miles from the Mormon capital. It was uncertain how long we might be detained, or what the real intentions of the Church toward us were.

After a few days, however, Captain Mott came to us again, accompanied by some Gentile emigrants, by whom I learned that my wife had been detected in her efforts to escape, and that she was to be detained.

I saw how useless it would be to remain longer for her, and our train then moved on for California. I had not yet heard of the death of Papa, and I entertained the hope that he would be able to carry out his proposed plan of her rescue. When I afterwards heard that he was dead, I felt that there was but small hope of her escape, at least not through the agency of any power outside the "Church." There were several Mormons at the city who pretended to be my friends, and through whose good offices I still hoped to regain my wife.

Our train advanced without further interference or delay, and we commenced our slow journey over the plains and sandy deserts, to Humboldt River, where we arrived in the fore part of June, without other accident than the loss of ten or twelve head of cattle, stolen as we supposed by the Indians, under cover of a stampede. How it was in our case we were unable to determine; but many, and perhaps most of these depredations upon the property of emigrants while crossing from Utah to California, as also those in the mountains, are the works of Mormons disguised as Indians.

The Mormons, as a people, have been greatly distinguished for enterprise, and for a rapid growth in wealth. Success undoubtedly has a tendency, with many of us, to cover a "multitude of sins;" but perhaps it has not occurred to those who profess to find in this *apparent* success of Mormonism, *as a social and political system*, evidence of industry and frugality, and as a consequence, a proof of that high state of *social virtue* and *moral rectitude*, which right aims (however much misguided), will often secure; to ask the question, *how a people could become so rich in so short a time who produce so little* of any article capable of a profitable exchange with the rest of mankind. The overflowing coffers of the "Prophet" are unquestionably more or less indebted to the liberal contributions of converts from foreign countries; but making a fair allowance for this "source of revenue," we are still unable to account for the unparalleled wealth of the "Church."

The "Church store" at Great Salt Lake city is always full, and the "Church brand" is borne by innumerable cattle, and the amount of public buildings, and roads, and bridges, and the work and money already expended upon the temple, is almost without a precedent in the history of human enterprise. It must be recollected that while all these public enterprises have been in successful execution, every member of the Church has had his own houses and barns to build, and his own farm to bring under cultivation, and when these things have been hastily put in order, he has been obliged to take his turn in filling a foreign mission, and hence, few of them can be producers at home.

The conclusion is unavoidable, that, from the very nature

of the facts of the case, and from the known character and aims of the people, there must be some important source of revenue, other than that which appears upon the surface of things in Utah. The Mormons are enterprising—fiercely and unrelentingly so—but theirs is not the energy of an honest purpose; nor are they *producers*, but *appropriators* of whatever comes in their way. "The earth is the Lord's, and the "Saints are to possess the earth." This is the key to Mormonism. What they cannot do by force, they will effect by fraud and cunning.

The "Prophet" has interdicted the working in the gold mines in California by his people; but the discovery of gold there, has been the saving clause with the "Church" in Utah. When everything else failed, there was one resource left. There were the California emigrants to rob and plunder; and they have been mercilessly robbed and plundered: and latterly, more than at first, it has been deemed safest to cut off all chance of detection, by killing the people they have robbed.

A full record of these robberies, often accompanied as they have been by assassination, would be perfectly appalling. It would be the darkest of those yet unwritten chapters of the secret history of the "Church in the wilderness." Nothing else, among the annals of the "West," can bear to it the shadow of a comparison. Age, sex, helplessness—the appeal for mercy—simple mercy from the defenceless; nothing—nothing could stay the hand that would sooner "forget its cunning," than disobey this pretended "Prophet of God."

Is it possible that Mr. Buchanan comprehended the character of the men between whom and the halter he has interposed his official protection? If he did, God help him.

We left Captain Mott at Carson Valley, and after recruiting our cattle for several weeks upon the rich grasses which abound in that vicinity, we crossed the Sierra Nevada into California, and arrived without material accident at Cosumnes, Sacramento county, where I sold my stock, and remained for eight months in the employ of Solomon Mizer. After this I worked in the mines at Spanish Camp, four months, and then went to Sacramento City, where I remained six months; when my brother, William J. Smith, came to me from Iowa, and we went to Live Oak City, and bought a mining claim together, which we worked thoroughly for three months, at a dead loss; for owing to the peculiarity of the soil, it failed to pay.

We then bought a farm on Cache Creek, which we worked with better success for two years, and were making money, when we were dispossessed by an order of the court in favor of other parties, claiming under a Spanish title. We then went to Suisun Valley, where we bought a rancho, and remained until July 19th, 1858, when I left California for the east.

During all this time, the one great aim of my life, to which all others were subordinate, was the rescue of Mary Ettie from her Mormon imprisonment.

While at Cosumnes, I met Riley Judd, as I supposed at the time accidentally, who was just from Salt Lake, and he told me my wife had made an attempt to escape, by disguising herself in men's clothing, but had failed. He professed to be friendly to us, and I sent her thirty dollars by him, ten of which he kept, telling Ettie it had been stolen from him. I soon after received a letter from my wife, acknowledging the letter, and part of the money sent by Judd, but telling me to send no more money after that, as the Mormons would manage to get it from her. I received after this one or two letters, but finally I failed to get anything through the mails that I recognized as being from her hand, but I had no difficulty in keeping up a correspondence with others at Salt Lake City, who had taken an interest in us. I frequently received letters from Wiley Norton, but his statements were so contradictory, and unaccountable, that they only served to increase my embarrassment.

Through these channels, the only ones now open to me, I was soon informed that Mary Ettie now regretted her marriage, and that it would be easy enough for her to get to me if she wished. In fact, that she had repudiated me, and was already seeking another husband.

At this time, and during my stay in California, it so happened, either by accident or design, that the Mormons always kept track of my whereabouts. Whenever I changed my place of residence, which I often did quietly to avoid them, some one from Salt Lake would soon appear at my new locality, though before unknown there, and inquire me out, on the score of old acquaintance, always professing the greatest friendship for me, and giving some new account of Mary Ettie having a tendency to estrange us.

Some time in September, 1856, I received a letter from my wife, and, at the same time, from others of her family, giving me the information that she had effected an escape from Utah, and was then at Perry, Pike county, Ill. The letter involved several contradictions, and the account it gave of her escape was not satisfactory. This, with the conflicting accounts before received from Utah, suggested the idea of looking further into the facts before deciding what to do. I therefore wrote to my brother, H. C. Smith, at Stringtown, Iowa, and awaited his answer. But soon after this I received another letter from her, saying, in a very few and hard words, that she had married a man by the name of Thompson. There were other things in the letter; but this was all I read. This was enough—too much.

I happened to be in Sacramento City the following winter (1857), and there met a Mormon with whom I had had a passing acquaintance in Utah, from whence he had just arrived. He said he was on his way to China as a missionary. Among other things, he told me—apparently without having any interest in the matter—that Mary Ettie had lately been married to a man named Thompson. He said he was well acquainted with her new husband.

Some time in the following spring, I received another letter, purporting to be from a Mr. Watkins, of Illinois, giving me the same pleasant information. I knew no such man; *

---

* It is now known that at this time Allen Cunningham was with Richard Cordon, and that the "stranger" from California (believed to be a Mormon), referred to by Warren Duzenbury in his letter to Mary Ettie (who was represented as saying, "I know R. P. Smith, and *know* he has married again"), was also, at this time, at Perry, Pike Co., Ill., and was living in the same house with Cordon.

The character of Cunningham will be understood by referring to pages 235 and 367 of the foregoing Narrative.

The fact that these three rogues were together, leaves but little doubt as to their "mission," and still less doubt as to who wrote this **Watkins** letter.

but the singular agreement of his statement with the information before received, as to the one important fact, viz., that Mary Ettie had been faithless, and was now lost to me, seemed to cut off all inducement for further investigation. The statement over her own signature appeared to be conclusive. It did not occur to me at the time, that possibly the letters bearing her name were forgeries; and it was long afterward, and under a more fortunate state of things, that Mary Ettie herself pointed out to me the fact, that the letter of Watkins, and the one bearing her own signature, had evidently been written by one and the same hand, and that neither were written by her.

Things were in this position until January, 1858, when my brother wrote me that he had made what investigation he could, but that he found himself embarrassed in coming to a determination as to the merits of the case, but that he was satisfied that one of two things was true, "Mary Ettie," he said, " is either the best or the most questionable of women."

He had not seen her, but she had not married again. This letter was followed by another from him, under date of June 12th, 1858, saying frankly and emphatically that he was now satisfied, that for reasons which were as yet not clear to him, interested parties were seeking to keep Mary Ettie and myself apart; but that he believed her every way deserving; that if he had such a wife, no earthly power should keep him from her.

I had before this determined to seek her out, and solve the mystery for myself, as soon as my business could be arranged; and yet I felt I had but small foundation for hope.

from all I knew of Mary Ettie, I believed her incapable of deception. She was frank to a fault. Had she not told me over her own signature that she had married again? And yet I wished to see and hear from her own mouth what explanation was possible; not so much that I yet clung to the hope that she was not altogether lost to me, as that she should, if she could, vindicate her sex: for I am free to acknowledge, that had I found her at last wanting in good faith, I should not have looked for that virtue elsewhere. But while in a state of mind wanting equally the determination to go, or to refrain from going, I received a letter which I at once recognized as being from under her own hand. It had about it the odor of other days, and at once determined me what to do. The letter reached me Saturday, July 17th 1858, and Monday, the 19th, two days after, I left Suisun Valley, California, on my way to find her.

It is often easier to do, than to decide what to do. The journey from San Francisco to New York, by the Isthmus, was accomplished in due time without accident, and on the 14th of August, 1858, I arrived at Old Forge, Luzern Co. Pa., where, as before narrated, I found Mary Ettie.

CHAPTER XXXVIII.

RISE, PROGRESS, AND PRESENT CONDITION OF MORMONISM.

"THERE is no God but God,"—might have been said for humanity,—being true: but when the great impostor added, "and Mohammed is His Prophet," he disclosed the self-seeker, in the shrewdest way, certainly, but he had taken the divinity out of his rallying-cry. Henceforth, he was the pretender, and his success became a question of arms, and of worldliness.

This element,—the yoking of a great truth to an absurd untruth,—has entered into all the successful delusions since that time: and it is not to the discredit of religion, that its indulgent mantle has been invoked to cover or mystify and give sanctity to the worst causes and the basest men.

"The Church of Jesus Christ of Latter-day Saints," is an enunciation of this sort.

It is a sadly interesting study,—this history of the world's delusion,—religious delusions, and the peoples, and the times, and other conditions necessary to the success of them.

If this subject were fully investigated, it would be developed, that important delusions have never, perhaps, been the outgrowth of any one mind; but, that the times and places of these exceptional commotions have been characterized by some peculiar want, or error, or extreme, among the people.

Forty-five years ago, a singular tendency had developed itself, in the State of New York, and perhaps in the neighboring States, in the direction of *extreme* opinions, touching religious beliefs;—" Bible doctrines," as it was the fashion to say,—with a certain finality of sanctified bitterness, from which no Christian sect was exempt, or excused.

The meeting-houses grew into religious debating clubs, and the newspapers of that section "took sides," and society was divided and tortured by conflicting uncertainties; and children were reared,—*not* under the kindly influences of "faith, hope, and charity," but under the hard and bitter dictums of a sect,—in which the "doctrines" were noisily paraded, as a threatening bulwark against all other Christian bodies; and salvation was clearly "on *our* side."

The religious confusion of this period was heightened by the advent upon the field of battle of Universalism.

Out of these tumults,—out of the depths,—came Mormonism.

In 1825, when this excited state of the public mind was at its boiling point, and in the very center of it, there lived a young boy, of mean parentage, and without acknowledged ability or education, or becoming ambition, whose character seems to have been the natural outgrowth of these conditions. This boy grew to be recognized as the founder of a new religion, which, in about forty years, has come to embrace in its membership, over 100,000 souls, claiming in fact to be several times more numerous still, which has been preached in all lands, and has a new bible, and a new dispensation, and possesses a secular kingdom, ranking as one of the powers of the earth, and still aspiring to greater dominion.

This boy was Joseph Smith, Jr., the coming Mormon "prophet;" his religion, Mormonism, as characterized by the "Gentile world," and by themselves, "the Church of Jesus Christ of Latter-Day Saints."

Joseph Smith was born at Sharon, Windsor County, Vt., December 23, 1805. His family removed to Palmyra, N. Y., when he was ten years of age.

At about fifteen, the future "prophet" became greatly exercised upon religious matters, as he alleges. This was in keeping with his surroundings, though less so with his own character, and that of his family; for the Smiths were idle, thievish, and unworthy citizens. This is admitted, even by the Mormons. Joseph was entirely uneducated, unable to read or write with ease, or well.

Nothing shows his character so clearly, as the accounts given of his religious experience.

Orson Pratt, one of the early magnates of Mormonism, who has given an elaborate account of Joseph's first inspirations, says, "he began seriously to reflect upon the necessity of being prepared for a future state of existence," but seemed undecided how to effect this. "He perceived that it was a question of infinite importance, and the salvation of his soul depended upon a correct understanding of the same. He retired to a secret place in a grove, and knelt down, and began to call upon the Lord," &c.

Joseph himself says of this first approach to divine honors: "My object in going to inquire of the Lord, was to know which of all the sects was right, that I might know which to join."

This was the burthen which *he* bore to the Lord, and it was in keeping with the circumstances.

Orson Pratt wrote afterwards, and saw the need of a consistent, religious experience.

"Joseph says, 'some few days after this vision, I happened to be in company with one of the Methodist preachers, who was very active in the before-mentioned religious excitement. I took occasion to give him an account of the vision I had had. I was greatly surprised at his behavior. He treated my communication not only lightly, but with contempt, saying, 'it was all of the devil; that there were no such things as visions and revelations in these days,'" &c.

The vision here referred to, was the opening of the young "prophet's" mission, and came after this wise:

While he prayed, "he was at first severely tempted by the powers of darkness," but having struggled against these, "he at length saw a bright and glorious light in the heavens above, which at first seemed to be at a considerable distance." But he continued praying, and the light at length descended in his direction, and he was disappointed and edified not to see the leaves of the trees over his head consumed by its brilliant glow, which illuminated the entire forest. He was now encouraged to hope he could look upon it and live. He was soon "enveloped in the midst of it," and "immediately his mind was caught away from natural objects, with which he was surrounded, and he was enwrapped in a heavenly vision, and saw two glorious personages, who exactly resembled each other in their features or likeness."

Orson Pratt says, Joseph was informed, at this point, "that his sins were forgiven," but Joseph himself seemed not to think this of importance; but both state what was said about the sects. They were all wrong, and Joseph must not join himself to any of them. Then followed the greatest of all. These "personages" promised that at some future time, "the true doctrine, the fullness of the gospel, should be made known to him."

But he fell away after this, into the world again. The heavenly vision, so great in promise, and wonderful in its glory of light, was forgotten. Joseph seems to have gone back to his sheep stealing again. He was human, and had human possibilities, as well as divine.

But, on the 21st of September, 1823, his prayer was again heard by the Lord. "It seemed as though his bones were filled with consuming fire," which "occasioned a shock of sensation visible to the extremities of his body."

Nevertheless, this was followed by the calmness of joy, and a "serenity of mind, that surpassed understanding, and in a moment, a personage stood before him," of whom, "though his countenance was as lightning, yet it was of a pleasing, innocent, and glorious appearance, so much so, that every fear was banished," and Joseph betook himself to "calmness."

In this connection, we have the amazing statement, that "The stature of this personage *was a little above the common size of men in his age;*" and that his garments were white, and "without seam."

But the celestial presence soon satisfied all curious inquiries, by declaring himself an angel, and was very communicative. This was the angel Moroni, and he appeared thus, three times, and gave him valuable instruction. God had a great work for Joseph. There were some golden plates hidden in the hill Cumorah, very near and convenient to him, in the town of Manchester, Ontario County, New York, on which were engraved, in peculiar and unknown characters, a record of the ancient inhabitants of America, and the dealings of God to them ward: that with this record would be found the identical and renowned Urim and Thummim of the ancients, by which alone these records could be translated,—stone spectacles, "set in two rims of a bow."

Not until four years after this were these treasures made available by Joseph. On the 22d of September, 1827, the angel gave them into his hands. They were about eight inches long, by seven wide, thinner than ordinary tin, and bound together by three rings, which passed through each plate, making a volume about six inches thick. A part of this golden document was sealed, and the remainder was written in a language called the reformed Egyptian, in hieroglyphic characters.

This, when translated by Joseph has given us the "Golden Bible," or the "Book of Mormon."

Mysteriously hidden behind a blanket, Joseph read from the golden plates, while Oliver Cowdery wrote from his "prophet" lips the wonderful record, as he translated it, by means of the stone spectacles.

Profane eyes were not permitted to see these plates. It were a dangerous profanation. Nevertheless the following papers are accepted by Mormons, as authentic. The first is the statement of the "Three Witnesses," and the latter of "Eight Witnesses."

"'TESTIMONY OF THREE WITNESSES.

"'Be it known unto all nations, kindreds, tongues, and people, unto whom this work shall come, that we, through the grace of God the Father, and our Lord Jesus Christ, have seen the plates which contain this record, which is a record of the people of Nephi and also of the Lamanites, their brethren, and also the people of Jared, who came from the tower of which hath been spoken; and we also know that they have been translated by the gift and power of God, for his voice hath declared it unto us; wherefore we know of a surety that the work is true, and we also testify that we have seen the engravings which are upon the plates; and they have been shown unto us by the power of God, and not of man. And we declare, with words of soberness, that an angel of God came down from heaven, and he brought and laid before our eyes, that we beheld and saw the plates, and the engravings thereon; and we know that it is by the grace of God the Father and our Lord Jesus Christ, that we beheld and bear record that these things are true, and it is marvellous in our eyes; nevertheless, the voice of the Lord commanded us that we should bear record of it; wherefore, to be obedient unto the commandments of God, we bear testimony of these things. And we know that if we are faithful in Christ we shall rid our garments of the blood of all men, and be found spotless before the judgment seat of Christ, and shall dwell with him eternally in the heavens. And the honour be to the

Father, and to the Son, and to the Holy Ghost, which is one God. Amen.

      "'Oliver Cowdery.
       David Whitmer.
       Martin Harris.

"'TESTIMONY OF EIGHT WITNESSES.

"'Be it known unto all nations, kindreds, tongues, and people, unto whom this work shall come, that Joseph Smith, jun., the translator of this work, has shown unto us the plates of which hath been spoken, which have the appearance of gold: as many of the leaves as the said Smith has translated we did handle with our hands; and we also saw the engravings thereon, all of which have the appearance of ancient work, and of curious workmanship. And this we bear record with words of soberness, that the said Smith has shown unto us, for we have seen and lighted, and know of a surety that the said Smith has got the plates of which we have spoken: and we give our names unto the world of that which we have seen; and we lie not, God bearing witness of it.

      "'John Whitmer.
       Christian Whitmer.
       Jacob Whitmer.
       Peter Whitmer, jun.
       Hiram Page.
       Joseph Smith, sen.
       Hyrum Smith.
       Samuel H. Smith.'"

The above papers, together with the mere assertions of the "prophet" himself, and certain others, make up in reality the evidence on which the Mormons rest their cause, and the authenticity of their religion.

Of course there are "miracles" and "revelations" in the case, but these are authenticated by similar proof,—by none.

Of the "witnesses," the Whitmers are unknown, and the three Smiths are of Joseph's family. Of Cowdery, nothing is to be said, but that he was the amanuensis of Joseph,* but all the "Three Witnesses" quarreled with Joseph afterwards, and publicly avowed their statements to have been false.

Martin Harris was a simple-minded farmer, who was made to believe there was money in the book, and he furnished the means for its publication,—an investment which he earnestly repented,—of whom Joseph speaks somewhat harshly: "There are negroes who have white skins as well as black ones; Granny Parish and others, who acted as lackeys, such as Martin Harris. But they are so far beneath my contempt, that to notice any of them would be too great a sacrifice for a gentleman to make."

This language seems to have been called out after the publication of the "Golden Bible," by the irreverent view taken of it, and of the "prophet," by these persons and his other neighbors. It appears Joseph was not always guarded or truthful, and he had made contradictory statements.

Peter Ingersall, his intimate friend, made oath: "Smith told me the whole affair was a hoax; that he had no such book, and did not believe there was any such book in existence; but, said he, as I have got the damned fools fixed, I shall carry out the fun."

---

* But Joseph had, in November, 1831, this prudent "revelation," which goes somewhat to the question of Oliver's veracity, if we accept the revelation:

"Hearken unto me, saith the Lord your God, for my servant Oliver Cowdery's sake. It is not wisdom in me that he should be intrusted with the commandments, *and the money* which he shall carry into the land of Zion, *except one go with him who is true and faithful.*"

The *italics* are a part of the "revelation," but it was all for Oliver's sake.

Many passages in the after life of Joseph, show him to have been a much greater man than the above would indicate, but we have here the key to his character. He never believed in himself, nor in Mormonism.

The "Golden Bible," or the "Books of Mormon," purport to have been written by prophets of different periods. It is in sixteen books, the last of these was by Mormon, whose name has been given to it, and to the whole as a series. Its numerous names are of Latin, Greek, Hebrew, and biblical origin, and imitations of these, and it is said to contain some three hundred passages from the common English Bible.

The religious character of the Book of Mormon is singularly toned by that of the public opinion in Western New York, before-mentioned. Infant baptism is denounced, and Universalism, Millerism, the Methodists, Calvinism, and the Roman Catholics are discussed; and Free Masonry, over which Western New York was excited in 1830, is condemned, as well as secret societies generally.

The story of the Book of Mormon is eminently American. The first book claims to have been written by a Jew, —Nephi, the Son of Lehi,—who lived in Jerusalem about 600 B. C.

Lehi was directed by the Lord, in a dream, to go to the desert of Arabia, with his family, which he did, and dwelt there for a long while; and being further directed by the Lord, traveled eastwardly for eight years, in search of a promised land, until he came to the sea.

After building a ship, he sailed, with his family and

others, to America, "guided by a compass." It is not stated upon what part of the continent the expedition landed, but by means of convenient "revelations" of later date, it is known to have been on the coast of Chili.

Lehi and his four sons, Laman, Lemuel, Sam, and Nephi, and their four wives, "two sons of Ishmael," and their two wives, and Zoram, a servant, and his wife; eight men with each a wife, made up the migrating party, except that Leh had also two sons born on the journey, Joseph and Jacob.

But Lehi soon died, and dissensions divided the brothers. Nephi and Sam, and the servant Zoram, with their wives, with the young brothers, Joseph and Jacob, went into the wilderness; while Laman and Lemuel, with the two "sons of Ishmael," and their wives, were condemned, with their posterity, by the Lord, for not following Nephi, to have dark skins, and to "become an idle people, full of mischief and subtlety, which did seek in the wilderness for beasts of prey."

Nephi had been appointed ruler by the Lord, and hence this severity against rebellion. Besides, it also proved the Hebrew origin of the American Indians. But Nephi was prospered and his people increased. He says, "And I did teach my people to build buildings, and to work in all manner of wood, and of iron, and of copper, and of brass, and of steel, and of gold, and of silver, and of precious ores, which were in great abundance. And I, Nephi, did build a temple; and I did construct it after the manner of the temple of Solomon, save that it were not built of so many precious things; for they were not to be found in the land;

therefore it could not be built like unto Solomon's temple. But the manner of the construction was like unto the temple of Solomon; and the workmanship thereof was exceeding fine. * * * * And it did come to pass that I, Nephi, did consecrate Jacob and Joseph, that they should be priests and teachers over the land of my people. And it came to pass that we lived after the manner of happiness. And thirty years had passed away since we left Jerusalem." After the death of Nephi, which occurred about fifty years after his arrival in America, his people were governed by a race of kings, bearing his name, for many generations. This people were called Nephites. The records were continued by Jacob, upon the golden plates, and by his son Enos, and then by Jarom the son of Enos, and Omni the son of Jarom, down to Mormon, the writer of the last book, who "many hundred years after the coming of Christ," gave all these plates to his son Maroni. Besides those mentioned, came in their order, Mosiah, Benif, Alma, Helaman, Nephi the second, and third. These various books give the history of the wars between the Nephites and the red men, i. e., the Lamanites, and relate to the affairs of North and South America, and particularly to the land of Zarahemla, located in the neighborhood of the isthmus of Darien, where was a great city. The crucifixion of Christ was announced in the days of Nephi the second, by an earthquake, three days after which, the Lord himself descended out of heaven upon one of the chief cities, and exhibited his hands and his feet, with the prints of the nails, where he remained forty days, and founded churches.

These Nephites, it seems, at once adopted the Christian era for chronological purposes.

For four hundred years after the coming of Christ among them, terrible wars were waged between the Lamanites and these Christian Nephites, to the disadvantage of the latter. Their civilized cities, which were numerous and large, were wasted and captured, and by degrees the Lamanites gained decided ground; and finally, a great and decisive battle was fought (singularly enough) in Western New York, in which the Nephites were entirely defeated. This was A. D. 384, upon the hill Cumorah, where the golden plates were found by Joseph. Two hundred and thirty thousand men were slain in this last conflict. Moroni, one of the survivors of this battle, wandered a fugitive, with these golden plates in custody, until A. D. 420, when he hid them on this hill, where they remained until 1827, as related.

Such is the Book of Mormon.

But there are two other persons bearing important relations to this book.

Solomon Spalding was born in Ashford, Conn., in 1761, and was graduated at Dartmouth, and ordained, and he preached several years; but relinquished the ministry, and went into business as a merchant at Cherry Valley, N. Y., and moved from there to Conneaut, Ohio, in 1809. In 1812, he removed to Pittsburgh, Pa., and thence to Amity, in the same State, and died in 1816.

It is well authenticated that he was addicted to the writing of a class of fiction too poor to find a publisher, but for which he had a passion. That while in Ohio he wrote one of these, which he was in the practice of reading to his friends, in which he attempted a plot to account for the origin of the American Indians, upon the theory that they were the descendants of the lost tribes of Israel. He called his book, "Manuscript Found," and mentioned it as a translation of the "Book of Mormon." He proposed to publish a fictitious account of its having been found in a cave in Ohio, as an advertisement.

It is in proof, that the manuscript of this romance was sent in 1812, to a printing office in Pittsburgh, Pa.; the year Spalding removed to that city.

The third important personage in this connection, is Sidney Rigdon. He was born in St. Clair, Alleghany county, Pa., February 19, 1793. When this manuscript was taken to the printing office, he was an employee in it. It was well known about the office that Rigdon had made a copy of Spalding's manuscript, and he admitted he had it. The original was returned to Spalding just before his death.

When the "Book of Mormon" was published by Joseph, the original manuscript was sent by Mrs. Spalding to Conneaut, Ohio, and there compared, at a public meeting, with the "Golden Bible" of Joseph, and the identity fully established. The widow Spalding says, "I am sure that nothing would grieve my husband more, were he living, than the use which has been made of his work. The air of antiquity which was thrown about the composition, doubtless suggested the idea of converting it to the purposes of delusion. Thus, a historical romance, with the addition of a few pious expressions and extracts from the sacred scriptures, has been construed into a new bible, and palmed off upon a company of poor, deluded fanatics, as divine."

It would be interesting to know how and when Rigdon and Joseph first met. It is certain that previous to their meeting, i. e., between 1816 and 1829, Rigdon took to preaching, and held peculiar views, and had drawn a church about him modeled upon a plan of his own. He does not appear conspicuously upon the stage, in connection with Joseph, until about the time of the first organization of the " Church of Latter-Day Saints," which was effected at Manchester, N. Y., April 6, 1830, by the union of Rigdon's followers with Joseph's. The first conference was held at Fayette, N. Y., in the June following, when the two "prophets" mustered about thirty adherents; from which insignificant following, what results!

There are many indications that the conjunction of these magnates was vital to the success of Mormonism. Rigdon was fierce, unscrupulous, original, and daring as a theorist and innovator, but he was indiscreet, and wanting in ability to influence and impress himself upon the masses. He signally failed to control men, or to win the hearts of the multitude.

Joseph was strong just where Rigdon was at fault. He was patient, and had unbounded perseverance, impudence, and dash in execution. He had the executive ability necessary to success in such a cheat; but he wanted originality. He was full of expedients for a given end, and had great personal courage, and his well-timed assumptions were audacious to sublimity.

But, nevertheless, as far as being the originator of a *"religion,"* he was a cheat. It was Sidney Rigdon who adapted the Rev. Mr. Spalding's romance to serve their joint purpose; and there is abundant proof that the idea of a *"new religion"* was Rigdon's and not Joseph's. Rigdon also introduced polygamy.

Among the proofs that the authorship of the "Book of Mormon" belong to Spalding, we find in the deposition of his brother John, that he saw the original, and heard Solomon read much of it, which he recognized; and says, "I well remember that he wrote in the old style, and commenced about every sentence with 'And it came to pass,' or 'Now it came to pass,' the same as in the 'Book of Mormon,' and according to my best recollection and belief, it is the same as my brother Solomon wrote, with the exception of the religious matter. By what means it has fallen into the hands of Joseph Smith, Jr., I am unable to determine."

Martha, the wife of John Spalding, and Henry Lake, the co-partner of Solomon in business, and John N. Miller, who was employed by Solomon, and lived in the family, all make conclusive statements to the same effect.

Miller says, "Many of the passages in the Mormon book are *verbatim* from Spalding, and others in part. The names of Nephi, Lehi, Moroni, and in fact all the principal names are brought fresh to my recollection by the 'Gold Bible.'"

Martin Harris, after advancing $50 to Joseph, for the publication of the "Book of Mormon," wishing to assure himself that everything was genuine, asked to see the plates, but Joseph was forbidden by a timely "revelation" to gratify his curiosity; but he gave a paper which he said was a transcript of a part of them, and proposed Harris should submit this to some learned person; and accordingly he went to New York for the purpose, and made the submission to Prof. Anthon.

The Mormons claimed afterwards the decision to have been that the characters were Egyptian.

When this question was under investigation in Ohio, Mr. E. D. Howe, of Painesville, received in reply to his inquiry, the following decisive answer. The "simple-hearted farmer" referred to was Martin Harris.

"NEW YORK, FEBRUARY 17, 1834.

"DEAR SIR,—I received your letter of the 9th, and lose no time in making a reply. The whole story about my pronouncing the Mormonite inscription to be 'Reformed Egyptian Hieroglyphics,' is perfectly false. Some years ago a plain, apparently simple-hearted, farmer called on me with a note from Dr. Mitchell, of our city, now dead, requesting me to decipher, if possible, a paper which the farmer would hand me. Upon examining the paper in question, I soon came to the conclusion that it was all a trick, perhaps a hoax. When I asked the person who brought it how he obtained the writing, he gave me the following account:—A 'gold book,' consisting of a number of plates fastened together by wires of the same material, had been dug up in the northern part of the State of New York, and along with it an enormous pair of 'spectacles!' These spectacles were so large, that if any person attempted to look through them, his two eyes would look through one glass only; the spectacles in question being altogether too large for the human face. 'Whoever,' he said, 'examined the plates through the glasses was enabled not only to read them, but fully to understand their meaning. All this knowledge, however, was confined to a young man, who had the trunk containing the book and spectacles in his sole possession. This young man was placed behind a curtain, in a garret, in a farm-house, and being thus concealed from view, he put on the spectacles occasionally, or rather, looked through one of the glasses, deciphered the characters in the book, and having committed some of them to paper, handed copies from behind the curtain to those who stood outside. Not a word was said about their having been deciphered by the 'gift of God.' Everything in this way was effected by the large pair of spectacles. The farmer added, that he had been requested to contribute a sum of money towards the publication of the 'golden book,' the contents of which would, as he was told, produce an entire change in the world, and save it from ruin. So urgent had been these solicitations, that he intended selling his farm, and giving the amount to those who wished to publish the plates. As a last precautionary step, he had resolved to come to New York, and obtain the opinion of the learned about the meaning of the paper which he had brought with him, and which had been given him as part of the contents of the book, although no translation had at that time been made by the young man with the spectacles. On hearing this odd story, I changed my opinion about the paper, and instead of viewing it any longer as a hoax, I began to regard it as part of a scheme to cheat the farmer of his money, and I communicated my suspicions to him, warning him to beware of rogues. He requested an opinion from me in writing, which of course I declined to give, and he then took his leave, taking his paper with him.

"This paper, in question, was in fact a singular scroll. It consisted of all kinds of crooked characters, disposed in columns, and had evidently been prepared by some person who had before him at the time a book containing various alphabets, Greek and Hebrew letters, crosses, and flourishes; Roman letters inverted or placed sideways, were arranged and placed in perpendicular columns; and the whole ended in a rude delineation of a circle, divided into various compartments, decked with various strange marks, and evidently copied after the Mexican Calendar, given by Humboldt, but copied in such a way as not to betray the source whence it was derived. I am thus particular as to the contents of the paper, inasmuch as I have frequently conversed with my friends on the subject since the Mormon excitement began, and well remember that the paper contained anything else but 'Egyptian Hieroglyphics.'

"Some time after the same farmer paid me a second visit. He brought with him the 'gold book' in print, and offered it to me for sale. I declined purchasing. He then asked permission to leave the book with me for examination. I declined receiving it, although his manner was strangely urgent. I adverted once more to the roguery which, in my opinion, had been practised upon him, and asked him what had become of the gold plates. He informed me that they were in a trunk with the spectacles. I advised him to go to a magistrate and have the trunk examined. He said, 'The curse of God' would come upon him if he did. On my pressing him, however, to go to a magistrate, he told me he would open the trunk if I would take the 'curse of God' upon myself. I replied I would do so with the greatest willingness, and would incur every risk of that nature, provided I could only extricate him from the grasp of rogues; he then left me. I have given you a full statement of all that I know respecting the origin of Mormonism, and must beg you, as a personal favor, to publish this letter immediately, should you find my name mentioned again by these wretched fanatics.

"Yours respectfully,
"CHARLES ANTHON."

But the new religion was now fairly enunciated, with its head-quarters at Fayette, N. Y. It had thirty members, and from the first it became obnoxious and demonstrative. It being necessary to erect a dam across a neighboring stream for baptisms, it was torn away by a mob. The young prophet was too near his own county to enjoy honors. He was assailed with charges of former bad character, and threatened with violence.

His answer was characteristic and able. He frankly admitted his past irregularities and crimes; but "the Lord had chosen him; had forgiven him all his sins, and intended in his own inscrutable purposes, to make him,—weak and erring as he might have been,—the instrument of his glory."

He cited high authority and example. Were not the followers of Christ unlettered and erring?

But in proportion as his enemies were defeated by Joseph's logic, they grew intolerant and determined.

Joseph had a "revelation" to go with his family and church to Kirtland, Ohio, in January, 1831. This was done, with a view of finding a place for the "New Jerusalem," to be established for a general rendezvous for the saints, where they at once began to assemble.

But attention was directed at an early day to the far west as the final resting-place of the faithful; and Joseph and Rigdon left the rapidly gathering saints at Kirtland to look out a fitting locality. Oliver Cowdery had already been sent into Jackson County, Mo., for this purpose, and his report had been so favorable, that the "prophet" directed his way hither,—three hundred miles of which weary journey was performed on foot by these two founders of a religious empire. From such small beginnings are the great things of the world originated. The strength and the daring. of the "prophet" was at once developed as the fruit of this journey.

Arrived at Independence, Mo., he was so enamored of the country, that he at once fixed upon it as the "New Jerusalem," and in order to silence all cavil as to this among his followers, he promptly had a "revelation," that took form in a document, which, for grasp, forethought, and boldness of design, stands forth among the extraordinary things of its kind.

It will be remembered, this was early in the history of Mormonism,—long before injustice, and persecutions, and dangers had sharpened his faculties by a rough experience. It opens:

"Hearken, O ye elders of My Church, saith the Lord your God, who have assembled yourselves together according to my commandments, in this land which I have appointed and consecrated for the gathering of the saints. * * * * Behold the place which is now called Independence, is the centre place, and a spot for the temple is lying westward, upon a lot which is not far from the court-house; wherefore it is wisdom that the land should be purchased by the saints; and also every tract lying westward, even unto the line running directly between Jew and Gentile."

And further on, his views are set forth with a business-like purpose and directness, not inferior to Brigham Young, after years of experience; in which the store-keeper and printer are named, and our friend, Oliver Cowdery, was assigned to the printing office, as an assistant.

The site of the temple was dedicated, and the place named New Jerusalem.

These two men then returned to Kirtland, Ohio, where they proposed to remain during five years, in order,—as they naively said, to "make money."

The prophet immediately addressed himself to business. A store, a mill, and a bank were organized; Joseph made himself the president, and Rigdon the cashier, of the latter,—without a charter,—and then the country was flooded with money in which the people of Ohio had little confidence. There were other dishonest dealings charged to the account of Joseph and Rigdon, and an excitement grew up and culminated on the night of March 22, 1832, in both being tarred and feathered.

The next year the Church was organized under the "First Presidency,"—a form of government which it still retains. The origin of the "Presidency" is singular, and came as follows:

While he was at Kirtland, the indiscretions of the saints in Missouri had given rise to suspicions that Joseph aimed at "empire," and apostacies were the result, and other dangers threatened the Church. By a fine stroke of policy, he disarmed his enemies by associating with himself, Sidney Rigdon and Frederic G. Williams, in obedience to a "revelation" to the effect that these saints "were forgiven, and were henceforth to be accounted as equal with Joseph Smith, Jr., in holding the keys of his last kingdom." Rigdon it seems had shown signs of ambition, and Joseph dare not place him in command at "Zion," but directed him to remain at Kirtland.

It was in this year that one of the most important conversions occurred, in the person of Brigham Young. He arrived at Kirtland, Ohio, at the end of the year 1832. He was born at Whitingham, Vt., June 1, 1801. It is related of him, that when he resided in Livingston County, N. Y., and was supporting himself as a field laborer, that once, at the end of a toilsome day, he leaned thoughtfully upon his hoe-handle for a long time, when suddenly, as if inspired by one of those bursts of genius, which has since so often served his purpose and made him famous, he threw his hoe into the corner of the fence and said, "There, by ——, that is the last day's work I ever do in Livingston County; I will go and join the Mormons." And he did so, and he has lived to save Mormonism more than once. He soon became prominent, and when the "Quorum of the Apostles" was organized, he was made one of the "Twelve," and was very successful as a preacher in the Eastern States. Brigham Young, next to Joseph, is the ablest man brought to the surface by the Mormon delusion, if not the ablest among the impostors of the world. These two men had much in common. Brigham has shown more shrewdness, and equal dash, audacity, and foresight.

Heber C. Kimball became a convert in 1832, and Orson Hyde in 1837.

The large and costly temple at Kirtland was finished in 1836.

The Kirtland bank failed in 1838, and Joseph and Rigdon found it necessary to flee, to avoid arrest, and they returned to Missouri, pursued by creditors, still directed by a divine "revelation."

It was on this march to Missouri, that the "prophet" first organized a military command, and a body-guard, and began to assume the prerogatives of his high mission, and to introduce system and discipline among his followers. He had about two hundred disciplined men at arms, out of which grew that fearful, secret band, afterwards known as the "Danites," or "Destroying Angels."

But he found the saints badly conditioned. Perhaps from motives of vanity, the saints had disclosed and made a boast of the intentions of the "prophet." Independence was the future capital of the "Latter-Day Saints," and the State of Missouri was soon to be in their hands, as well as the whole country. And the facts seemed to justify the boast. Most of Jackson County was already in Mormon hands, and the saints were still flocking thither. They were also charged with crime.

A public meeting was held at Independence, which at length grew into a western mob, and the Mormons were forcibly and cruelly driven across the Missouri river into Clay County, and thence into Caldwell County, where Joseph and Rigdon joined them. Farwest and other "stakes," which they had established, characteristically grew into important places under Mormon hands.

Mills, and workshops, and farms, and various industries, sprang up in the wilderness about their temporary resting-places. The master-mind of the "prophet" was shaping and moulding the rudest material into a great, enthusiastic, religious power.

Then grew into fact, one of those wild and romantic histories, which could have been enacted only upon a western frontier in America, and outrages which could have been provoked only by the demonstrative spirit of Mormonism.

To complicate affairs, a schism occurred in the Church. The President of the "Twelve," Thomas B. March, and Orson Hyde, also an "apostle," apostatized, with others.

The following affidavit was made by March, before a justice of the peace, in Ray County, on the 24th of October, 1838:

"They have among them a company, consisting of all that are considered true Mormons, called the Danites, who have taken an oath to support the heads of the Church, in all things they say or do, whether right or wrong. * * * The plan of said Smith, the prophet, is to take this State; and he professes to his people to intend taking the United States, and ultimately the whole world. This is the prophet's plan and intentions. The prophet inculcates the notion, and it is believed by every true Mormon, that Smith's prophecies are superior to the law of the land. I heard the prophet say, that he would yet tread down his enemies, and walk over their dead bodies; that if he was not let alone, he would be a second Mahomet to this generation, and that he would make it one gore of blood from the Rocky Mountains to the Atlantic Ocean."

This was corroborated by Hyde's affidavit.

On the 4th of July, 1838, Sidney Rigdon preached a sermon, in which he said to the saints:

"We take God and all the holy angels to witness this day, that we warn all men in the name of Jesus Christ, to come on us no more forever. The man, or the set of men, who attempts it, does it at the expense of their lives. And that mob that comes on us to disturb us, it shall be between us and them a war of extermination, for we will follow them till the last drop of blood is spilled, or else they will have to exterminate us. For we will carry the seat of war to their own houses, and their own families, and one party or the other shall be utterly destroyed."

Rigdon was, from first to last, distinguished for his zealous indiscretion, without executive ability.

Near the close of this year, the excitement against the Mormons increased, and the militia of the State of Missouri was called out by the Governor. Joseph, Rigdon, Hiram Smith, and others were arrested by the military authorities.

The wild drama which followed was under the leadership, in part, of one "Major-General Clark," who seems to have been less civilized, and as much the fanatic as the rudest Mormon. In a brutally threatening address to his *prisoners*, he used this extraordinary language: "And, oh! that I could invoke the spirit of the unknown God to rest upon you, and deliver you from the awful chain of superstition," &c., and had the bad taste to say, before trial, that nothing could save the leaders; "their fate is fixed,—their die is cast,—their doom is sealed." He also kindly informed his prisoners: "The orders of the Governor to me were, that you were to be exterminated, and not allowed to remain in the State."

But, he had "discretionary powers," and he would allow them to withdraw, and the State would take their lands to pay the cost of the war. The Mormon property thus taken by the State, has been estimated at between one and two million dollars. These acts are without justification. The Mormons were clearly entitled to the protection of the laws. Nevertheless, there had been much provocation. The Mormons were probably the first wrong-doers. But a mob, backed by the State militia, called out under the pretence of enforcing the laws, was not a good remedy. It has told badly upon Missouri. She still suffers by reason of her former want of respect for law and justice.

Hiram Smith thus describes the situation of the Mormon leaders under arrest:

"When I arrived at the camp, I was put under the same guard as my brother Joseph, and my other friends, who were taken the day previous.

"That evening a court-martial was held, to consult what steps should be taken with the prisoners, when it was decided that we were to be shot the next morning, as an example to the rest of the Church. * * * When I heard of these unjust and cruel sentences, 'my heart was fixed, trusting in the Lord.'

"The next morning came on, when we were to be shot. * * * The time at length arrived when their sentence was to be carried into effect, but in consequence of Gen. Doniphan protesting against the unlawfulness of the proceedings, and at the same time threatening to withdraw his troops, the court rescinded their resolution."

A monument to Gen. Doniphan.

With the leaders in arrest, and pressed by a superior force, the Mormons submitted to the conditions imposed, and withdrew from the State into Illinois, where the "prophet" joined them, after having broken jail. Rigdon had been discharged before, for whom this confinement seems to have been too much; for he never afterwards displayed his usual courage, and his unbecoming habit of complaining about it, was afterwards urged as a proper ground for charges against him on his Church trial, afterwards had. The true Mormon saint is too heroic and self-forgetful to indulge in childish complainings.

The following amazing statement is copied from a late popular work:

"The story of their exile,"—the Mormons,—"their persecutions, and their sufferings, is most painful. Of course, I take their own accounts, for the other side of the story has never been written, or if it has, I have never seen it. But it will be written, and we shall then have both sides of the story. I am assured that the other side view will be very different, and will make fearfully against their own history. We shall see. But, taking *their* version, I hesitate not to say, that the treatment they received in Illinois was not merely unjust and unkind, but was cruel to a degree that ought to make savages blush."

As relating particularly to affairs in Missouri, to which the author also refers in this connection, the following from the message of the Governor of that State in 1840, gives us a hint of the "otherside view." He says:

"These people,"—the Mormons,—"had violated the laws of the land by open and avowed resistance to them; they had undertaken, without the aid of the civil authority, to redress their real or fancied grievances; they had instituted among themselves a government of their own, independent of and in opposition to the government of this State; they had, at an inclement season of the year, driven the inhabitants of an entire county from their homes, ravaged their crops, and destroyed their dwellings. Under these circumstances, it became the imperious duty of the executive, to interpose, and exercise the powers with which he was invested, to protect the lives and property of our citizens, to restore order and tranquillity to the country, and maintain the supremacy of our laws."

The foregoing is a fair statement, within the facts of history, as far as it relates to the aggressions of the Mormons. It does not cover the facts as to the influences and outrages of the mob, and the subordination of the law and the executive to it. It is but fair to say, the "otherside view" involves the statement, that Mormonism is incompatible with the institutions of civilized life, and cannot exist with it; and the Mormons seem, practically, to coincide with this view. But the important propositions relating to this subject are:

First, civilization cannot afford to suppress Mormon irregularities by other than the recognized law remedies,— civil or military.

Second, it cannot afford to ignore nor neglect to suppress them.

The same author says: "What it was that so exasperated the community, I cannot see. It was *not* polygamy, for at that time they had no revelation allowing more than one wife. In their 'Book of Doctrines and Covenants,' containing the revelations made to Smith and many others, men and women, they say positively, page 331, 'Inasmuch as this Church of Christ has been reproached with the crime of fornication and polygamy, we declare that we believe that one man should have one wife, and one woman but one husband, except in case of death, when either is at liberty to marry again.'"

Dr. Todd could have truthfully quoted the Mormon Bible to the same effect. This later "revelation" had been *entirely uncalled for*, if polygamy had not existed in fact, in the church, at this time,—which was intended to cover up an existing state of things, and it had that effect, until the indiscretions of the heads of the church made it impossible longer to hide it. Polygamy "*was*" one of the very things which "exasperated the community,"—and more, it led to the schism of 1844, and was the direct cause of the death of Joseph, and his brother Hiram, and the Mormon exodus from Illinois.

None of the facts of Mormonism are better established, than that polygamy existed among the heads of the church, and the trusted Mormons, long before their settlement in Illinois; that it was one of the charges early brought against them in Missouri; that Sidney Rigdon originated its introduction into the church; that Joseph sanctioned it by a "revelation" in 1843, and practiced it before that time; that it was re-affirmed by a "revelation" to Brigham Young in 1852.*

---

* My attention has been called to the following, which not only confirms what is said above, but in a remarkable manner vindicates the truthfulness of Mrs. Smith's narrative,—in the mention of her brother Howard, and the facts there given, as to Emma.—*See ante p.* 34-5.

POLYGAMY IN SALT LAKE CITY.
The War between Brigham Young and the sons of Smith.

A correspondent of *The San Francisco Bulletin* gives the following account of the recent contest in Salt Lake City on the subject of polyg-

Joseph arrived in Illinois, from his imprisonment in Missouri, at the darkest period in the history of his church. But his prospects immediately brightened. Injustice in Missouri seemed to have done them good service in Illinois. Dr. Isaac Galland owned a large tract of land at Commerce, Carthage County, and he made Joseph a present

---

amy. Joseph F. Smith, son of "Hiram the Martyr," and cousins of his opponents, David and Alexander Smith, sought to prove in a public meeting that the original Joe Smith actually received a revelation establishing polygamy, and that both he and Hiram his brother, practiced polygamy secretly, and in the face of their positive denials contained in *The Times and Seasons*, a Mormon paper published at Nauvoo. The first witness introduced to the congregation by Joseph F. Smith was "Elder Howard Coray." All who have read Mary Ettie V. Smith's book, "Fifteen Years Among the Mormons," will at once recognize this name as that of the "older brother Howard," often mentioned by her. He stated that his wife had a dream, in which "Brother Thompson sealed her on the five points of fellowship;" that she told part of her dream to Hiram Smith, but felt a delicacy about telling it all; and that Hiram Smith then explained to Coray and his wife the entire revelation authorizing polygamy. He further said that Hiram Smith's sister-in-law soon after moved to Hiram's house, and another sister had her house built alongside of Hiram's, so there was a passage to his bedroom. Joseph F. Smith manifested great nervousness and excitement throughout the meeting. He commenced by stating that many would run after David and Alexander Smith simply because they were the sons of Joseph. In view of this fact, it had been determined to hold a series of meetings to answer the statements of David Hiram, and before they were through they purposed to present testimony to convince any honest mind who heard it, and damn any who rejected it. He stated that he would present the affidavits of twelve women now living that they were the spiritual wives of Joseph Smith, and so continued to the time of his death; that he had the evidence of hundreds of men who had been taught the doctrine by Joseph and Hiram, and that he knew to a certainty that his father, Hiram Smith, had two other women while his mother was still alive. As an excuse for the published denials of his father and Joe Smith, he said: "I cannot help the posi-

of a part of it, with the view of opening a market for the remainder; and immediately a new "revelation" indicated this to be the "center spot," and commanded the saints to assemble there to build a city, to be called Nauvoo; and a temple, and a "hotel," where the "prophet" and his family could "have place from generation to generation, for ever and ever."

---

tion this places my father and Joseph in as to their denials. I only know these facts. But everybody knows the people then were not prepared for these things, and they had to be cautious. They were in the midst of their enemies, in a State where this doctrine would have sent them to the penitentiary. There were traitors on every hand; the right-hand man of the Prophet, one Marks, was a traitor of the blackest dye. When Joseph and Hiram left Nauvoo, intending to come to the Rocky Mountains and pick out a refuge for the people, when the mob were after them, that man Marks and Emma Smith joined in writing them a letter urging them to come back. They came back, delivered themselves up, and were murdered. And the blame rests upon that woman, their mother, Emma Smith. And I say the blood of Joseph and Hiram is upon the souls of Marks and Emma Smith, and there it will remain until burned out by the fires of hell."

If Joseph F. Smith proved that polygamy did exist—and I think he did—he thus proves his father and Joseph Smith to have been deliberate liars.

On Sunday evening, Joseph F. Smith, the avowed champion of polygamy, again occupied the stand. He made no quotations from the Book of Mormon, that authority being against him; nor from the Book of Doctrine and Covenants, that being equally so; but he quoted from the Bible. Many passages in the singular number referring to marriages were construed by him to mean the plural also. He said: "It has been said that I have proved my father a liar. I will show that he has not lied. There is a difference between telling a lie and not telling the truth. Webster says: 'Polygamy, a man having several wives, or a woman having several husbands.' The latter part my father meant to deny, and not the former; therefore he did not lie."—*N. Y. Semi-Weekly Tribune, Sept.* 14. 1869.

The land given to Joseph was divided into lots, and sold to the saints, by which he realized over $1,000,000.

The city of Nauvoo immediately grew into importance, as the saints were called to it from the four quarters. The legislature granted it a liberal charter, with extraordinary privileges, including the authorization of a military body, afterwards known as the Nauvoo Legion. The "prophet" was the Lieutenant-General of this corps, to which all Mormons able to bear arms belonged. He was also made the Mayor of the city.

Joseph was now approaching the zenith of his great power and fame. He was, as by the "revelation" of April 6, 1830, "seer, apostle of Jesus Christ, and elder of the church." But the Lord had said of him, "The church shall give heed to all his words and commandments which he shall give unto you; for his words shall ye receive as from my own mouth, in all patience and faith."

This was a sufficiently broad commission, and no good Mormon doubted its binding force. Among his people he was both the State and the Church;—some fifteen years before, a common thief,—now a Mayor, a Pontiff, and Lieutenant-General, and very rich.

It was on the 6th of April, 1841, that Joseph laid the foundation of the great temple, on which occasion he appeared at the head of his legion, and surrounded by a numerous staff. The temple walls rose as by magic, as each Mormon was required, by a "revelation," to contribute one-tenth of his substance and time to this object.

Nauvoo had become to Mormons, the capital of the

world, whither they flocked with their families and means, while it challenged the attention of mankind.

An observing officer of artillery, of the U. S. Army, has given an intelligent account of the city and its institutions, as he saw them at this time.

"Yesterday," he says, "was a great day among the Mormons. Their legion, to the number of two thousand men, was paraded by Generals Smith, Bennett, and others, and certainly made a very noble and imposing appearance. The evolutions of the troops, directed by Major-General Bennett, would do honor to any body of armed militia in any of the States, and approximates very closely to our regular forces. What does all this mean? Why this exact discipline of the Mormon corps? Do they intend to conquer Missouri, Illinois, Mexico? It is true they are part of the militia of the State of Illinois, by the charter of their legion; but then there are no troops in the States like them in point of enthusiasm and warlike aspect, yea, warlike character. Before many years this legion will be twenty, and perhaps fifty, thousand strong, and still augmenting. A fearful host, filled with religious enthusiasm and led on by ambitious and talented officers, what may not be effected by them? Perhaps the subversion of the constitution of the United States; and if this should be considered too great a task, foreign conquest will most certainly follow. Mexico will fall into their hands, even if Texas should first take it.

"These Mormons are accumulating like a snow-ball rolling down an inclined plane, which, in the end, becomes an avalanche. They are enrolling among their officers some of the first talent in the country, by titles, or bribes, it don't matter which. They have appointed your namesake, Captain Bennett, late of the army of the United States, Inspector-General of their legion, and he is commissioned as such by Governor Carlin. This gentleman is known to be well skilled in fortification, gunnery, ordinance, castrametation, and military engineering generally, and I am assured that he is now under pay, derived from the tithings of this warlike people. I have seen his plans for fortifying Nauvoo, which are equal to any of Vauban's.

"Only a part of their officers, regents, and professors, however, are Mormons, but they are all united by a common interest, and will act together, on main points, to a man. Those who are not Mormons when they come here, very soon become so, either from interest or conviction.

"The Smiths are not without talent, and are said to be as brave as lions. Joseph, the chief, is a noble-looking fellow, a Mahomet every inch of him. The postmaster, Sidney Rigdon, is a lawyer, philosopher, and saint. Their other generals are also men of talent, and some of them men of learning. I have no doubt that they are all brave, as they are most unquestionably ambitious, and the tendency of their religious creed is **to** annihilate all other sects; you may, therefore, see that the time will come when this gathering host of religious fanatics will make this country shake to its center. A western empire is certain. Ecclesiastical history presents no parallel to this people, inasmuch as they are establishing their religion on a learned footing. All the sciences are taught, and to be taught in their colleges, with Latin, Greek, Hebrew, French, Italian, Spanish, &c. The mathematical sciences, pure and mixed, are now in successful operation, under an extremely able professor of the name of Pratt, and a graduate of Trinity College, Dublin, is president of their University.

"Now, Sir, what do you think of Joseph, the modern Mahomet?

"I arrived here *incog.*, on the 1st instant, and from the great preparation for the military parade, was induced to stay to see the turnout, which I confess has astonished and filled me with fears for future consequences. The Mormons, it is true, are now peaceable, but the lion is asleep. Take care and don't rouse him.

"The city of Nauvoo contains about ten thousand souls, and is rapidly increasing. It is well laid out, and the municipal affairs appear to be well conducted. The adjoining country is a beautiful prairie. Who will say that the Mormon Prophet is not among the great spirits of the age?

"The Mormons number, in Europe and America, about one hundred and fifty thousand, and are constantly pouring into Nauvoo and the neighboring country. There are probably in and about this city and adjacent territories, not far from thirty thousand of these warlike fanatics, this place having been settled by them only three years ago."

Notwithstanding the public denial of the spiritual wife dogma, the heads of the church had secretly taught and practiced it. These irregularities attracted the attention of Emma, the wife of Joseph, and to pacify her, he had a "revelation" justifying and authorizing it. This was July 12, 1843. But this "revelation" was soon whispered about, and scandals followed. Joseph had made advances to so many married and single women, whose virtue was proof against his inspired lechery, that he was denounced, and a schism and tumult arose among his own people. The wives of Dr. Foster and William Law were conspicuous, as having resisted the embraces of Joseph. Their husbands publicly renounced Mormonism, and established the "*Expositor*," a newspaper, in opposition to Smith. This was boldly done at Nauvoo. The first number gave the affidavits of sixteen women, who had been thus approached by Joseph, Rigdon, and others, with offers of spiritual marriages with themselves, respectively.

But Joseph was not likely to tolerate opposition within his own stronghold. The office of the "*Expositor*" was destroyed, including the building and press. Law and Foster fled to Carthage, the county seat, and obtained warrants for the arrest of the heads of the church, and others,—eighteen in all. The execution of the warrant was resisted, and the officers of justice driven out of the city. The military power of the county was invoked, and civil war was inaugurated by the arming of the Mormons.

The wonderful foresight of the "prophet," which was never at fault, suggested to him the necessity of an isolated home for his people. He was already on the way, in company with Hiram, to seek out such a place among the mountains, when the specious letter of his wife Emma, overtook and called him back,—and in obeying it, he made the first fatal mistake of his life, judged from his point of view, —except in the matter of polygamy, perhaps.

The brothers returned, and submitted to arrest, and were taken to the Carthage jail, with others.

An otherwise reliable account, says, "the governor of the State persuaded the two Smiths to surrender, and take their trial." But the previous statement is now well authenticated.

The people of Missouri had neither forgotten nor forgiven the Mormons, and were mainly instrumental in inciting the mob, which, on the 27th of June, 1844, made an attack upon the jail, and after overpowering the guard, shot Joseph and Hiram. The Smiths died manfully. Joseph defended himself with his revolver, as long as the bullets in his "carnal weapon" were available; and then fell dead, in the act of leaping from the window. He was heroic in a sense seldom allied to meanness or deception; and yet, all the circumstances of his death, as well as his life, clearly attest the cheat,—but he was one of no ignoble order.

The Governor of Illinois acknowledged he had given his official pledge for the protection and safety of the prisoners; and was actually on his way to Carthage, with a military force, when he heard of the outrage.

The shooting of the brothers Smith was murder, if that is not too brave a name for an act so craven and cowardly.

Confusion at first succeeded the death of Joseph. Few recognized in Mormonism the strength to survive the loss of its "prophet." But this was a mistake. The elders acted with great discretion. They wisely counselled peaceable measures. The people of Carthage expected an attack from Nauvoo, but this was disclaimed. Their published addresses to the saints, at home and abroad, evinced remarkable wisdom and self-respect.

This seems to have been the critical period in the history of Mormonism, and the question promptly resolved itself into this, viz: On whom the mantle of the "prophet" was to fall.

But the issue was met by the assembled magnates with resolution and sagacity.

Sidney Rigdon assumed the functions of the "prophet" as of right; and had a "revelation" directing the saints to repair to Pittsburgh, Pa. He had many and strong claims. He had originated Mormonism, and made polygamy a part of it. He had apparently been recognized by Joseph, and had seen visions, and received "revelations." He had in his custody, important secrets, which he threatened to divulge.

But, on the other hand, he was unpopular. He never had the confidence of the people; nor held that mysterious key by which he could unlock, at will, the wonderful fountain of Mormon enthusiasm, and hence, was not the proper successor of Joseph; and above all, he was not respected among the elders. He was distrusted.

When Joseph had thundered and ruled by majestic "revelations," Sidney had blustered indiscreetly, or resorted to unmanly tricks. He had no elevated faith. The history of men and of causes, disclose the hopeful and important fact, that the element of faith,—though mistaken,—is necessary to any measure of success, in ruling men.

Rigdon was put upon trial, and cut off from the faithful, and "handed over to the devil, 'to be buffeted in the flesh for a thousand years.'"

Brigham Young was elected by the same assembly, "First President," and invested with the "keys." These two measures saved Mormonism.

Rigdon immediately withdrew, and has since maintained a studied reticence, which goes far to vindicate his claim to some discretion.

Brigham's first circular letter to the saints fixed his status; it was calm, hopeful, practical, and masterly.

But nothing could bring reconciliation with the "Gentiles." It was evident the Mormons must leave.

The charter of Nauvoo was repealed by the legislature of Illinois in 1845.

In the midst of all these complications, the Mormons gave a sublime example of faith.

Joseph had predicted the completion of the temple. In order to the fulfillment of this "revelation," the Mormons made unheard-of exertions; and succeeded, even to the last ornament, and to the dedication. The approaching exodus had been delayed for this purpose.

In the winter of 1846, the movement commenced. It is stated, upon seeming good authority, that this was under a stipulation between the State government and the Mormons, that hostilities should be mutually suspended; and time given those who remained at Nauvoo, to sell their property, under the State protection.

The van-guard established "stakes" at various points along the route, and a main one at Council Bluffs; and in the spring, put in crops for the coming swarms. There is no proof to justify the suspicion, which gained currency in Illinois, that the Mormons intended to hold Nauvoo; but to the contrary.

But, without justification, and in violation of State faith, the militia drove the defenceless men, women, and children from their homes, in September, of this year, at the point of the bayonet, after having actually "*bombarded the city for three days.*"

While these atrocities, alike humiliating to our common humanity, and to the State of Illinois, were being visited upon the weak and defenceless ones in the rear, the heads of the church, under the astonishing leadership of the new "prophet," were preparing to found a city, and an empire, in the wilderness.

Brigham Young arrived, with a company of followers, at Utah, on the 24th of July, 1847; and the great body of the saints, in the fall, 1848.

Lands were surveyed, and put under cultivation, and Great Salt Lake City was founded; and then followed an era of enterprises and successes, as wonderful as they were anomalous and contradictory.

While the people established "stakes" in every direction, and subdued and irrigated the land for cultivation, and built up the city, and the temple, and established mills, and shops, and stores, and all available industries, under the personal direction of the ever-watchful bishops, missionary corps were organized for foreign lands, under the seventies, and an emigration fund established, which resulted in a swarming emigration to Utah, from all parts of Europe.

It is noticeable, that a committee of the British Parliament has recognized the wisdom of the Mormon system of emigration, by consulting with the managers of it, in England. From the moment the new converts,—mainly from the working classes,—leave their homes, until they reach, and are settled at the "stake," or upon the little farm to which they are assigned in Utah, they are under a regularly organized system of government and police,—by which the percentage of casualties, and cost of transportation are greatly lessened, and health and cleanliness secured.

So early as March, 1849, a convention was held at Great Salt Lake City, for the organization of a State, which was done under the name of "Deseret,"—said by the Mormons to mean "the land of the honey bee."

Congress refused to accept the constitution which was adopted; but erected the country into a territory, in September, of that year; and President Filmore appointed Brigham Young its governor.

But troubles soon intervened.

The judges were driven out of the territory by the "prophet" governor; and the latter was removed by the President, and Col. Steptoe, of the U. S. Army, put in his place. He arrived in Utah, with his command, in August,

1854, but by reason of its smallness, perhaps, he deemed it not prudent to assume the functions of his office, and consequently, after wintering there, went to California with his troops.

The effect of this mis-judgment, or mistaken armament, was unfortunate. From that day to this, the Mormon "prophet" has successfully defied or outwitted the federal authorities.

When gone, a "revelation" gave the credit of the departure to Brigham, and everything tended to consolidate his people.

Brigham said in a sermon, after the departure of Col. Steptoe: "I am, and will be governor, and no power can hinder it, until the Lord Almighty says, 'Brigham, you need not be governor any longer.'"

In February, 1856, Judge Drummond, of the U. S. District Court, was driven from the bench by an armed Mormon mob, at the instigation of the heads of the church, and he was forced to adjourn his court.

All the United States officers, except the Indian Agents, were forced to leave the territory.

Other outrages, both public and private, characterized this period, many of which are given in the foregoing narrative.

Things were in this condition until the spring of 1857, when Alfred Cumming, superintendent of Indian affairs on the Upper Missouri, was made Governor of Utah by Mr. Buchanan; and Judge Eckles, of Indiana, Chief Justice. Col. Sidney A. Johnson, afterwards a Confederate General, and killed, while in command, at the great battle of Shiloh, was sent with a force of 2,500 men for their protection.

The expedition was fitted out with some show of good faith and efficiency, and civilization took note of the event. It was September before the army reached the confines of Utah, and was not joined by Col. Johnson until it was overtaken by the snows of approaching winter. But on the 5th and 6th of October previously, the supply-train had been attacked by a party of mounted Mormons; and soon after, eight hundred oxen were cut off from the rear, and actually driven into Salt Lake City. These were daring acts of war,—enough it would seem, to have justified war measures.

The army went into winter quarters in the middle of November at Ford Bridger, and on the 27th, Governor Cumming issued his proclamation, declaring the territory to be in a state of rebellion.

But this was just before the great slave-holder's rebellion, when no opportunity was to be lost, by which that cause could to be served.

Thomas L. Kane, of Pennsylvania, who, although he had been with the Mormons during the exodus, never had been able to discover them to be other than excellent saints, and most worthy citizens, and had rendered them essential service, by lecturing in their behalf on the Atlantic coast, now came again to their succor. He arrived in Utah in the spring, with letters from President Buchanan, and succeeded in bringing the belligerent "saints," and the governor, sent to subdue them, into relations of harmony and pleasant fellowship.

Mr. Kane was hotly pursued by two "peace commissioners," who arrived as early as the end of May, bearing from the President of the United States a proclamation, "offering pardon to all Mormons who would submit to federal authority." The bearers of this "grace of pardon," were Gov. Powell, of Kentucky, and Maj. McCulloch, of Texas. Before these gentlemen had arrived at the camp, Mr. Kane had hurried on to the Mormon capital, and thus was in time to secure a reconciliation, the conditions of which were accepted by the heads of the church.

With becoming consideration for a "subdued people," the army was stationed forty miles away from the capital, where it remained until the spring of 1860, when it was withdrawn.

During the long winter, when Col. Johnson's army was hedged in by impassable snows, at Fort Bridger,—living upon short rations,—the Mormon people were exultant and hopeful. They trusted in the "prophet," and echoed his spirit and words, and nothing could harm them. Brigham has exhibited the rare union of reckless daring with the subtlest prudence. He recognizes a point beyond which he may not go,—which Joseph failed to do. Though lacking the lion-like personal courage of the first "prophet," he is nevertheless, his equal, and more, in moral heroism; and in the mysterious control he exercises over his people.

The following letter is an illustration of Mormon feeling at this time. It was written from Utah while the army was in winter-quarters; and has been singularly verified as a prediction of the then coming rebellion.

This is the letter.

LETTER FROM SALT LAKE CITY.

The Providence *Journal* publishes a letter from one of the Mormon women at Salt Lake City, written to her daughter in Rhode Island, from which we take an extract to show the strength and character of the delusion that prevails in Utah. Different from Mrs. Smith, whose narrative of Mormon life has just been published, she seems to have the most complete faith in Brigham Young, and to live contented under his rule. She describes her situation there as very comfortable, and writes with full confidence of the security of the saints under the protection of the prophet; she scouts the idea that they can be harmed by the United States troops. She says:

"I expect you have heard the loud talk of Uncle Sam's great big army coming up to kill the saints. Now if you did but know how the saints rejoice at the folly of the poor Gentiles. There are about four thousand on the border of our territory, with six hundred wagons,— one naked mule to draw them,—all the rest having died. The men are sitting in the snow, about a hundred and fifteen miles from us, living on three crackers a day, and three-quarters of a pound of beef a week. Thus you see the old prophet's words are fulfilled,—'whoever shall fight against Zion shall perish. The time is very near when one man shall chase a thousand, and ten shall put ten thousand to flight.' Zion is free; she is hid in one of the chambers of the Lord. We are a free people. We do not fear Uncle Sam's soldiers. We only fear our Father in Heaven. We are learning his commandments, every day, from his prophet, and I am determined to keep them. If you were here, and could hear the prophet's voice, as I do, and hear the lion of the Lord roar from the mountains, as I do, and know how near the scourge of the Lord is upon the Gentiles, you would flee to the mountains with haste. The time has come when the Lord has called all the elders home, and commanded them to bind up the law and seal the testimony. They are now coming home as fast as possible. What comes next? The judgment, hail storm, thunder, lightning, pestilence, war; and they that will not take up the sword against their neighbor, must flee to Zion for safety. Will you come, oh! my dear children?"

During the war for the suppression of the great rebellion, the Mormons were in a measure overlooked; but since then, the public attention has been especially turned in that direction, by the continuance of violence, and by the increased facilities of travel,—the Pacific Railroad having brought Utah to our doors;—and by the writings of numerous tourists, attracted thither by these new conditions, which have already disturbed, and threaten further, the isolation of the "saints."

While many distinguished citizens have availed themselves of the opportunity of looking silently in upon Salt Lake, and upon her exceptional social system, it has been only by the grace and forbearance of the "prophet," and of his people.

Visitors have been made to comprehend, that Utah was not common ground, nor polygamy a debatable subject. No traveler has presumed to tell the Mormon elders, "face to face," what the outside world's opinion of them was, until lately; but this has come at length, in a peculiarly impressive and authoritative way.

On the 5th of October, 1869, the Vice President and his traveling party found themselves at Salt Lake City, and having been called out, Mr. Colfax made,—from the portico of the Townsend House,—one of those well-poised, and closely reasoned speeches, for which he is widely distinguished.

The opportunity,—and the fearless, but kindly manner of embracing it, were as anomalous, as the strange people he addressed;—while, as a statesman, he uttered the common sentiment; and as a leader, pointed a way the politician may not again blunder or "compromise."

It will be seen, ante p. 248, what happened in 1853, when a Judge of the United States attempted to "interfere with the affairs of our Zion;"—and the Springfield *Republican*, of the 15th of the same month,—the accomplished editor of which, was one of the Vice President's party,—indicates that violence was apprehended on this occasion. It says:

"Such a speech ought not to be considered unexpected or remarkable in any public man visiting that territory, and observing the peculiar features of its polity. That it was so regarded there by both Gentiles and Mormons,—that his friends felt doubtful of his being permitted to express such sentiments in that presence, and anxious for his personal safety afterward,—is the best illustration that perhaps could be given of the character of the rule of Brigham Young and his associates, and the feeling that it has inspired in that community. * * * No public man has ever said anything like this before, while on a visit to Utah; and it had come almost to be thought that no public man would dare thus to attack the distinguishing features of the civilization that has grown so bold and aggressive on that theater. * * * Mr. Colfax's words will have a wider welcome than lips dare utter in Utah."

The following is the principal part of the speech, as copied from the same paper:

CONDITION OF MORMONISM.

THE VICE-PRESIDENT IN UTAH.—MR. COLFAX'S SPEECH AGAINST POLYGAMY IN SALT LAKE CITY.—THE TRUTH TOLD TO THE MORMONS FACE TO FACE.

FELLOW CITIZENS:—I come hither in response to your call to thank the band from Camp Douglas for the serenade with which they have honored me, and to tender my obligations to the thousands before me, for having come from their homes and places of business "to speed the parting guest."

As I stand before you, to-night, my thoughts go back to the first view I ever had of Salt Lake City, four years ago last June. After traveling with my companions, Gov. Bross and Mr. Bowles, who are with me again, and Mr. Richardson, whose absence we have all regretted, over arid plains, and alkali valleys, and barren mountains, day after day, our stage coach emerged from a canon one morning, and we looked down upon your city, covering miles in its area, with its gardens green with fruit trees and shrubbery, and the Jordan, flashing in the sun beyond. And when, after stopping at Camp Douglas, which overlooks your city, to salute the flag of our country, and to honor the officers and soldiers who keep watch and ward over it at this distant post, we drove down with your common council to the city, and saw its wide streets, and the streams which irrigate your gardens, rippling down all of them in their pebbly beds, I felt indeed that you had a right to regard it as a Palmyra in the desert.

* * * * * * * *

I am gratified too, that our present visit occurred at the same time with your territorial fair, enabling us to witness your advance in the various branches of industry.

* * * * * * * *

I have enjoyed the opportunity, also, of visiting your tabernacle, erected since I was here before, the largest building in which religious services are held on the continent, and of listening to your organ, constructed here, which, in its mammoth size, its volume of sound, and sweetness of tone, would compare favorably with any in the largest cities in the Union. Nor did I feel any the less interest on my present, than on my former visit, in listening to your leading men in their places of worship, as they expounded and defended their faith and practice, because that faith and practice differed so widely from my own. Believing in free speech, as all of us should, I listened attentively, respectfully, and courteously, to what failed to convince my mind, and you will doubtless hear me with equal patience, while I tell you frankly wherein we differ.

But first let me say that I have no strictures to utter as to your creed on any really religious question. Our land is a land of civil and religious liberty, and the faith of every man is a matter between himself and God alone. You have as much right to worship the Creator through a president and twelve apostles of your church organization as I have through the ministers and elders and creed of mine. And this right I would defend for you with as much zeal as the right of every other denomination throughout the land. But our country is governed by law, and no assumed revelation justifies any one in trampling on the law. If it did, every wrong-doer would use that argument to protect himself in his disobedience to it. The constitution declares, in the most emphatic language, that that instrument and the laws made in conformity thereto, shall be the supreme law of the land. Whether liked or disliked, they bind the forty millions of people who are subject to that supreme law. If any one condemns them as unconstitutional, the courts of the United States are open, before which they can test the question. But, till they are decided to be in conflict with the constitution, they are binding upon you in Utah as they are on me in the District of Columbia, or on the citizens of Idaho and Montana. Let me refer now to the law of 1862 against which you especially complain, and which you denounce Congress for enacting. It is obeyed in the other territories of the United States, or if disobeyed its violation is punished. It is not obeyed here, and though you often speak of the persecutions to which you were subject in the earlier years of your church, you cannot but acknowledge that the conduct of the government and the people of the United States towards you, in your later years, has been one of toleration, which you could not have realized in any other of the civilized nations of the world.

I do not concede that the institution you have established here, and which is condemned by the law, is a question of religion. But to you who do claim it as such, I reply, that the law you denounce, only re-enacts the original prohibitions of your own Book of Mormon, on its 118th page,* and your Book of Doctrines and Covenants,

---

* The Book of Mormon denounces David and Solomon for having "many wives and concubines, which thing was abominable before me saith the Lord." "Wherefore I, the Lord God, will not suffer that this people shall do like unto them of old. Wherefore, my brethren, hear me and hearken to the word of the Lord; for there shall not any man among you have save but one wife, and concubines he shall have none, for I, the Lord, delighteth in the chastity of women."

in its chapter on marriage; and these are the inspired records, as you claim them, on which your church was organized.

The Book of Mormon, on the same page, speaks twice of the conduct of David and Solomon, as "a grosser crime," and those who follow their practice as "waxing in iniquity." The Book of Doctrines and Covenants is the discipline and creed of their church; and in its chapter on marriage, it declares, that as the Mormon church has been charged with the crimes of fornication and of polygamy, it is avowed as the law of the church, that a man shall have but one wife, and a woman but one husband, till death shall part them.

I know you claim that a subsequent revelation annulled all this; but I use these citations to show you that the congressional law, which you denounce, only enacted what was the original and publicly proclaimed and printed creed on which your church was founded. And yet, while you assume that this later revelation gives you the right to turn your back on your old faith, and to disobey the law, you would not yourselves tolerate others in assuming rights for themselves, under revelations they might claim to have received, or under religions they might profess. The Hindoos claim, as part of their religion, the right to burn widows with the dead bodies of their husbands. If they were to attempt it here, as their religion, you would prevent it by force. If a new revelation were to be proclaimed here, that the strong men should have the right to take the wives of the weaker men, that the learned men should take the wives of the unlearned, that the rich men should take the wives of the poor, that those who were powerful and influential should have the right to command the labor and the service of the humbler, as their bond-slaves, you would spurn it, and would rely upon the law and the power of the United States to protect you.

But you argue that it is a restraint on individual freedom; and that it concerns only yourselves. Yet you justify these restraints on individual freedom in every thing else. Let me prove this to you. If a man came here and sought to establish a liquor saloon on Temple street without license, you would justify your common council, which is your municipal congress, in suppressing it by force, and punishing the offender besides. Another one comes here and says that he will pursue his legitimate avocation of bone-boiling on a lot in the heart of your city. You would expect your council to prevent it, and why? Because you believe it would be offensive to society and to the people around him. And still another says, that as an American citizen, he will establish a powder-mill on a lot he has purchased, next door to this hotel, where we have been so hospitably entertained. You would demand that this should be prevented, because it was obnoxious to the best interests of the community. I might use other illustrations as to personal conduct which you would insist should be restrained, although it fettered personal freedom, and the wrong-doer might say only concerned himself. But I have adduced sufficient to justify Congress in an enactment they deemed wise for the whole people for whom they legislated. And I need not go further to adduce other arguments as to the elevation of woman; for my purpose has been in these remarks, to indicate the right of Congress to pass the law, and to insist on obedience to it.

One thing I must allude to, personal to myself. The papers have published a discourse delivered last April by your highest ecclesiastical authority, which stated that the President and Vice-President of the United States were both gamblers and drunkards. (Voices in the crowd, "He did not say so.") I had not heard before that it was denied; but am glad to hear the denial now. Whether denied or not, however, I did not intend to answer railing with railing, nor personal attack with invective. I only wished to state publicly in this city, where the charge is said to have been made, that it was utterly untrue as to President Grant; and as to myself, that I never gambled to the value of a farthing, and have been a total abstinence man all the years of my manhood. However I may differ on political questions or others from any portion of my countrymen, no one has ever truthfully assailed my character. I have valued a good character far more than political reputation or official honors, and wish to preserve it unspotted while life shall last.

A few words more and I must conclude. When our party visited you four years ago, we all believed that, under wise counsels, your city might become the great city of the interior. But you must allow me to say that you do not seem to have improved these opportunities as you might have done. What you should do to develope the advantages your position gives you, seems obvious. You should encourage, and not discourage, competition in trade. You should welcome, and not repel, investments from abroad. You should discourage every effort to drive capital from your midst.* You should rejoice at the

---

* By order of the church all Mormon stores, shops, etc., have a sign inscribed, "Holiness to the Lord; Zion's Co-operative Mercantile Institution;" and the members of the church are instructed to trade there only. The result is that many Gentile establishments have closed up and removed elsewhere. A few, with large capital, still remain, but with diminished business.

opening of every new store, or factory, or mechanic shop, by whomsoever conducted. You should seek to widen the area of country dependent on your city for supplies. You should realize that wealth will come to you only by development, by unfettered competition, by increased capital.

Before the completion of the railroad, your isolation could be maintained. Now, however, you are brought into close juxtaposition with the remainder of the nation and with the civilization of the continent. You can persist in the policy you have adopted, but if you do, the only result will be to dwarf and destroy your own prosperity and to build up the rival cities near you that pursue a truer and wiser policy. You will decrease and they will increase; and you will have no one to blame but yourselves.

Here I must close. I have spoken to you face to face, frankly, truthfully, fearlessly. I have said nothing but for your own good. Let me counsel you once more to obedience to the law, and thanking you for the patient hearing you have given me, and for the hospitalities our party have received, both from Mormon and Gentile citizens, I bid you all good night and good-bye.

This timely and unexpected utterance of Mr. Colfax has been well received by the country. It has put into earnest, unwarped words, the popular will.

It is the rugged statement of the national faith, touching its relations to "revealed" polygamy.

But not less unexpected, has been the result in Utah, where it seems to have broken the spell of the "prophet's" authority, and thrown his people into the wildest excitement.

The advent of a schism, and of newspapers to support it, are already announced.

But, on the other hand, the Mormon magnates do not yield the argument. The "prophet" stands his ground. One of the leading minds among the elders, and his ablest writer, has been called in to answer Mr. Colfax; and this brief account of Mormonism cannot be otherwise more fittingly closed, than by giving it in full.

The following letter of John Taylor is copied from the *N. Y. Semi-Weekly Tribune*, of November 19, 1869.

A MORMON'S REPLY TO MR. COLFAX.

To the Editor of the Tribune:

Sir :—I have read with a great deal of interest the speech of the Hon. Schuyler Colfax, delivered in Salt Lake City, October 5th, containing strictures on our institutions, wherein there is an apparent faith and sincerity manifested. Permit me, sir, to make the following remarks. Mr. Colfax says:

"I have no strictures to offer as to your creed, on any really religious question. Our land is a land of civil and religious liberty, and the faith of every man is a matter between himself and God. You have as much right to worship the Creator through a President and Twelve Apostles of your Church organization, as I have through the Ministers, and Elders, and creed of mine, and this right I would defend for you, with as much zeal as the right of every other denomination throughout the land."

This, certainly, is magnanimous and even-handed justice, and the sentiments do honor to their utterer. They are sentiments that ought to be engraved on the heart of every American citizen. He continues:

"But our country is governed by law, and no assumed revelation justifies any one in trampling on the law."

That our country is governed by law we all admit, but when it is said that no "assumed revelation justifies any one in trampling on the law," I would respectfully ask: What, not if it interferes with my religious faith, which you state "is a matter between myself and God alone?" The assumed revelation referred to, is one of the most vital points of our religious faith; it emanates from God, and cannot be legislated away; it is part of the "everlasting covenant" which God has given to man. Mr. Colfax continues:

"I do not concede that the institution you have established here, and which is condemned by the law, is a question of religion."

Now, I think that if Mr. Colfax had carefully examined our religious faith, he would have arrived at other conclusions. In the absence of this I might ask: Who constituted Mr. Colfax a judge of my religious faith? Mr. Colfax has a perfect right to state and feel that he does not believe the revelation on which my religious faith is based, nor in my faith at all; but has he the right to dictate my religious faith? I think not. He does not consider it religion. It is nevertheless mine. If a revelation from God is not a religion, what is it? His not believing it is from God makes no difference. I know it.

"But to you who do claim it as such I reply, that the law you denounce only re-enacts the original prohibition of your own Book of Mormon, on its 118th page, and your Book of Doctrine and Covenants, in its chapter on Marriage."

In regard to the latter of these, I would state that it was only considered a portion of the discipline of our Church, and was never looked upon as a revelation. It was published in the appendix to the Book of Doctrine and Covenants long before the revelation concerning celestial marriage was given. That, of course, superseded the former. The quotation from the Book of Mormon given by Mr. Colfax is only partly quoted I cannot blame the gentleman for this; he has too many engagements to carefully examine our doctrines. I suppose this was handed to him; had he read a little further he would have found it stated "For I will, saith the Lord of Hosts, raise up seed unto me; I will command my people; otherwise they shall hearken unto these things." In answer to this I say, the Lord has commanded it, and we obey the command. I again quote:

"And yet while you assume that this later revelation gives you the right to turn your back on your old faith and to disobey the law, you would not, yourselves, tolerate others in assuming rights for themselves under revelations they might claim to have received, or under religions they might profess."

Mr. Colfax is misinformed here. All religions are tolerated with us, and all revelations, or assumed revelations. We take the liberty of disbelieving some of them, but none are interfered with; and in relation to turning our back on our old religion, we have never done it.

Concerning our permitting the Hindoos to burn their widows, it is difficult to say what we should do. I hope, however, that we shall not be condemned for crimes we are expected to commit. It will be time enough to atone for them when done. We do acknowledge having lately started co-operative stores. We think we have a right to buy and sell of, and to whom, we please. We do not interrupt others in selling, if they can get customers. We are certainly rigid in the enforcement of law against theft, gambling, drunkenness, debauchery, and other civilized vices. Is this a crime? If so, we plead guilty. Mr. Colfax says that we complain of persecution. Have we not cause to do it? Can we call our treatment by a milder term? Was it benevolence that robbed, pillaged, and drove thousands of men, women, and children from Missouri? Was it Christian philanthropy, that, after robbing, plundering, and ravaging a whole community, drove them from Illinois into the wilderness among savages? Did Government make any amends for these outrages, or has it ever done so? Is it wrong to call this persecution? We have learned to our cost "that the king can do no wrong." Having said so much in regard to Mr. Colfax's speech, let me now address a few words to Congress and to the nation. And first, let me inquire into the law itself, enacted in 1862. The revelation on polygamy was given in 1843, nineteen years before the passage of the Congressional act. We, as a people, believe that revelation is true, and came from God. This is our religious belief; and, right or wrong, it is still our belief. The Constitution is to protect me in my religious faith, and other persons in theirs, as I understand it. It does not prescribe a faith for me or any one else, or authorize others to do it, not even Congress. Now, who does not know that the law of 1862, in relation to polygamy, was passed on purpose to interfere with our religious faith?

We are told that we are living in a more enlightened age. Our morals are more pure (?), our ideas more refined and enlarged, our institutions more liberal. "Ours," says Mr. Colfax, "is a land of civil and religious liberty, and the faith of every man is a matter between himself and God alone,"—provided God does not shock our moral ideas by introducing something that we don't believe in. If He does, let Him look out. We won't persecute—very far be that from us—but we will make our platforms, pass Congressional laws, and make you submit to them. We may, it is true, have to send out an army and shed the blood of many; but what of that? It is so much more pleasant to be proscribed and killed, according to the laws of the great Republic, in "the asylum for the oppressed," than to perish ignobly by the decrees of kings, through their miserable minions, in the barbaric ages. Let me here respectfully ask: Is there not plenty of scope for the action of Government at home? What of your gambling hells? What of your gold rings, your whisky rings, your railroad rings, manipulated through the lobby into your Congressional rings? What of that great moral curse of the land—

that great institution of monogamy—Prostitution? What of its twin sister—Infanticide?

We can teach you a lesson, polygamist as we are. You acknowledge one wife and her children. What of your associations unacknowledged? We acknowledge and maintain all our wives and all of our children. We don't keep a few only, and turn the others out as outcasts, to be provided for by orphan asylums, or turned as vagabonds on the street, to help increase the fearfully growing evil; our actions are all honest, open, and above board. We have no gambling hell; no drunkenness; no infanticide; no houses of assignation; no prostitutes. Our wives are not afraid of our intrigues and debauchery; nor are our wives and daughters corrupted by designing and unprincipled villians. I am sure you would not, on reflection, reverse the order of God and exchange the sobriety, the chastity, the virtue and honor of our institutions, for yours that are so debasing, dishonorable, corrupting, defaming, and destructive? We have fled from these things, and with great trouble and care have purged ourselves from your evils; don't try to legislate them upon us, nor seek to engulf us in your vices.

JOHN TAYLOR.

Salt Lake City, November 2, 1869.

"I know it," says John Taylor; and we are willing to go to the people with him, upon his own argument; meantime, calling attention to the "twin-sister,—infanticide," by the following:

The *Corinne* (Utah) *Reporter* says of an item from the *New York Evening Post*, relating to the mortality among the Mormons: "We are sorry to say that the *Post's* information is too true in regard to the mortality among Mormon children. It is not, however, very well informed, or else wishes to draw it very mild, for instead of some of the bosses of large harems, like Heber Kimball's, burying only forty-eight children, we can show the *Post* polygamous graveyards of one family, as they call them here, that will foot up nearer one hundred and forty-eight. As this is certainly the healthiest climate known to tourist and explorers, equalized and modified as it is, the year round, by the salutary influences of the Great Salt Lake, it is an easy matter to point to this mortality evil—it is polygamy, and nothing else. —*N. Y. Tribune, January* 18, 1870.

At the moment of going to press, several current topics, which have been by necessity crowded out of the foregoing brief sketch, for want of available space, seem to demand, at least, a passing notice here.

It has already been mentioned, that very recent events at the Mormon capital indicate the existence of agitation, and of a growing schism in the church. The later accounts indicate a very high state of excitement among the adherents of Mormonism, as well as the " Gentile " population, by which business was at one time mainly suspended.

The schismatics are under the leadership of Messrs. Harrison and Godbe, both of whom have been promptly cut off from the church; and they in turn, have established a paper, and organized a "liberal" movement, which addresses itself to the Mormons themselves.

The following, from the *N. Y. Tribune*, of December 1, 1869, indicates its nature:

" The persons who head the liberal cause in Utah propose to issue a new paper to be called the *Mormon Tribune*, publishing the same every Saturday at Salt Lake City. The *Tribune* will aim to break down bigotry and fanaticism, and to foster ideas in harmony with the spirit of the age, and of course in direct opposition to polygamy."

Ordinarily, these altered conditions would be accepted hopefully; but it is to be noted, that the " liberal " tendency of the schism has only this extent: to bring Mormonism into "harmony with the spirit of the age,"—an admitted absurdity. New " revelations" by those in opposition to the "prophet" are already announced. Thus nothing is gained in principle, since we have only a war of counter " revelations."

The civil laws which govern other communities, and other communions, must set free the *deluded victims* in Utah. "The gospel of the day," is the admirable speech of Vice President Colfax, through which "the spirit of the age" has found an intelligent utterance.

The need of legal protection to the women of Utah is made sadly evident by a single incident which the newspapers have widely mentioned; in substance, as follows:

THE MORMON WOMEN IN COUNCIL.

The Mormon women held a mass meeting in the Tabernacle at Salt Lake, on the 13th inst., to denounce the bill for the suppression of polygamy introduced in Congress by Mr. Cullom. About three thousand women attended, and all the proceedings were conducted by the sex. One of their number presided, and a round dozen of them made speeches sharply condemning the Cullom bill as an infringement on their right to choose their own husbands, and exercise the religion which their judgments approved. Polygamy was stoutly defended as of divine commandment. A series of resolutions embodying these ideas was adopted, though it is said many of those present did not vote either way. The gathering was conspicuous for the absence of young women, and the lively demonstrations of numerous babies, whose outcries nearly drowned the voices of the oratresses at times.—*Amherst (Mass.) Record, January* 27, 1870.

The most truthful and touching delineation given by Miss Anna Dickinson, in her widely pouplar lecture, entitled, "Whited Sepulchres," now being delivered through the country, is where she sets her true woman's heart and wits at work to get at the bottom of this very matter. She says she went into their homes, and talked with the wife-pluralities themselves, at polygamous firesides, and in *all cases* their occupants said, with calm demeanor, and with seemingly *free tongues*, they were satisfied with polygamy, with their home relations, and believed in it; would not change it; while the woman's heart, which could not lie, told a different tale, through the eye, and in the tones, which no true woman could fail to detect, and which Miss Dickinson did detect. I write from memory, and do not profess to give her language.

The public endorsement of polygamy, by the "willing" victims of it, thus described, were an easy thing for the "prophet" to have managed; and that this line of policy is extended beyond the limits of Utah, is shown by the following:

The *Deseret News* published, a short time ago, a letter from a Mormon woman traveling in the East, in which she said, "You would shudder to hear of the impropriety that is going on between men and women here, and boys even are boasting of their unholy deeds with the other sex; you would feel to glory that you are in Zion. Yes, it is well named. I would not exchange my home and standing there. All the people you meet here seem dead to all religion and the things of God."

A correspondent of the *Tribune*, who was a member of the "Mormon Zion" for many years, and now lives in Massachusetts, enters a forcible protest against such statements, as follows: "I cannot but say with one of old, 'Thou hypocrite.' Have you never heard of anything in Utah to make you shudder? Is there no impurity where a man marries grand-mother and grand-daughter? For you know there are many such cases in Utah; and often they have but a shanty with a single room where they all herd together. I could name many 'green' girls who have been deluded into marriage, and who afterwards complained to Brigham Young, and obtained of him a 'divorce' for $10, after he had himself 'sealed' them for time and eternity." The writer warns people against the missionaries who have recently been sent over the country, and concludes: "I myself was caught years ago and gathered into the fold, but was very glad to get back to the people who this lady says are 'dead to religion and the things of God.'"—*New York Semi-Weekly Tribune, January 14,* 1870.

While this kind of discipline is being stamped upon a crushed womanhood in Utah, the subtle genius which directs that vast centralized power, is making extraordinary efforts to organize further agencies to bring other victims to his harems.

See the following:

"Two Mormon apostles are traveling in Massachusetts, trying to make proselytes, and complain bitterly because Dr. Todd, who preached in their temple, refuses to admit them to his pulpit. They say they belong to a corps of two hundred missionaries sent by Brigham Young to States having more women than men."—*Id., December* 10, 1869.

And,—

"The Mormon bishops and elders are making great exertions to extend their faith in Long Island. A conference was begun at Hempstead on Friday last, and was closed on Sunday."—*Id., January* 25, 1870.

What the Mormons are doing in Massachusetts and New York, they are doing everywhere.

All this vast machinery is directed by a single mind,—by Brigham Young, of whom Miss Dickinson makes the statement: "he is the third largest depositor in the Bank of England;" who controls the largest emigration fund in the world; who, in the interest of that fund, took contracts for building the Railroad extensively, in both directions from his dominion, and performed most of the labor through the poor emigrants indebted to it. Whose emissaries appeal to the poor, and homeless, and destitute, and ignorant, and misguided of all lands, with the offer of a home, and a free passage to it.

And on the other hand, it was Brigham Young, who, through his trained assassins, disguised as Indians, did the Mountain Meadow massacre; and by whose order, William Hickman, the disaffected leader of this band, has lately acknowledged he had committed over four hundred murders in Utah.

And yet, while the little sinners of the land are punished, Brigham is treated with the consideration due a "political offender;" and while we organize powerful agencies for the conversion of the heathen abroad, we neglect to interpose an enlightened Christianity in behalf of his victims at our doors.

There is much difference of statement as to the actual Mormon strength. The sect claim to number in Utah from 80,000 to 100,000; but it is represented by other inhabitants of the territory, as not greatly exceeding 50,000. They have adherents scattered over the country in small numbers,—about 200 in and about New York; and claim in the old world a membership of 100,000,—mostly in Europe, —but also scattered through Asia, Africa, Australia, and Polynesia.

Utah has 65,000 square miles, or 41,600,000 acres, only about 500,000 acres of which can be cultivated, even by irrigation,—about one acre in eighty-three. It has 130 cities and villages, one of which,—Salt Lake,—has 20,000 inhabitants. It has 160,000 acres of land under cultivation, 94,000 of which is by irrigation, the water-rents for which,—paid by the people to the heads of the church,—

amount, annually, to $274,000. Of cultivated lands, 80,000 acres are in grain, 2,000 in sugar-cane, 6,800 in roots, 200 in cotton, 900 in orchards, 1,000 in peaches, 75 in grapes, 195 in currants, and 30,000 in grasses.

The Mormons claim to have expended in Utah, for canals and similar works connected with irrigation, the sum of $10,588,000; and nearly half that sum through its emigration fund; and $70,000 for the city hall at Salt Lake, and both the city and territory are out of debt.

Of school districts, they claim to have 186, and 226 schools, and 18,000 children in them, with 306 teachers, for which $61,000 is expended annually.

A canal is proposed, at a cost of half a million of dollars, from Utah Lake to Salt Lake City, by which 50,000 acres will be added to the productive lands of Utah, by irrigation,—there being about 1,000 miles of canal for this purpose, already constructed.

They have 150 grist and saw mills, three cotton and four woolen factories, twenty-five tanneries, and other industries in wonderful abundance and perfection.

The land surveys are made upon an uniform system; the first tiers, for village or city lots, of five acres, and these, in the towns, into house lots of one and a quarter acres each. The next tier into lots of ten acres, and the third twenty, and so on, up to forty acres, which is the highest number of acres one man may own.

As the leading endeavor, in this hastily prepared history of Mormonism, has been to bring the prominent facts of

Mormonsim before the reading masses in a way to indicate the work to be done, if this moral blight upon our institutions is not to remain, marked attention has been given to unusual sources of information; and especially to the newspapers, from which nothing, save a want of space, has prevented more copious extracts.

www.ingramcontent.com/pod-product-compliance
Lightning Source LLC
Chambersburg PA
CBHW051857300426
44117CB00006B/434